The Reflective Professional in Education

of related interest

Mental Health in Your School
A Guide for Teachers and Others Working in Schools
Young Minds
ISBN 1 85302 407 4

Educational Psychology Casework
A Practical Guide
Rick Beaver
ISBN 1 85302 364 7

Group Work with Children and Adolescents
A Handbook
Edited by Kedar Nath Dwivedi
ISBN 1 85302 157 1

Meeting the Needs of Ethnic Minority Children
A Handbook for Professionals
Edited by Kedar Nath Dwivedi and Ved P Varma
ISBN 1 85302 294 2

Child Psychiatric Units
At the Crossroads
Edited by Rosemary Chesson and Douglas Chisholm
ISBN 1 85302 329 9

How and Why Children Fail
Edited by Ved Varma
ISBN 1 85302 108 3 hb
ISBN 1 85302 186 5 pb

How and Why Children Hate
A Study of Conscious and Unconscious Sources
Edited by Ved Varma
ISBN 1 85302 116 4 hb
ISBN 1 85302 185 7 pb

The Reflective Professional in Education

Psychological Perspectives
on Changing Contexts

Edited by Carmel Jennings and Elizabeth Kennedy

Foreword by Bob Burden

Jessica Kingsley Publishers
London and Bristol, Pennsylvania

Figure 6.1 'Internal and external consultation'
is reproduced with the kind permission of Karnac Books.

The right of the contributors to be identified as authors of this work has been asserted by them in accordance with the Copyright, Designs and Patents Act 1988.

First published in the United Kingdom in 1996 by
Jessica Kingsley Publishers Ltd
116 Pentonville Road
London N1 9JB, England
and
1900 Frost Road, Suite 101
Bristol, PA 19007, U S A

Library of Congress Cataloging in Publication Data
A CIP catalogue record for this book is available from the Library of Congress

British Library Cataloguing in Publication Data
The reflective professional in education : psychological
perspectives on changing contexts
1. Education – Philosophy 2. Education – Aims and objectives
3. Educational sociology
I. Jennings, Carmel II. Kennedy, Elizabeth
370.1

ISBN 1-85302-330-2

Printed and Bound in Great Britain by
Cromwell Press, Melksham, Wiltshire

Contents

List of Tables and Figures

Acknowledgements

During the time it has taken to write and compile this book, a constant concern has been that the changes we were writing about would overtake us, affecting the impact and topicality of the written contributions. We have been involved in several such tensions while gathering together these important examples of specialised work within the broad context of education. This reflects the current socio-political context and the legislation, and we expand more fully on some of the metamorphoses which have taken place in the Introduction.

We are grateful to our families who have encouraged us through each stage of the process of writing and editing. We would also like to thank Jane Rayner, Irene Henderson and Teresa Lorenzo for their skilled help in typing some of the manuscripts. Mark Pickthall kindly assisted with some of the graphics and diagrams.

Finally, we would like to express our gratitude to all the contributors, who have kept some of the important professional issues and perspectives of the book alive in their work. They have managed to keep a creative space for thought in the midst of their hectic working lives and, more impressively, to shape, reflect on and write about the worthwhile practices they are involved in. We hope that this gives our readership encouragement for the survival of skilled professional expertise and services as described in the book, and that some of our readers will feel inspired as we have been to develop and incorporate some of these ideas within their practice.

A Note on Confidentiality

We have included examples of situations which we think help to illustrate how staff in various settings can work with children, families and other agencies. Some of these refer to details which may seem familiar to our readership, but we would like to clarify that all the examples we have included are fictitious. Where case studies are included, we have altered all the details to preserve the anonymity of those involved.

Foreword

In recent years the concept of a 'helping professional' seems to have undergone something of a sea-change. On the one hand, the move towards greater accountability, however sensible and well meaning in its original purpose, has led to an emphasis on measurements, which not unnaturally has itself given rise to a search for that which can be measured. It is but a small step from here to the identification of 'competencies' as the key elements of good practice. This is as true of educational psychologists as of social workers and of all helping professionals.

Whilst it is entirely laudable that the rights of clients should be given greater prominence than has sometimes been the case in the past, and that greater explicitness in what is being offered should make the process of evaluation far easier, in some respects at least, there are attendant drawbacks. The most insidious danger is that only that which can be measured will be considered worthwhile, thereby leading to a reversion to the worst excesses of behaviourism and a blinkered focus on behavioural objectives. At this extreme, professionalism may be constructed as connecting bundles of competencies, and the training of professionals as helping applicants to reach a minimum level of competence.

At the same time, British educational legislation from 1981 onwards relating to children with special needs, despite its apparently inclusive intent, has led to a narrowing of role for educational psychologists in particular. The most recent Code of Practice may well improve the lot of children with special needs, but it will also undoubtedly increase bureaucratic procedures and, by focusing so explicitly upon these procedures, it seems likely to narrow the range of school-based involvement by educational psychologists and to threaten the very nature of consultancy work.

Under such circumstances there is a need for members of the helping professions, and particularly those involved with education, to stand back and reflect upon exactly what they consider professionalism to mean and how this applies to their own profession. In this instance it is important also not to lose sight of the significant paradigm shift that has occurred in the social sciences in recent years, from positivist to constructivist and social interactionist ways of making sense of human behaviour. In such times there is also a great need for practice to be underpinned by strong theory and not merely to reflect current fashion or, worst of all, political expediency.

In brief, systemic ways of coming to understand what happens in schools and other social institutions are in danger of being overlooked or pushed aside because they don't fit comfortably with the more linear, empiricist approaches demanded by recent legislation. If this should happen then I for one – and I'm sure I'm not alone in this – will see it as an enormously retrograde step in growth process of educational psychology.

There is a need, therefore, for a resistance movement, for a group of dedicated social science professionals who are willing and able to articulate both the need for such resistance and ways in which systemic and other 'new paradigm' ways of thinking and writing can benefit the helping professions. This I see as one of the main aims of this book. Such books are urgently needed to redress the balance and to add to that small but growing number of texts which speak eloquently for more complex ways of understanding. In this respect above all others I commend it to you.

Bob Burden
Exeter University June 1995

Introduction

Carmel Jennings and Elizabeth Kennedy

This introductory chapter sets out some of the dilemmas and challenges in the education services arising from the circumstances of rapid change brought about by recent legislation. An overview is presented of the legislative and structural changes, as well as their procedural and experiential impact. Including some of the reactions experienced at an individual, group and institutional level helps us to examine ways in which the legislation has challenged the notions of collective social responsibility inherent in the philosophies underpinning the welfare state. We also explore the ethical and practical dilemmas for education professionals working in the unfamiliar world of the market place.

The Age of Irony: Political, Economic and Legislative Context

It is tempting to think that historians writing one hundred years from now about the 1980s and 1990s might call this period 'The Age of Irony'. Alongside central government claims regarding increased choice, efficiency and quality, the professions have seen a massive growth in bureaucratisation, centralisation, and over-determination of professional roles. The advantages of this have included requirements from greater openness and accountability. Responsibility has shifted away from central government and onto the various professional groups, at the same time as their ability to determine the content and processes of their work has increasingly been restricted. The subjugation of education and health services to market forces has also taken place against a backdrop of frameworks, practices and procedures from business and industry. Ironically, this has been happening at the same time as the commercial world has increasingly been embracing ideas, tools and practices from the social sciences, particularly psychology.

Much of the legislation has determined that the public sector ('human services') is driven by a model of a free-market economy. This model, formerly applicable to the transactions of goods and commodities, is now thought to regulate social issues involving beliefs and values, as well as some of the functions of the state. At a conceptual level, there is an apparent lack of fit between the economic model of entrepreneurism and some of the more complex socio-cultural mechanisms that regulate society at the end of the twentieth century. Professionals working in public service contexts have felt increasingly constrained by political and economic realities. These realities have sometimes led to a feeling of compromise with their traditional commitments to a more humane society.

The concept of 'performance management' is relatively new to the pubic sector professions. Because of the nature of the work in these settings, performance targets have tended to emphasise the quantitative rather than qualitative aspects of the work (league table figures, number of immunisations etc.). This has felt to be at the expense of the less objective, measurable and visible tasks central to the nature of the work. Such measures have increased the visible accountability of the professions at the same time as central government has progressively abdicated responsibility for maintaining a supportive social infrastructure.

Delegation to 'independent' bodies (such as quangos) and increasingly fragmented groups has been accompanied by a narrowing of task definition and domain in some professions. Traditionally, groups who found themselves collaborating in the service of the wider tasks such as 'community health and social services' can now find themselves in direct competition for resources. A 'culture of complaint', exemplified by the consumer chartering movement, has accompanied this diversification and left these so-called independent groups acting as a buffer against holding central government to account.

The virtue of self determination through increased public choice is a much vaunted pillar of this government's political programme. Expectations of a greater freedom of choice have been raised through vigorous publicity promotion. The harsh realities of world recession, a fragile economy and decreasing public expenditure in real terms, whilst widely known, are less frequently acknowledged as limiting 'real' choice.

In many ways it has been the professionalism and the commitment of professionals that has obscured the harsher aspects of political and economic change. Most professionals have seen their employment bases altered and their contractual obligations changed. Longer hours, greater demands, fewer supports, are common to workers in education, health and social services. The irony is that this is largely unacknowledged and often accompanied by a seeming devaluing of professional experience and expertise.

In this political climate, quality in the public sector is predicated on the notions of increased choice and greater accountability through subjection to market forces. The way in which this argument has been articulated seems to have located the resistance to change and indifference to quality assurance practices within the professions. The government has grasped the initiative and claimed ownership of the wish to provide quality services. These paradoxes have alienated many professionals, ironically creating polarised attitudes where there had previously been, if not unanimity of purpose, then at least a broad measure of agreement.

Legislation and The Education System

Recent legislation has demanded changes at every level of the education service, initiated by central government. The 1980s were punctuated by interventionist statutes which not only fundamentally altered structures and relationships, but also dictated the content in education (1981, 1986, 1988, Education Acts, The Children Act 1989). This has continued into the 1990s with the largest piece of education legislation on the statute book, the 1993 Education Act. The impact of such profound and rapid change has been enormous on those delivering the education service, in all phases from higher education to primary schools.

Of the legislation mentioned above, the most influential to date has undoubtedly been the Education Reform Act of 1988. This Act should be viewed as of constitutional importance, as it fundamentally shifted the balance of power between different organs of the state. But not only was the content of the Act important (the introduction of the National Curriculum, open enrolment, local financial management, grant maintained status for schools, provisions for further and higher education), the manner in which it was introduced and subsequently managed has also proved to be of enormous significance. Many education personnel experienced the changes as a challenge to their training, experience and integrity; they were greeted with a mixture of enthusiasm and concern, but sometimes with resentment. Some professionals found the external imposition of, for example, teaching content, as an under-mining of their expertise, and this was exacerbated by a perceived lack of consultation. Together these issues were, on occasion, felt as a diminishing of the professionalism in education, and of the teaching profession in particular.

The prevailing climate has tended to emphasise the marketing and costing forces of service delivery, sometimes at the expense of the human resources involved. Thus powerful feelings of excitement and promise on the one hand, and fear, anxiety and stress on the other, have permeated the education system. The pace and sweeping nature of the changes both at the organisational and the human level have been experienced by some as overwhelming. Frequent alterations and additions have made consolidation unlikely and consistency difficult to sustain. Little time has been left for reflection and, not surprisingly, there has been a high human cost to implementing the changes. The philosophical underpinning of market forces has led to uncertainty and rivalry receiving legislative sanction, and there has been much worry that the centrality of the pupils' experience has been lost as education's primary task (see Kennedy, Chapter 4).

Against this turbulent background, in which the primacy of the individual is emphasised relative to that of the group, it seems vital to examine the impact of the changes at both the individual and the systemic level. This book is an attempt to introduce a possible framework for understanding the experience of people working in and with schools. No one currently working in education has been immune to the changes described. From Secretary of State down, practices are different – the intervention of the then incumbent Kenneth Clark in the management of an individual school (Stratford) is just one example. Local Authorities are stripped of many of their former powers and functions and face an uncertain relationship with the Funding Agency For Schools. Many aspects of the traditional role of Her Majesty's Inspectorate (HMI) and local inspectors in inspecting, monitoring and supporting schools have been taken over by OFSTED and its functioning. Headteachers have found themselves in a newly conceived management role with little specific training, and against a background of traditional ambivalence to the managerial aspects of education (Handy and Aitken 1986). Teachers, many of whom welcomed the introduction of a national curriculum, have felt overwhelmed as well as excited by the broad base, rapidity, and frequent modification to school organisation, administration and classroom practice. Governors, a disparate lay group, hold much of the power and responsibility for the management of schools, demanding of them new levels of involvement and commitment.

Parental rights have been strengthened (particularly under the 1993 Education Act in relation to special needs children) and publicised, challenging some of the fundamental aspects of the relationships at the school boundary. Of the impact on the children, the evidence is equivocal, but it seems as if they have been protected from the worst excesses of change by the professionalism of their teachers.

Developments in Interprofessional Work with 'Children in Need'

At the same time, legislative·changes have occurred in the contexts of health and social services as a response to the 1990 NHS and Community Care Act, creating different demands in the shape of services which are offered to children and young people. The philosophical underpinning of market forces behind the legislation has led to the creation of internal markets between these different sectors concerned with children's mental health and well-being. New employment practices by health trusts now make it possible for the work of child educational psychologists, and that of other staff groups offering specialised services to children, to be 'bought in', offering the potential for more flexible professional collaboration across different service boundaries.

The Children Act 1989 places a clear 'duty' on local authorities to safeguard and protect 'children in need', which must include 'all aspects of development including emotional, behavioural and mental, as well as physical health'. Similarly, recent education legislation in the Code of Practice (Department for Education 1994) includes provision for preventative and early interventions work to ensure that children's emotional and psychological difficulties are recognised and treated. Under the 1989 Children Act, social services departments are obliged to identify children in need, children with disabilities, abused children, and those suffering emotional deprivation, and to provide appropriate services for them in co-operation with health and education. Furthermore, agencies are urged to follow the principles of partnership and close working so that professional knowledge, expertise and commitment to quality practices for children are co-ordinated with coherent local services.

It is to be hoped that many of these good intentions towards 'children in need' which have been enshrined in recent government policies can be realised by effective collaboration between the professional groups involved. For this to occur, there will need to be a strengthening of resources and infrastructures to support services at local community levels. The last five years have seen services to children in education, community health and social care being diminished, as professionals have found that they are in competition for increasingly scarce resources. Existing teams, especially those working from child guidance units, have been threatened with disintegration, yet are often overwhelmed with referrals and requests for supportive consultation. Moreover, many services have been delivered by agencies operating in separate, yet overlapping, conceptual and statutory frameworks, and from different institutional bases. If staff are to be enabled to work together effectively, greater government co-ordination is required to ensure that local agencies create projects for the effective sharing of monies and services for children and their families at a local level.

The concept of 'child and adolescent mental health' was introduced in the 1992 'Health of the Nation' (Department of Health 1992) document, and now, it is hoped, seems set to become a more significant force for change. As there is an increasingly evident need to inform and educate the key purchasers in the market place, two further documents have been issued in 1995. The Department of Health handbook 'Child and Adolescent Mental Health' and the NHS Advisory Service's 'Together We Stand' both promote and set out local strategies which are aimed at commissioners, purchasers and providers of services for children. These documents set out, for the first time, a vision of a comprehensive and integrated child and adolescent mental health service, consisting of several tiers of service involving different levels of intervention, consultation, liaison and treatment. Both documents stress that an effective multi-disciplinary service is at the heart of effective provision for children and young people. There is an important implication for child educational psychologists, who have had an established tradition in working across professional boundaries, developing and maintaining communication across a wide range of agencies, and contributing to interprofessional support systems and trainings.

As part of the challenge and integrity of their professional practice, educational psychologists and other staff groups need to be able to produce broad-ranging and creative solutions across all aspects of their working contexts, and to have this potential recognised by their employing institutions. This book provides examples of collaborative thinking and practices which it is hoped will help staff reconnect with the interdisciplinary aspects of their roles, in providing specialised and coherent services to children in need. Whilst not necessarily accepting the rationale for some of these changes, it is evident that professional staff groups working within education will need to become more outward-looking and responsive to the changing occupational and external environments.

The Reflective Professional

A common response to rapid and extensive change is to function through custom and habit. Although adaptability, flexibility and the application of common sense can ensure survival and continuation of the preordained task in the face of upheaval, it can be a recipe for not having to think.

This book is an attempt to highlight the general benefits of reflective practice. It is our shared belief that frameworks that have a 'search for meaning' as their central tenet are of particular value at a time when the drive to 'act' rather than 'reflect' is so powerful. The contributions are all from workers informed in their practice by psychodynamic and systemic ideas. Reflection in these disciplines is characterised by attending to the emotional experiences of workers as well as clients. In our view, the reflective professional tries to keep in mind simultaneously the different levels of their work, including themselves, their clients, the groups within which they work, the groups in which their clients have to function, and the wider organisational responses to the work and workers in their own target organisations. Understanding the intrapersonal and interpersonal aspects of interactions will, we believe, furnish the individual practitioner with the resources to cope with and change puzzling and problematic situations.

'The distinctive quality of a setting – a classroom, a nursery or a family – is that if people are to learn and grow, someone needs to be there who is capable of *thinking* about what is going on, and of helping others to do so.' (Rustin 1991, p.48). This book looks at the processes involved in working effectively in complex organisations and the training, evaluation and supervision issues involved (see Jennings, Chapter 1). We know from our own experience how profound are the effects of the various encounters and relationships which are formed in school, and how long lasting they are. We hope that a focus on the overt and covert aspects of 'educational life' will illuminate some of the subtleties of the relationships within and between individuals and groups and their impact on performance. We argue strongly for thinking time to be sustained in the face of ever-increasing demands on individuals, groups and systems.

Conceptual Framework

Carmel Jennings and Elizabeth Kennedy

The Introduction has outlined some of the unprecedented changes which have occurred in education and other public services during the last decade. The impact of such change and uncertainty on staff and services has now changed the cultures in many organisations. In the deconstruction of professional practices which some of the changes have imposed, the complexities of various practitioner roles have been overlooked, as well as their more creative and developmental possibilities. The effects of entrepreneurial models on professional approaches to work has also meant an invasion of values and ethical concerns. This section outlines some of the conceptual and theoretical frameworks which we have found help staff groups to find a more acceptable fit between some of these constraints and the more reflective aspects of their practice.

Contributors to the book have drawn on a number of interwoven strands of theory, which together provide the conceptual framework on which their work is based. The book hopes to address some of the challenges which have been outlined by giving examples of specialised work which requires the professional to take a more active and dynamic stance. Delivery of good quality educational and social care systems also leads naturally to staff from different agencies and disciplines being able to work together effectively. Yet it is now much more difficult for staff to work together coherently across the boundaries of their organisations to provide integrated cross-disciplinary services to children and their families. In Chapter 1, it can be seen how the training context now has a tremendous potential for influencing understanding of each other's roles and practices. The training models and supervisory processes described here can also help to create awareness of social and institutional environments which are favourable to growth at the level of individual staff and clients, of the staff team, and of the organisation as a whole.

This brings us to the institutional context in which the book has been compiled, and which has influenced some of the varied applications of theory and practice in the different chapters. Different theoretical perspectives inform the work described here, mirroring some of the overlapping theoretical approaches which have emerged during the 75 years of the Tavistock Clinic's history. It is now widely known that the Tavistock offers psycho-analytically-based therapy trainings within the Kleinian tradition, and family therapy trainings in systems-based theories (Campbell, Draper and Huffington 1988). Much of the training in psychodynamic and systemic thinking and application is also focused on staff groups who want to enhance their ordinary working skills. They are trained in a way of thinking, understanding and developing awareness of emotional and social capacities which can be widely learned. We are all dependent on the qualities of the relationships which surround us, and conditions which are favourable for the development of children and adults can also be incorporated within styles of work in our institutions and become part of our legitimate expectations of them.

Developing reflective and proactive styles of work within the educational context, which is now increasingly at odds with personal professional belief systems, is a central theme and challenge of the book. Implicit in this approach is that the professional is able to adopt a 'meta' stance and to contribute towards creating a climate in which uncertainty and difficult issues can be thought about. Sue Holt summarises this approach in Chapter 9, in the form of a more reflective questioning of 'What is going on here?' rather than the prescriptive tendency towards 'I know what to do here.' She looks at some of the misguided belief systems often instigated by academic psychology departments, which have set psychodynamic theory and practice in opposition to empirical and 'scientist-practitioner' based models. This leads to stereotyped thinking and often serves a defensive function in deflecting psychologists away from a more genuine understanding of themselves and their clients. There is now, for instance, a much greater mutuality between developmental psychology and psycho-analytically-based approaches to the observation and study of infants (see Stern 1985). There is also a tremendous interest in psychodynamic approaches among incomers to clinical psychology and other practitioners who are allied to education.

Many of the professional groups who are likely to form the readership of this book are now finding they need more in-depth understanding of their relationships with clients, in order to balance some of the restrictions entering into their practice. In several chapters we illustrate how the emotional dynamics of work with clients can reverberate throughout the professional network and influence the outcomes of assessment and intervention work. Chapter 1 includes examples of psychoanalytic and systemic terms and concepts which can enable reflective understanding. There is also a practical discussion of supervision systems in the workplace in this chapter, setting out the need for clear contracts and review processes.

Reflective professional styles of work therefore require a mastery of skills-based approaches and professional techniques but also an appreciation of the particular nature of the mental and emotional pain with which the child, parent, or teacher is likely to be struggling. We are not suggesting here that practitioners need an extensive knowledge of particular psycho-analytic theories, but that they become more broadly oriented towards different styles and levels of communication which their client groups express, and able to take up issues which can often seem ironical and irrational. Reflection on practice is likely to involve a suspension of certainty, or of a wish to arrive quickly at a formulation. This has several implications in the working context, as there are often pressures on professionals to deny ignorance and anxiety and to display pseudo-competence at a more superficial level of understanding.

Ethical Concerns

When professionals are restricted to working within existing areas of statutory work and contractual demands laid down by their employers, there is often a cost at other levels of their work. Changes in the power structures of the human services have been responsible for importing models of service delivery which are often incompatible with professional responsibilities towards children and parents. When fiscal considerations assume priority, staff need to struggle with the ethical implications of vulnerable client groups being overlooked in the competition for scarce resources. As much of the recent legislation focuses on individuals rather than on social groups, this has led to some of the most disadvantaged client groups being marginalised. Professionals need to ensure that the presence of vulnerable clients, and particularly the perspective of children, is still thought about, and their voices are still heard.

In such a climate, professionals also need to sharpen the debate about what they collectively believe in. As part of their role as public employees, they are sought out as experts by different client groups and have power and authority invested in their roles. They are invested with professional responsibility to contribute to an ongoing discussion about the role of their profession in a wider society, and need to be prepared to articulate the changes which are required. This involves being sensitive to inequality issues and of how they think about their own power in their professional role. Conversely, the client may have a corresponding lack of power, and of choice about whom they see. Professionals may need to ask themselves how this might affect the quality and flexibility of services they offer and to be prepared to introduce the social context more directly into their professional discourses. Effective feedback mechanisms can then help to ensure that disadvantaged client groups have a choice of services, which can be determined by sensitive evaluation of local needs.

Some of these ethical aspects of the professional role can be considered within the perspective offered by inter-group relations training. Group Relations Conferences were originally set up by the Tavistock Institute of Human Relations (TIHR) in 1957. These conferences are still held regularly, and provide participants with an educational opportunity during the life of the conference to focus on themes of authority, task, context, power and leadership. It is possible to explore some of the dynamics of difference which surround these themes, and to legitimise them in application to everyday practice and working roles. Several chapters in this book are based upon theoretical applications of this approach, and a fuller exposition of some of the far reaching influences and practices of the style of work can be found in Obholzer and Roberts (1994).

In Chapter 2 of this book Anton Obholzer illustrates how concepts from group relations and organisational consultancy can enhance understanding of institutional processes within the educational setting. A capacity to think about an institution and to stay on the margins without being drawn in to some of the powerful shared assumptions has several benefits. Roger Booker provides a working model in Chapter 3 of 'open systems' functioning at the level of service development within an Educational Psychology Service (EPS). The primary task is likely to involve adapting valued professional skills if the service is to survive beyond a minimal statutory role, and this means addressing the needs of clients who are in distress in a more creative way. Another side of the professional leader's task is to ensure that organisations uniquely value professionals' expertise and skill, and to identify resource niches where professional expertise may be developed.

Since the 1950s, the TIHR has undertaken a large number of both research and consultancy projects combining perspectives from both the social sciences and psycho-analysis, which has been known as 'action research'. The staff members' stance in these styles of work has been to construe their observations and experiences as consultants in a way which facilitates helpful changes for the institution (Miller and Rice 1967). Chapters 4 and 5 illustrate how staff in the respective roles of educational psychologist and psychotherapist can readily transfer such applications of group functioning to their everyday work and help to disseminate understanding about the quality of social environments and staff–children relationships which are conducive to learning and development. Elizabeth Kennedy describes group influences in school settings, presenting a broader framework for understanding subtle aspects of teaching and learning which can extend beyond and enrich the usual focus on special needs procedures and statutory demands.

In Chapter 6, Clare Huffington defines the roles of the internal and external consultants in the current context, giving particular consideration to service development. She sees consultative approaches as helping organisations to be clearer about their primary tasks and describes how consultation can become a vehicle of empowerment. This occurs through the sense of involvement and ownership which is offered to those participating in the process, including managers, practitioners and service users. Developing consultation skills often enhances professional practice, as it can expand staff members' basic functional roles in new ways, generalise to different situations and prepare staff for different practices and interventions.

In Chapter 7, Eileen Orford describes working as an external consultant with support teachers, within a framework which is influenced by Bion's perspectives on group functioning. She illuminates how disturbed and anti-task behaviour at the level of the individual child is often part of a wider system of irrational and negative emotions which also surface at the whole school level, and are reflected in the classroom dynamics. What the teacher experiences with the child is critical to further understanding of the child's difficulties, and can be communicated to the child through the curriculum. It is crucial that such facilitative styles of work, in which one group of practitioners offers support and containment to another staff group who work directly with children, are preserved within the educational context. As some of these indirect aspects of staff roles are often invisible to outsiders, it is important that they are costed, marketed and publicised as part of overall service delivery.

It is now more widely recognised in society that professional services are needed to provide a co-ordinated response in the aftermath of trauma and disaster. In Chapter 8 Joyce Iszatt and Enid Colmer describe a sensitively planned intervention following a tragedy in a girls' comprehensive school. This involved a process of consultation drawing on Critical Incident Stress Debriefing, and both psychodynamic and systemic perspectives to help staff make sense of their experiences. It was then possible to offer direct work with the class group who had been most directly affected by the tragedy. The authors portray how the sessions seemed to reflect the process from traumatic shock reactions through to a discomforting accommodation, and on to the progression of grief and its uneven integration. This specialised intervention depicts how joint work from a multi-professional perspective can extend the support systems offered to a large institution at a time of crisis. Combined roles and perspective helped staff to recognise underlying processes in the group work they undertook, and to draw on each other's complementary skills and expertise to offer a flexible service.

In both of the above examples, it was possible to draw on professional expertise for the specialised work because the settings were still in place which enabled the staff to work together, providing in-built models of reflective practice and mutual support. When staff are able to work flexibly in this way, their complementary skills often generalise to all sorts of situations. This prepares them to set up different practices and to take risks about venturing in to new and challenging areas of work. In the present context, there is a need to create more preventative services for young children and adolescents (see Chapter 5) and their families. This may mean setting up different models of inter-agency working, as well as enhancing traditional models, such as child and family guidance units.

Chapter 10 acknowledges some of the challenges to traditional structures of inter-professional collaboration which are inherent in the implementation of the Children Act. This chapter concentrates on the group of children in need because of sexual abuse, although there is often also a lack of services for the larger group of 'children in need' whose health and development is impaired. The chapter starts with the perspective of the school based practitioner and suggests that the intervention in instances of suspected child sexual abuse is considered as a continuum of involvement. The aim is to contextualise concerns about abuse so that the teacher is able to differentiate the separate child-protective, therapeutic and legal strands which overlap in this sensitive area of work. The teacher also needs to be able to share her concerns with the professional network in a way which does not further jeopardise the child's safety and well-being. Dr Judith Trowell is a nationally recognised expert in this field who has contributed significantly to the understanding of both treatment and management issues for children who have been sexually abused. She refers in the chapter to the wide range of theoretical knowledge which is required if staff are to conceptualise how concerns about children overlap, requiring perspectives which are interactive.

This leads us back to acknowledging the range of theoretical influences throughout the book. Most of the core theoretical influences originate in different models of learning and developmental theories (Stern 1985; Bion 1962; Bruner 1966), attachment theory (Bowlby 1988; Barrett and Trevitt 1991), family systems theory (Street and Dryden 1988; Carter and McGoldrick 1991), as well as work relating to group relations and organisational development which has already been discussed. The work of John Bowlby on attachment and attachment disorders is included in Chapter 9, where Sue Holt describes how the family, school and psychologist worked towards a shared understanding of the child.

However, it is misleading to think about theoretical influences as derivative without considering the leading position the Tavistock has occupied in both the model of training and research it offers, and its social mission in disseminating psychotherapeutic influences, ideas and treatment. The Tavistock has been built on principles analogous to those of the National Health Service (NHS), namely that therapeutic services should be free of charge to those who need them, and many of its members, including John Bowlby, have contributed directly to different phases of state welfare policy. The working philosophy has been to promote the health of families and children growing up in the community, to further understanding of the conditions necessary for healthy and effective development, and to train professional personnel in integrative approaches to understanding and managing some of these processes in their own work (Dicks 1970).

Since it was first established in 1920, the Tavistock has been person- or task-centred, rather than theory-centred, and committed to understanding the whole social context in inter-disciplinary approaches which cross different boundaries. Many creative innovations have arisen from the cross-fertilisations which occur between clinical work, research and internal and external training activities. Some of the deepest and most far-reaching improvements which have come from the Tavistock are likely to be in the preventative aspects of its work, with regard to a wide range of settings, for example in children's relationships with staff in day nurseries; their experiences in schools; the treatment of children and families in hospitals; the effects of sudden change, loss or divorce on parents and children; bereavement; work with refugees; and many other aspects of human stress situations. The task of developing adequate approaches to the assessment of therapeutic results has been an integral part of the 'problem-centred' research tradition, and this is now continued in audit methodology and therapeutic-outcome research (Aveline and Shapiro 1995).

The identity of much of the work which is presented in this book stems from this ongoing and distinctive integration of skills and ideas which are applicable to a wide variety of different professional roles. There is now perhaps a greater need than ever for some of these common principles to be allied to the role of the reflective professional in the educational and social care settings. We hope that reflective practices as described in this book can continue to be actualised and diffused in the everyday working lives of both practitioners and their clients.

CHAPTER 1

Training the Reflective Professional
The Practice of Supervision

Carmel Jennings

The Current Context

During the last ten years, the framework for training professionals across all phases of education, from primary schools to universities, has changed significantly. Many staff groups in both education and the public services have needed to change their approach to work as a result of legislation and the creation of internal and external markets. Recent legislation (1986, 1988, 1993), has provided a more over-determined view of professional roles and tasks, with a greater emphasis on accountability and clarity of service delivery. The Department for Education (DfE) is now a more significant source of influence in the whole sphere of education, and is setting requirements which are centrally directed and advocate a stronger vocational base. All of these fundamental changes in the orientation of services have had implications for the styles of training involved for different professional groups in education.

Many of these initiatives have been concerned with delivering more 'cost-effective' services to consumers, and trying to ensure that both the professional services and specialised knowledge involved become more accessible. In the training context, this has meant that courses have been restructured to take more account of the aims of the workplace. These trends were introduced by the DfE, and began by making the focus of initial teacher training more school-based (DfE 1992). Although there have been some concerns that this was a retrograde step, universities and training institutions have since responded to some of these changes by redefining and often relocating professional learning. Work-based learning now takes greater precedence in educational settings, and is often interspersed with theoretical input and reflection on practice in a more progressive, developmental way (Peckett and Shepherd 1994).

Some of the developments which have taken place include an emphasis on more individualised approaches to learning. These may take the form of negotiated learning contracts and portfolios, and opportunities for more flexible, distant, modularised part-time courses. Such modifications enable students to make firmer links with ongoing work experience, to take a more active role in determining their own learning, and to strengthen opportunities for reflection on practice.

Some of these trends have reflected shifts in the socio-political context of education. They have precipitated awareness of the need to reflect on what is meant by client-centred practice, and on the general meaning of one's profession in society. When the nature of professional expertise and education is explored more closely, it is apparent that different views have emerged about the nature of professional knowledge.

This leads to a closer exploration of the nature of professional expertise and development. If some of the distinctive needs and experiences of seasoned professionals can be identified, then they may inform the design of trainings which are simultaneously intellectually challenging and of direct benefit to clients and practice.

It is difficult to capture professional practice, which by its nature is distinctive and involves both generalisable knowledge and specific knowledge to be freshly acquired about individual clients and problematic situations. Eraut (1992) has described some of the features of professional decision-making as involving 'a sufficient repertoire of possible causes of action and ways of adapting them to individual circumstances, and the experience and wisdom to make an optimal set of decisions, adjusting to new information as it becomes available'. This enactive view of professional learning acknowledges the considerable overlap between personal, interpersonal and professional areas of understanding which influence professional work with clients and institutions. Gains in self-knowledge are essential to working perceptively and sensitively with clients, and the relationship between skills, qualities and understanding is complex. The implications for the training context are that models of training need to mirror the processes which constitute professional work, and use teaching and learning methods which parallel the development of different roles.

The 'Core Competencies' Framework and Reflective Practice

The representation of professional expertise has also been attempted in the 'core competencies' framework, which has been adapted from the National Certificate of Vocational Qualifications (NCVQ) model to portray professional practice at Level 5. As the model was originally based on the specification of work performances, its application to the development of professional thinking and judgement presents several dilemmas. These are disussed in more detail by Figg (1994).

A challenge for some professional groups, including the different branches of applied psychology, has been to integerate the different levels and components of this model to provide a dynamic and overarching representation of professional psychology for the late 1990s. This has involved producing a framework for the knowledge base, together with specifications of the range and levels of performance, which emphasise the process as well as the product aspects of professional competency and development. The Standing Committee of the Division of Educational and Child Psychology has been proactive in this respect, and has tackled the work in two phases. The first phase of the work involved mapping out some of the content of the core curriculum to represent a 'scientific practitioner' approach, based on the development of professional learning objectives (Figg 1994).

Subsequently, a newly formed committee has evolved this model into a more dynamic document which has included views from consultation with the profession of practising psychologists. Interpersonal effectiveness is now a theme which runs throughout, and there is a key emphasis on the development of the self in professional applied psychology as a 'reflective practitioner'. Within the limitations of a one dimensional model, competencies have been represented as multi-faceted, interactive and relevant to all the sections of applied psychology. The document depicts characteristics which child psychologists need to help them analyse complex problems, and to take reponsibility for managing change. It also provides a working model from which a core curriculum for initial professional training can be derived, and continuously updated with scope for interpretation and review about the learning processes and levels of skill which are involved.

This has been achieved by positioning the competency statements at a meta-evaluative level of practice. A reflective professional approach is equated with this 'meta'-level of practice which is based on a cycle of initial hypothesising, consideration of alternative modes of intervention, and a process of evaluation and review. There are clear analogies with other models of professional practice, including the personal problem-solving model described by Miller (1991) and the 'professional artistry' of Schon (1987).

The working model thus combines integrative features and a capacity for adapting the elements for different contexts. It encapsulates the need for continuing professional development to be both professsionally effective and personally meaningful. There is scope for inbuilt evaluation procedures to prompt further understanding of the important interactions between professional knowledge, skills, and the personal relationships involved. A challenge has been to move away from viewing the competencies of professional work as merely practical activity and to suggest how the imtegration of knowledge, skills and personal understanding occurs within reflectively critical practice.

It is this skills or 'competencies' view of teaching and other professional work as essentially practical activity which has dominated recent changes. It is accompanied by a view that learning of practical skills is often conveyed by experienced practitioners. This has led to a more collaborative partnership

between training institutions and schools in devising effective learning programmes which enable people to 'learn on the job' by building in various
support mechanisms.

Some of these separate but complementary trends can coalesce through the
agency of the 'mentor' or work-based tutor. There is some overlap between the
terms which are used, and one of the aims of this chapter is to consider
developments in mentoring approaches alongside other supervisory practices.
Peer tutoring and partnership models often imply more agreed and equitable
approaches to learning. Topping (1992) reviews some of the objectives of
co-operative learning and points out that partnership involves more than
support and collaboration. There is a need to differentiate between the cognitive, social and affective aspects in educational evaluation and to monitor the
processes and outcomes of effective individual learning.

The role of the 'mentor'

A mentor is defined as an 'experienced but trusted adviser' by the Oxford
Dictionary. The emphasis in the role of mentor is that of facilitator of learning,
and implies a capacity to join the learner in a sense of mutual challenge and
process of enquiry. The educative aspect of mentoring implies that the mentor
is likely to understand how people learn, and will be skilful in helping to
accelerate the conceptual aspects of learning. This involves mentors in helping
practitioners make the links between current work, previous experiences and
theoretical understanding.

Mentors now occupy positions in all areas of life. In the educational setting
they are usually involved in appraisal systems and assume the responsibilities
of facilitators of learning. In secondary schools there is now a DfE requirement
that two thirds of student time on PGCE courses must be physically based in
schools. Mentors have an important role in induction of newly qualified teachers
(NQTs), appraisal, OFSTED inspections, and other forms of school-based
training. Many aspects of existing courses are now being adapted to be used
by mentors in a school-based context. They are likely to monitor the Learning
Contracts, which form a major component of the students' Professional Development Portfolio, which is a central focus of assessment. If mentors are to
maximise their effectiveness in this crucial role, it is important that they are able
to integrate knowledge and understanding with learning processes which
contribute to effective relationship building.

Transformations in the style of learning can therefore be involved. The
trainer is less likely to be a transmitter of expert knowledge, and more likely
to be positioned in a more open, collaborative role which promotes self-reflec-
tion. It is pertinent to ask whether some individuals are more suited to the role
of mentor than others. We have possibly all observed how some individuals
seem to possess a natural ability for conveying insights and accumulated wisdom
from their own practice, in ways which help the learner make a shift, and take

ownership of their learning. Responding sensitively to the needs of the learner demands personal qualities of flexibility, tolerance, acceptance and the ability to integrate a broad range of perspectives and levels of awareness about the learners's work and its context. The feelings and attitudes of the mentor towards their own work are probably a critical determinant of their suitability for this formative role. Student placements can often be jeopardised by placing an impressionable and committed learner with a disillusioned and burnt-out staff member. Some staff may unwittingly need to unburden their dissatisfactions and express their own needs for affiliation with the student. It is helpful if other staff support systems can be in place for the experienced staff, as discussed later in the chapter.

Reflective professional learning

It is also necessary to cultivate a shared understanding about some of the different learning processes involved. As well as the prescribed items of knowledge which are set out in the Learning Contracts, students need to be able to develop an awareness of learning as an ongoing process of reflection, intervention and evaluation. This view of the learner as actively involved in her or his own learning and development can be expressed in representations of the learning cycle, as originally presented by Kolb (1970). This helps professional staff to make their own their own cognitive strategies explicit to themselves, and to address different points of view by 'switching frames', as described by Schon (1987). Schon illustrates how professionals at various levels of their development tend to operate on the basis of incorporating the perceived needs of a situation within their own existing system of beliefs, attitudes and values. Developing these aspects of multi-layered thinking and professional judgements requires a framework where the individual can bring some of their own subjective dilemmas into shared discussion about practice.

It is proposed here that effective models of training are those which incorporate the development of cognitive, personal and professional capacity simultaneously, and are likely to mirror the practices involved in work performance. Knowle's (1978) concept of the adult learner, and Schon's (1987) elaboration of the 'professional artistry' of the reflective practitioner both provide models of the development of of these forms of professional education. They imply that adults characteristically draw on their accumulated experiences in problem-solving, reflect on them and re-evaluate them in a new work context.

The psychology of adult learning as described by Knowles (1978) has implications for both course design and for assessment in higher education. Training needs to emphasise the learner's active involvement and learning intentions, and to promote the development of participants as self-directed learners. This means utilising learning activities which are rooted in the learner's existing knowledge and experience, as well as drawing on academic knowledge, which needs to be preceded by problems and issues of concern. The implications for assessment are that adults will assume increasing responsibility for identifying their own learning needs and objectives, and for planning their own learning processes. Self-monitoring with consultation, review and evaluation mechanisms are an important part of initial, as well as of continuing professional development. This 'formative' rather than 'summative' approach to assessment also needs to be reflected in the evaluation frameworks of university-based courses. It directs attention to the important role of 'informal'

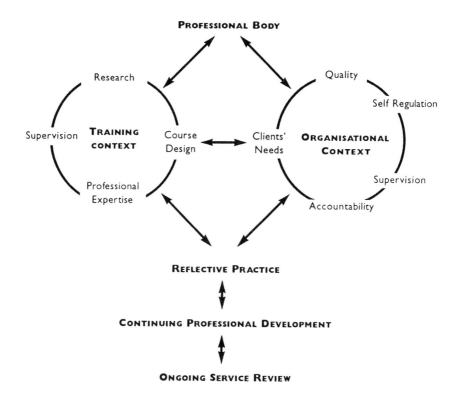

Figure 1.1 Joint influences on reflective professional practice

self-monitoring systems with clearly defined criteria, alongside the more 'formal' written assignments and examination-based assessments.

'Mentoring' and supervision

One of the aims of this chapter is to consider some of these recent developments in mentoring approaches within a broader framework of *supervisory* practices. Although both terms may connote common aims and practices, supervision is more likely to develop some of the interpersonal skills and attributes which are an important part of professional learning. Both approaches may mutually inform each other. However, supervision is often thought to have a more formative significance than other relationships, and to strengthen the possibilities for becoming aware of one's own subjective self. Equally, there may be a strong pull against attempting to do this, which is why consideration of the dynamics of the relationship is considered important in supervision. The terms of 'mentor' and 'supervisor' often refer to different levels of work, and different views about some of the realities which can emerge during the process of reflection. Supervision helps to provide a meta-analytic, superordinate framework to help professionals become reflectively critical about their own practice, and about the context in which they work.

A reflective practitioner in education will need to integrate their skills and professional role within themselves as a person, rather than merely acquiring a set of techniques. This is a complex, ongoing process, and a central requirement of supervisory practices is to provide the necessary conditions for a developmental, lifespan view of learning to occur. For teachers, educational psychologists and other staff groups in education who will be considered in this chapter, a commitment to understanding and helping others is a core feature of the work they undertake. Yet many staff have rarely had an opportunity to apply a model which offers help and understanding within their own training. The supervisory model may go some way in helping to resolve this contradiction.

In both the roles of mentor and supervisor, approaches to the acquisition of skills and the development of understanding may be combined. This is based on a recognition that complex thoughts and feelings about work can be embedded in the supervisory relationship itself, and that skills are not always detachable commodities which can be given away. Practitioners in education exercise their expertise by talking, listening, observing, sharing each other's live practice, giving feedback, shifting perspectives and making decisions at many levels. Many of these aspects of professional learning reside in the creative interplay between different personalities, as well as in considerations of the context and the meanings of the beliefs of the organisation in which supervision is taking place. Considering some of the different roles and responsibilities of different staff groups in education will help to elaborate on the different learning opportunities, and I will do this later in the chapter. It is important to consider opportunities for training first, as this is an area of un-met needs in some groups of practitioners.

As the process of learning and exploration is mutual for both the supervisor and the supervisee, it is important that supervisors receive training for the new and ongoing aspects of being a supervisor, so that they are clear about what they are providing and may prepare for how to function. Without formal training, it is likely that they may feel uncomfortable and ill-equipped, particularly in the way they interpret the authority aspects of the role. Hawkins and Shohet (1991) point out that the commitment to learning from both parties is crucial, and that if the supervisor is not learning from the supervisee, a power or dependency imbalance is likely to occur. In the contemporary context, supervisors of child psychologists may wish to develop their services through specialised work in child advocacy, consultation and organisational development. Experienced practitioners are likely to require models of supervision which mirror their own professional approach and are attached to different models of specialised work.

Training Opportunities in Supervision

One of the few systematic surveys which has been carried out in this country into different aspects of the frequency and availability of supervision for a particular staff group (Lunt 1993) established that supervision as a means of learning and support among educational psychologists was becoming more valued and widespread. The training of supervisors among this group is a more recent development, and tends to take place in the company of clinical psychologists, counsellors, social workers and other mental health workers. While this can be helpful in overcoming some of the biases associated with particular modes of work, there is also a suggestion that more in-depth studies of the needs of particular groups are required, and of the features and applications which are specific to their own practice and agency needs.

Another factor which is possibly related to the limited training opportunities available for supervision in the educational context was the view expressed by the more experienced members of the above sample, that they had earlier negative memories of supervision. Osborne (1993, personal communication), has found that asking participants in a workshop about their own previous experiences of supervision can be a destructive experience, as memories of unfinished business surfaced which then affected their abilities to be more open and receptive to the subsequent training which was offered. This finding is confirmed by Clulow (1994), who also reports a high level of negativity towards supervision in the implementation of a training programme for managers of probation officers. He suggested that the three work-specific issues which helped account for this were ambivalence towards authority, fear of disclosure, and 'problems with triangles' in the client and management structure.

The ambivalence was also likely to be connected with the nature of probation work, and the client group of the service.

When such ambivalence is present in educational settings, it is likely to reflect some of the more didactic or disempowering situations people have encountered in the past. Memories of being reprimanded by an unsympathetic teacher, for instance, can evoke similar cautions in the present. There is often a need to understand some of the anxieties which accompany the supervisory relationship, and how they may be managed so that the relationship remains a productive one.

Dryden and Feltham (1994), for instance, report that supervisees found scrutinising and styles to be unfavourable, and were best helped by a purposeful agenda which included high levels of support. Many people new to supervision may have experienced earlier debilitating effects of teaching and learning in the classroom. They may be reminded of obstacles and interruptions in their cycles of learning and require encouragement to engage in exploratory and associative thinking, as well as intellectual analysis of a more rigorous type.

A *needs analysis* (Binsted 1986) among the staff group, is more likely to help supervision meet a range of personal professional development goals, as well as integrating learning processes with routine work. Given the scarcity of time as a resource in the educational setting, it is important that supervision is demonstrated to be effective in terms of both time and effort which is invested. Such considerations can be addressed directly if training workshops for supervision are set up within the service context.

Negotiated contracts can also help in the setting of goals which will reflect both individual and service level agreements. It is helpful to adopt a systematic approach if supervision is to be introduced into a service, and to pay careful attention to the different phases which are often involved. More experienced staff are likely to need reassurance that supervision is made separate and distinct from other modes of appraisal which may be operating in the heirarchy. This will require careful management of the context of supervision, and detailed thought in the setting up of a supervisory alliance which may offset some of these factors. It raises the likelihood that some professional groups have complex levels of decision-making and accountability within the larger organisational framework which will need to be mirrored in the supervisory approach which is offered.

The 'Primary' Tasks of Supervision

There are several different tasks implicit in the supervisory process. At a meta-evaluative level, the meanings of these tasks will need to be explored in relation to the overall primary tasks of the organisation, and the particular department in which the work is likely to take place. This is particularly important when restructuring takes place, and working practices are modified to take account of ongoing changes. However, it is difficult to use a simple notion of goals in educational organisations, as schools have diffuse and unclear goals. Obholzer (1994) supports this view and emphasises that within an organisation, people may pursue different kinds of primary tasks.

The primary task is defined as the task an institution must perform if it is to survive. Obholzer distinguishes between the:

> analysis of the primary task (official task), the existential primary task (the meaning attached to the task by members), and the phenomenal primary task (the task which may be inferred from behaviour and may be subconscious).
>
> Analysis of the primary task in these terms can highlight discrepancies between what an organisation or group says it sets out to do. (p.30)

Examples of different primary tasks in the educational context are those of preparation for life; nurturing the young; teaching essential skills of literacy and numeracy; managing change; and promoting knowledge and understanding. In supervision, a lack of clarity regarding the primary tasks of the organisation can result in anti-task behaviours being manifest. This is more likely to occur where staff groups already have multiple, overlapping or confused roles and may detract from the potential of the learning processes in supervision.

One central dilemma in the current educational context is defined by Booker in Chapter 3. This is to ensure the survival of services beyond a minimal statutory role. The task is likely to involve adapting valued professional skills by addressing the needs of clients in a more creative way. The examples he draws upon are from an EPS context, which is also embedded within the larger system of the local education authority (LEA). The challenges of considering service development may invoke a sense of implicit and external threat, as there is a need for staff to think through the essential parts of their roles in relation to offering understanding and support to clients who are in distress. It is only when the impact of some of these feelings has been discussed and acknowledged at different levels of the service context, and incorporated with some of the more tangible aspects of statutory work, that supervision can be introduced as an opportunity for development. It is then more likely to be seen as a way of valuing individual staff and helping them to develop new skills. Accountability issues can also be set within more generally agreed and open service goals before they are positioned within the supervisory relationship. As supervision aims to enable and support staff and to maximise the learning which is inherent in practice, it is important to consider the impact of the contemporary organisational climate.

Organisational Learning and Staff Support in Supervision

Rapidly changing legislation, combined with funding restrictions, has had far-reaching effects on organisational structures within local authorities (LAs) and the public services. The effects have already permeated some of the internal 'cultures' of organisations and have affected the climates in which staff work. The introductory chapter outlined some of different levels of the metamorphoses which are occurring – those of society, the organisation, the individual and the group. If training issues are also considered within this extended framework, it is possible to increase awareness and understanding of some of the complex and subtle forces which determine attitudes and responses to work at different levels of the primary tasks.

All of these influences are likely to impinge on supervision, as it is possible to explore in supervision how individuals form an internal model of the working groups and the whole organisation to which they belong. The model of self-review which is implied in supervision can also be paralleled by an organisational capacity for renewal of work and review. Organisations are now increasingly accountable to outside bodies, and are required to evaluate their work in a number of different ways; in league tables, qualitative studies, performance indicators, different modes of appraisal and consumer feedback. If organisations are to meet some of these challenges constructively, they will need to find ways of evaluating which can sustain healthier modes of functioning, whilst enabling continuous learning and mutual work review to take place.

Within the larger enterprise of organisational development, exploration of work 'culture' often provides a way of accessing some of the less tangible influences on working practices and beliefs. McLean and Marshall (1988) have defined 'culture' as 'the collection of traditions, values, policies, beliefs and attitudes that constitute a pervasive context for everything we do and think within an organisation' (p.32). Implicit in descriptions of culture is an awareness that many practices and beliefs are likely to operate below conscious levels of awareness. Helping the organisation to develop a more conscious capacity for working with hidden influences often leads to an acknowledgement that some practices and beliefs serve as important defensive processes which need to be unravelled. The role of the external consultant is an important source of leverage in bringing about approaches to change along some of these dimensions.

Models of management are another significant influence on whether organisations can function as entities of learning and development. Management styles which are based on cultivating the human resources of staff rather than on 'top down' heirarchical approaches are more likely to espouse some of the values and techniques which facilitate ongoing learning and review. Sometimes, a distinction needs to be made between 'leadership' and management. Hirschorn (1988) has illustrated how, paradoxically, management training programmes frequently conceal and disguise the interpersonal dimensions which are essential to an understanding of the tasks of leadership. Deflection of relationship issues is likely to occur as it involves getting in touch with affects and emotions which are uncomfortable, and may provoke anxieties. If managers are to be enabled to address the integration of people and tasks in frequently changing settings, they need ways for considering the potential that all different work situations have for individual and collective learning.

In the current context some of the models of management which have been imported are incongrous for the belief systems and primary tasks within the education and social care professions. This has occurred as LAs have become increasingly tied to marketing models of service delivery which emphasise accountancy, end products and recording systems over the importance of more vital and purposeful interpersonal contacts. Successive legislation has now eroded some of the overarching, mediating and containing functions of the LA as a repository of values and arbitration in relation to the local community. This mirrors an intrinsic dynamic in recent legislation, which is a severance and denial of any link between the individual and society. Yet professionals in the human services are still caught in the paradox of investing their commitment in groups in society who are becoming increasingly vulnerable, disadvantaged and further marginalised by the legislation. They are likely to be struggling with a sense of incompatibility between different ethical and belief systems, excacerbated by an awareness of shrinking funding and an inability to meet the perceived needs of clients.

If practitioners are to be able to work effectively, they need to feel valued so that they can also value their clients and be enabled to provide the best services which are available for them. A key issue which needs to be addressed is how forms of work organisation and tasks can be designed which are compatible with efficacious styles of work for the professional groups involved. Again, this reflects the need for a vehicle for implenting the management of change at an organisational level. Leiper (1994) has highlighted the fact that this process is likely to be managed by placing a 'respected outsider' in relation to the system to help promote staff reflection, encourage innovative action, and to develop the organisation's capacity to think and to sustain change. 'This emphasis on learning, reflection and thought stresses that the problem is not so much obtaining information to assess the current service, but getting the information "into the mind" of the organisation in such a way to enable learning and change.' (p.202). He adds that this requires the development of a spirit of enquiry, and the conditions which provide the necessary security for learning from experience; especially the containment of both personal and organisational anxiety.

The model of supervision which is described here attempts to embrace some of these functions. The supervisory task is distinguished by its main concern with the professional relationships which are formed between the staff and their clients. This assumes that contacts with clients carry important messages about stresses, beliefs and values, which may determine the staff's outlooks and responses to many levels of their work. The supervisory relationship is also likely to mirror fundamental tensions in the organisation's task, and can be a key to understanding institutional processes. As supervisors are likely to be caught up in these processes themselves, they will also need support from senior management in helping to respond to issues which arise. It is suggested that these tensions are explored at the level of senior management, with an outside consultant, before a supervision programme is implented.

Supervision can be a place for considering implementation of the management of change at an organisational level, and for engaging individual staff in an ongoing process of discussion, consultation and review. The changes in climate and policies within which services operate has created a demand for structures to monitor the quality of the staff's work. This may lead to the supervisory function being seen as a vehicle for managing changes in corporate aims, practices and values. As recent legislative changes need to be absorbed and implemented within daily work, staff frequently experience high levels of uncertainty, particularly when the organisation itself is also changing.

These sobering reflections on some of the combined functions of supervision can mean that it is viewed with ambivalence by some staff groups. Some staff have reservations about the use of the term 'supervision', as it can be perceived as implying a lack of competence or equality in the relationship. They may prefer to adopt models of peer-based learning (Topping 1992), which are set within a framework of partnership practices with their clients.

Supervision and the setting
Some of the systems in which supervision is carried out in an educational framework include:

- supervision on an institution-based training course
- supervision on a fieldwork placement, and for the 'practice' elements of some trainings, for example initial teacher training models
- supervision as part of an induction process
- supervision for the ongoing work of experienced practitioners, particularly in the setting up of psychologically-based interventions, and brief, focused therapeutic input for children
- tiered models of supervision, where models of support and understanding are built into 'staged' approaches to work. Support may be offered by one group of practitioners to another, as in the Code of Practice, or at a service level between different sub-systems
- supervision in community-based agencies, for health and social care practitioners concerned with child protection issues.

Each of these contexts will influence the style of supervision which is carried out, the model used and the intervention strategies adopted by the supervisor.

Different Staff Groups and Specialised Work in the Education System

Many practitioners in the education services are likely to have a particular component of their work which is specialised and requires supervision, whilst performing other roles which involve different skills and functions. In the case of teachers, this means that as well as planning for whole class groups, they usually need to develop differentiated curricular approaches for individual children with special educational needs (SEN). They will therefore need training and consultation to help them become aware and informed of the ways in which other staff groups who are based in the community work with these children. The Children Act of 1989 has offered a framework for protecting children in need under the auspices of the LA, and urges closer collaboration and partnership between different groups of professional staff. Multi-agency work of this nature depends upon successful liaison and the ability to adopt multiple perspectives to one's work, and is considered in more detail later in the chapter.

Several staff groups and professional disciplines within the LA are now required to offer approaches based on listening, counselling, and offering support to families and children in need (Jennings 1995). Although some groups, such as educational and clinical psychologists, social workers, counsellors and therapists are likely to have had specialised counselling components in their basic generic trainings, the responsibilities of this work also fall to other personnel. At the pre-school level, it is vital that professionals in the health, education and social services are able to offer an understanding of the emotional and social effects of disability upon the child's longer-term development. Helping the families of 'children in need' to adapt to the consequences of these and similar stresses, and to reshape their lives, is another important area of responsibility. Davis (1993) has developed a systematic approach to establishing close teamwork and collaboration between professionals, by building in training and supervision for health visitors and community medical officers (CMOs).

Work with under fives – 'partnership' models and supervisory practices

Many of the principles of partnership work have been integrated within some aspects of primary school practice since the Plowden recommendations of 1967 (Plowden Report 1967). Understanding of how to translate the general aims and philosophies of partnership into practice in other areas of education is often nebulous and it is difficult for staff to adopt a continuous model of practical help and support to families. In partnership approaches, the model of involvement with clients is based on their need to be understood on their own terms. They are then more likely to be empowered to rely on their own thinking and resources. This client-centred approach is particularly important in work with parents of children under five. Evidence shows that early interventions may help longer-term prognosis, and establish more favourable adaptations for the whole family (Rushton and Davis 1992).

Educational psychologists usually regard partnership approaches as integral to their work with parents of children with SEN (Wolfendale 1988). At the pre-school level, Portage is an extension of a model of parental involvement which is based on negotiations with parents, to help them establish learning objectives for their child within the home setting. Davis (1993) has developed the partnership model in a specific way, based on clear contracting at the outset between parents, health visitors and psychologists. This involves helping parents clarify their own constructions (Kelly 1955), asking them to imagine the futures they would like to foresee, and setting specific behavioural and developmental goals which can then be evaluated.

Supervision is an essential part of the training programmes which are set up to assist staff in developing the requisite counselling techniques and support for their work. Within partnership frameworks, there is usually a tendency to see supervision as group-based, collaborative and set within a clearly negotiated and explicitly structured framework. As well as being advantageous in terms of time, group supervision offers a forum for staff to pool ideas and resources. Peer-based consultation (see McCarthy 1992 for a discussion of these and similar approaches) is likely to take precedence, and the group is able to provide a supportive atmosphere where staff realise that others are facing similar issues. The group can therefore maximise the range of skills and perspectives to consider. This combined model of training and support is often thought to approximate more closely to the particular ethos of partnership practice, where people learn from their colleagues as well as the supervisor.

It often happens that issues of expertise, autonomy, aspects of 'in-depth' understanding and the use of critical, balanced feedback are less likely to be addressed directly in this model. This may be because drawing attention to the 'here and now' experiences in the life of the group is sometimes mistakenly equated with disempowering the members. It is important that the prospective 'supervisor' of such a group is respectful towards the views of participants in selecting a model of group work which attunes with their concerns and perspectives. Nevertheless, it is necessary that the person charged with the responsibility for convening such a group recognises and understands the group dynamics. Group processes including rivalries and sub-groupings can be powerful underlying forces which affect the work of the group, and the group leader needs to understand, contain and address them so that the supervisory process is not undermined.

Teachers and specialised work

Teachers have recently been under considerable pressure to extend their roles. They are now more accountable to a diverse range of different interest groups, including parents and governors, as well as the children in their charge. In managing the requirements of the National Curriculum, they now need to be aware of children's performance and progress relative to the achievements of others within the school, and also within the wider community. The need to adapt the curriculum for some groups of children and the requirement for teachers to work within the staged framework of the Code of Practice present a tremendous challenge in the range of skills and expertise which are involved. Teachers now need to monitor, observe, assess and record children's progress within a consistent framework before they call upon the expertise of psychological and other support services.

One dilemma is that LEAs now have considerably fewer resources for children with SEN, and identifying children with SEN does not help resolve the levels of need and the means of allocating additional resources. Many teachers may experience these pressures as resources have been taken away, and feel deskilled and overwhelmed by the perceived withdrawal of support services when they had been accustomed to relying on them. Changes of this nature in policy can also present opportunities to set up and identify models of good practice within the Code. This is likely to involve different models of co-operation and innovation between psychological services and other external support services and schools. Psychological services, whose hands have been tied with statutory assessment work, are given an opportunity within the Code to deliver training and support programmes in a structured and effective way, so as to empower teachers and reaffirm their skills. Educational psychologists may help to promote and maintain a balance between detailed observation and assessment work, the setting up of focused therapeutic interventions, and the provision of psychological support to teachers. Suitable vehicles for this type of work involve approaches based on developing teachers' psychological insight and understanding of children.

Barrett (1994) has described some ongoing work of this nature with teachers which is based within a consultation model and the sharing of 'case' material. The ability to change perspectives and experience a problem from different angles can be explored through discussion of case material and role play. By considering that the child, parent or teacher might experience issues differently, it is possible to engage with several views of reality, rather than looking for the 'right' approach. Sometimes the teacher can engage with another professional in a consultative and training capacity before requesting their direct help and intervention with a child and family. An educational psychologist (EP) working in this way may perceive their role as that of a facilitator of learning and staff development. By adopting a supervisory capacity, the EP may be able to help a teacher become sensitively aware and sufficiently confident to work with a child in making sense of bewildering experiences. The following example illustrates how a teacher can help a child make sense of issues of loss and bereavement which can arise following the separation of the child's parents.

Case Example

Mrs A had noticed that John, aged eight, returned from his school holidays looking listless and sad, and that he was not concentrating on his school work. His parents had separated some months previously, and John told her that his pet cat had disappeared that weekend. Mrs A was worried about John, as she thought he had not had a proper opportunity to express how much his family life had changed recently. She wondered whether he was blaming himself, as he was expressing a lot of angry feelings in his drawings, in the form of destruction of houses by fire and bombs. She had also noticed that John had become increasingly isolated in the playground.

Mrs A realised that John was confused by the mixture of conflicting feelings he was experiencing. She wondered who might be the most appropriate person to talk with him, and discussed her dilemma in a regular workshop which was convened with the school educational psychologist. The EP supported her in arranging a joint meeting, to which both parents were invited. The parents were both suffering themselves from the loss of familiar routines, and John's mother had been under a lot of pressure at work, leading her to feel preoccupied in the evenings. John's father recognised that the partings with John at the weekends were difficult for them both, and was also concerned to find a way of talking about this with his son.

The adults looked at John's drawings, and realised that he was unable to risk expressing these angry, destructive feelings more directly. Sometimes children fear on a less conscious level that their anger might lead to the other parent leaving and that their security might be shattered. The EP explained that it was important for someone whom John trusted to help him clarify these emotions. Mrs A was supported in setting aside some times to talk with John about his drawings and the feelings they contained. She appreciated the need to emphasise that his feelings were not unusual, but that feeling lost and destroyed, and compensating by being good, were all reactions which children were likely to feel in these circumstances. The teacher subsequently read John a story in which some of these ideas were differentiated. John's parents also found some more open ways of discussing their own distress with him which helped John to feel less burdened by carrying these unacknowledged experiences around by himself. The adults thus took on the capacity safely to contain some of these emotions for John, so that he was less inhibited and more able to move on in his own development.

In the above example, it was particularly important for the teacher to have access to a professional with specialised knowledge and experience of work of this nature. The EP was then able to provide a supportive, supervisory capacity for helping the teacher and parents discuss potentially harmful and damaging feelings in a way which felt safe, both for themselves and the child concerned. Lindsay and Miller (1991) provide a range of examples of different styles of collaborative work between primary school teachers and EPs which aim to promote children's positive mental health and well-being, as well as their successful learning and socialisation.

In the secondary school setting, it is likely that teachers may have designated roles which combine different skills and functions. An example would be an SEN Co-ordinator, or a year head with a counselling role, who would need to combine the dual roles of teaching with small group work or counselling. Jones (1984), writing from the perspective of school counsellor within a comprehensive school, describes some of the challenges and constraints arising from this joint application of roles. One of the tasks is to work towards extending the input of counselling beyond the immediate sphere of activity, so that some of the attitudes associated with counselling become accepted as part of the school 'culture'. This would reflect the joint nature of the primary tasks of education, which are concerned with learning and nurturing. However, sometimes there are incompatibilities with other primary tasks within the institution, which can make it difficult for work to be supported at the appropriate levels.

Noonan (1988) has described how the role of a student counselling service within a university setting can come to represent some of the 'split off' aspects of the ordinary functioning of the institution. In a university, the intellectual tasks and outcomes tend to be given precedence, whilst the emotional ones can represent failure, illness, and disturbance. This is similar to the role of off-site support units in the life of secondary schools. A belief system may operate to support the view that if children whose behaviour is problematic are removed, then other manifestations of these disruptive influences are less likely to surface within the main institution. This process of 'splitting' may disguise a more overt conflict of values between the academic and personal areas of development, which is substituted by stereotyped thinking in such views as 'it's the students who create the problems and who always get away with things'.

A teacher or professional who occupies a specialised role in education may also need to fulfil a consultative capacity, and to try to bring some concerns in their role to the attention of management. This is often more helpful than employing particular short-term strategies which may resolve the more immediate and pressing needs. In supervision, it is possible to address issues of combined role and to think through some of the implications of addressing individual, group, or organisational needs as they arise. It helps the individual concerned to clarify their own particular responses as well as being of benefit to the institution as a whole.

The 'Clinical' Aspects of Supervision

Professional applied psychologists and other staff groups in education have an important concern with the psychological well-being and mental health of children, young people and their parents. This means they offer emotional understanding and support to clients who are in distress. They therefore need an opportunity to discuss their work therapeutically, as well as in terms of the skills they acquire. Prospective supervisors need to be able to understand and contain anxieties which arise from such work, and this involves engaging with clinical perspectives and frameworks.

By its nature, the supervisory relationship is likely to carry intense feelings, and it is important that these are permitted and managed within a framework which is sufficiently containing. Consideration needs to be given to the different levels of the relationship, conceptual understanding and technical practicalities. In order to help with the establishment of safety and mutual trust it is important to protect the way supervision is set up, with attention paid to consistency and reliability of time-keeping. Respect needs to be given to the setting of boundaries of time, space, role and professional task. This can be particularly difficult in the crisis-ridden atmosphere of many busy services. If the supervision times can be set aside as sacrosanct, this can also be a powerful message about the way staff who help others are valued and need similar support systems for themselves.

Although the experience of reflective practice involves being open to intuition and emotion, its structure must also be made explicit so that it can be critically examined and assessed.

Supervision is also a forum where discrepancies can be observed between people's belief systems, espoused theories and 'theories in use' (Argyris and Schon 1987), as the external frame of reference in supervision provides a critical perspective to the ongoing work. There are additional reasons for adopting a more structured approach to work-based supervision in the contemporary climate, where supervision systems may no longer be regarded as optional and informal extras. Some of these reasons include the evaluative aspects of the work. It is important that management-related issues are made explicit so that the supervisee can feel less inhibited about exploring issues of personal and professional development.

Contracts are economical ways of acknowledging that approaches based on skills and competencies are integral to experientially-based approaches. Both models of learning can be successfully intertwined within supervision. If the individual's learning needs can be reviewed and built into the contract at the beginning, this enables a more informed process of discussion and review to occur. It is also easier to keep track of the various strands which are likely to enhance the supervisee's learning. Constructive feedback can be aired about some of the negative feelings arising from the work. These are likely to include feelings about ways in which the supervisory time is used and stresses arising from the work as a whole.

The use of critical feedback

A function of supervision is to be able to address negative feelings and to be able to challenge working practices which are unsatisfactory; in practice, however, this is difficult. Trainees have indicated in some surveys that they value clear feedback, rather than vague reassurances that they are doing well, and paradoxically, it is often the supervisor who finds it difficult to give critical feedback. Ashcroft and Gray (1993) noted that supervisees are more likely to be receptive to feedback if it is presented in a balanced way. Good practice would suggest that feedback is preceded by discussion of some of the positive features of supervisee's work, as this also opens up the way for further exploration. Bion (1974) drew our attention to the need to respect some of the deep uncertainties which are inherent in thinking about how to present negative feedback: 'In every consulting room, there ought to be two rather frightened people' (p.42).

This urges us to stay with states of uncertainty which may arise, as they can often lead to further understanding of some of the negative and unpleasant aspects of work and relationships which can then subsequently be articulated. Sue Holt and Roger Booker in Chapters 9 and 3 respectively of this book both point out that addressing difficult emotions is becoming an increasingly necessary survival skill for professionals who work in inhospitable contexts, and that 'creating a climate in which difficult issues can be thought about and held on to is an important function of the psychologist' (see p.149, Chapter 9).

Agreeing on the context and theoretical models to be discussed in sessions

The supervisor needs to model a capacity to free both parties for the task of exploring new skills and different forms of understanding. Involved in this is the ability to hold uncertainty so that creative thinking can occur, and the challenging if not changing of assumptions. As well as justifying a particular intervention in terms of the strategy and context involved, there is also a need to ask what was valued about the anticipated outcome, and to ask what beliefs underlie these values.

A number of different theoretical models may be drawn upon to contain some of the working styles and assumptions which are involved in supervision. The approaches I am concerned with are the theories of adult learning described earlier (Schon 1987; Knowles 1978), psychodynamic approaches at the individual and organisational levels (Symington 1986; Obholzer and Roberts 1994) and a joint systems approach to working with families and schools (Dowling and Osborne 1994). For further reading about the 'clinical' aspects of supervision, I would recommend Noonan (1983), Hawkins and Shohet (1991), and Dryden and Thorne (1991).

Psychodynamic approaches

Psychodynamic theory is compatible with models of reflective professional practice, as it enriches the possibilities for developing personal and professional capacities simultaneously. There is a key emphasis on considering how people are influenced by less rational feelings and beliefs in their relationships with others at work. If staff become more aware of these constructs and belief patterns on either an individual or a collective level, they become more able to make informed choices between alternative modes of action.

Developments in psychoanalytic theory have led away from earlier mechanistic views of instincts seeking gratification, and now focus more on notions of growth. Alvarez (1992) says: 'Psychoanalytic theory is nowadays better equipped to account for change, development, novelty and mental growth in ways impossible before' (p.8). Bion has pointed out that right from the beginning of life there seems to be a desire for knowledge, and for getting to know someone, which is independent of emotional and bodily needs. This is borne out in recent research by developmental psychologists, who find that the new baby is pre-structured to be keenly interested in her mother's face, voice and pre-speech dialogue with her, as she is in her purely need-satisfying functions (Stern 1985).

To understand the interaction between beliefs, feelings and relationships in a work setting, we need to draw upon the notion that individuals invest emotional significance in people and events from the beginning of life, and throughout subsequent stages of development. All our experiences are filtered through ways in which we structure the world, make sense of it and give it meaning. Psychoanalytic understanding helps to access our implicit theories of the world which govern our actions and value judgements. It can thus lend itself to the goals of reflective practice by helping practitioners clarify the basis of their beliefs, enabling an understanding of themselves based on their own realities and so creating an environment for increased meaningful choice.

As the tasks of supervision are different from those of counselling and therapy, the focus is likely to be on the dynamics which permeate the particular work situation, rather than the supervisee's personality. Psychodynamic theory lends itself to this blend of educative–therapeutic endeavour, as it is immediately concerned with personal relationships, and helps us to look descriptively at issues of process which are inherent in discussions about work.

If these are unacknowledged, the dynamics can be set in motion in other areas of the working context.

Supervision provides a context which readily lends itself to the process of modelling and learning by identification. Interviewing techniques, the setting of personal and professional boundaries, issues of confidentiality, ethical concerns and other aspects of the protection of clients can all be encompassed within the relational structures of supervision. Attitudes of tolerance and acceptance towards the supervisee's mistakes help them to avoid punitive or patronising attitudes towards clients. A capacity to learn from mistakes and to avoid failure can be modelled in sessions, which reassures against the notion that there are absolute answers to everything, and that anxieties must be responded to in a unilateral way. The supervisee needs to learn the importance of sensitivity to others, even when asking innocent questions and seeking fairly neutral information. The concern and empathy of the supervisor when providing critical feedback may serve as a connection with the way anxieties are held, and this is often internalised as a model for future work.

The dynamics aspect of reflection can be extended into a model of how the processes at work between the client and supervisee are paralleled or reflected in the relationship between the supervisor and the supervisee. This acknowledges that sometimes an expression of the problem can occur by re-enactment within the 'here and now' relationship. If the supervisor is able to identify and describe what is happening it may become available to conscious exploration and learning. This phenomenon was originally described by Searles (1955) as 'parallel processing'. It is similar to the process of 'projective identification' in psychoanalytic understanding, where the first person, in wanting to get rid of an unwanted feeling, treats the other person as if that person were experiencing the feeling state.

Parallel processing is similar to 'mirroring' in family systems work, when patterns of interaction suggest different levels of connection, meaning and insight. Hawkins and Shohet (1989) have demonstrated how the idea of 'parallel processing' is helpful in suggesting ways of elucidating the material which is brought to the supervision setting. The moods, responses and feeling states which are identified in the parallel foci of supervision need to be located, so the source of them can be identified and fed back to the supervisee, as in the following example.

Case Example

While you describe your concern about the interview with Lee's mother, I can sense some of the depression in the situation, which is probably affecting Lee's ability to concentrate at school. I notice you haven't said anything about what it's like in the evenings at home. Is anyone there to play with Lee and take an interest, because he seems to spend a lot of his time alone? You've also noticed that in the classroom, when you've observed him. Lee seems to keep a distance from people, and I think you may need to talk with his mother again to explore why Lee is so solitary, and also with the teacher to help him to become more involved at school.

This brief example illustrates an attempt to encourage the supervisee to experience a problem from a different angle, of the parent, child or teacher, rather than looking for the 'right' solution. It leads on to the importance of considering work with families and schools as 'joint systems', as a child's difficulties can be perceived in very different ways by parents and teachers.

Working with contextual issues in supervision: systemic perspectives

In individual, team, organisational and multi-disciplinary settings, the need to be able to understand the world from another's point of view is a key to good professional communication and relationships. Intersystemic understanding, as described by Dowling and Osborne (1994), provides a conceptual framework for considering some of these relationships. Specific techniques involve mirroring; shifting from a linear to a circular perspective; exploring different perspectives in an interactive way; and modelling this with the supervisee within the session. Sometimes it is also necessary to challenge some of the belief systems which are brought to the forum of supervision.

When content material is presented in supervision, it can sometimes be conceptualised in terms of a one-dimensional level of contact between the supervisee and the client. In many situations in the educational setting it is more likely that several levels of work may simultaneously be presented as broader aspects of the context. Usually, the supervisee brings dilemmas which contain the client's needs and values; teachers' and schools' responses and concerns'; the statutory framework involving different agencies; the supervisee's own working models; interventions; and possible future strategies. There is thus a rich and varied scope in how some of the themes and material can be elicited and unpacked.

A family systems model is helpful in moving from the individual model to an interactional one. This helps to emphasise circular causality, and looks to how, rather than why, something may occur. Within this framework, the supervisee may be encouraged to look for broader themes, such as the meanings attached to separation issues when a child has frequently changed schools, rather than to detail the specific content of anxieties. It is particularly important to understand the meanings which underlie the relationship created between the 'problem bearer' and the consequences for the wider system of seeing things that way.

Summarising complex inter-agency interactions may be particularly difficult in the time available in a 'non live' supervisory setting. The supervisor may find it helpful to conceptualise parallel process by focusing on some of the roles of different agencies. For professional staff who work with different agencies concerned with children it is important to bring in some of the other interactions, as these may reveal important clues about the dynamics which are occurring. As described above, the circular framework in a joint systems approach is different from the linear model of the special needs framework. It acknowledges that the child is sometimes caught between two systems and may be 'carrying' issues for the adults involved. The notion of circularity can complement the more linear approach which is epitomised by the idea of a child progressing through the Code of Practice, and can lead to creativity in devising interventions which fit in which the whole context of the referral process.

This model is also helpful in considering issues of interprofessional working which are required by the Children Act of 1989. The need to collaborate can create additional stresses for staff, as the boundaries between different agencies are now less clear. This is partly due to purchaser/provider distinctions and new community care systems in which the responsibilities for service delivery are often blurred. There may be increased competition and rivalry between different sectors and professional groups, sometimes centring upon access to increasingly scarce resources. Supervisors need to be able to recognise these dynamics, as it is easy to become unwittingly caught up in them. Although contexts are rapidly changing, effective supervision can address and capture some of the recurring patterns of interaction.

In the following example, it can be seen how some of the retaliatory fears of staff contributed to the action of excluding a boy from school, with the likelihood that his transition to secondary school could be damaged by the reputation which became attached to him. The educational psychologist involved in the work attempted to shift the focus of concern away from the child by 'reframing' the issues within the wider context of the family and community. Although she was able to prevent Tim from being isolated as the 'problem bearer' and sent to a special school, it was still difficult to protect his reputation before he transferred to secondary school.

Case Example

Tim, aged 11, became the subject of an ongoing 'disagreement' between the school and his family after his parents were involved in an argument with neighbours at a school disco. Towards the end of the evening, a fire was started on the school premises, and Tim's father was blamed for this with apparently little clear evidence. Subsequently, when Tim became involved in a fight in the playground, he was seen as a danger to others and excluded from school.

In listening to this account by the Headteacher, the educational psychologist was struck by the sense that feelings were inflammatory, and becoming out of control. His teachers had already warned the secondary school of Tim's impending arrival, and suggestions were made that a place be found for him in an off-site unit, where he could be safely contained. By helping teaching staff to reconsider the situation from the child's perspective, it became possible to see that

Tim was defending his family, and particularly his unemployed father. Tim was seen as having shown extreme loyalty to his family, particularly as he had not been seen as a potential bully or troublemaker before this particular incident took place. It was necessary to place the incident in the wider context of the neighbourhood relationships with the school, before Tim's part in it could be reframed.

Nevertheless, this process of 'labelling' Tim had damaging repercussions on his subsequent reputation at his new school as word had got around that a troublemaker would be arriving, and Tim was placed on a report sheet in his first week of term.

Some of the important work of containing complex issues and process in supervision may involve helping to ensure that they are not re-enacted between and within the professionals and their different agencies. For example, sometimes children and families may be referred to two or three different agencies for help and advice. This may result in professional rivalries surfacing, so that the client is unwittingly able to play off different aspects of the professional network and to 'split off' their concerns between different aspects of their roles. The client may unconsciously work, for example, to keep educational and medical professionals part, and staff will need to integrate their work if the whole picture is to be kept in mind.

The supervisee may find it helpful to be aware of the different systems, contexts and boundaries around their interactions, as well as the immediate impact of the needs being expressed between teacher and child, or parent and teacher. They may be encouraged to view themselves as a participant-observer, rather than a main player in the situation. The process consists of listening on different levels for the concerns of the other participants, and seeing how the different meanings can contrast and be juxtaposed. Insights which are thus derived can be used to further the understanding of the realities of the child or family.

Kraemar (1988) has illustrated some of the dynamics which occur in the wider system of professionals when issues to do with the management and treatment of child sexual abuse arise. He vividly portrays how thinking mechanisms shut down on a collective and individual basis in response to some of the unthinkable anxieties involved in incest, and the necessity to protect the child. This leads to a form of professional 'stupidity' which undermines the capacity for honesty of judgement and all but the most authentic professional skills:

> one effect of this is oversimplification and polarisation (for/against, us/them, possible/impossible, either/or etc.), so that only half of the opposing ideas can be considered at a time. This split is reflected and repeated in groups and in society as a whole, and makes for inflexible, half-headed thinking at all levels. (p.254)

There is an important and task-oriented role in supervision, and this often needs to be given an overt and work-specific focus by relating it to the broader action framework which surrounds the work. Both participants may experience this as a movement between two different frames, where an explicit, reality-based interventionary style punctuates the listening, reflecting, discussion of feelings, and consideration of predicaments. It is usually the responsibility of the supervisor to use reframing skills in a proactive way, by summarising, asking for examples, encouraging good practice, and asking the supervisee to focus on action plans. By linking some of the content of the session to the client and agency setting, the material becomes translated into practice, and the supervisee is able to feel that her experiences have been managed, contained and legitimised in work with the client. Managing the supervisory boundary in this way, as well as making links between what is happening in the supervisory and work contexts, provides an opportunity for translating action into insights, as well as the other way round.

Personal Professional Development

In the preceding sections, I have shown how personal understanding and resourcefulness is an integral part of establishing effective professional relationships with clients and co-workers. I have illustrated some of the conceptual frameworks which can enrich the possibilities for developing personal and professional capacities simultaneously. As the qualities and attributes required for making effective professional judgements often overlap with personal characteristics, it is sometimes difficult to distinguish between the two areas. For example, qualities involving good communication skills, flexibility, resilience, breadth of vision, open-mindedness, sensitivity, tact, thoughtfulness, enthusiasm and self-motivation all refer to aspects of personal and professional development. If supervision is used to create a parallel with work situations, a model can be provided of the holistic nature of professional expertise (Jennings 1994).

The overlap between personal and professional selves is a central theme of supervisory practice. In the working context of education, this should not mean that supervision is equated with counselling or therapy. A closer approximation between supervision and therapy can occur in some settings, usually in counselling and therapy trainings. The 'personal' element of learning referred to in the educational context does not usually include explicit discussion in a therapeutic sense. It relates to the development of awareness that our own subjective reactions can be a reliable source of understanding children, clients and complex situations. Empathy, sincerity, openness and sensitivity to the needs of others are an important basis for exploring these personal dimensions, and can be developed in supervision.

When supervision is introduced in the educational context, it is likely that the supervisee has previously been exposed to other contrasting styles of learning. Different approaches may emphasise the didactic aspects of the professional role, the empowerment of others, or the 'scientist-practitioner' model. It can therefore seem quite a risk to shift to a focus on personal feelings and vulnerabilities, and it may also seem unsafe to explore the connections between personal and professional life. As being professional can mean suppressing subjective experiences in some contexts, it is often difficult to realise a clear divide and to establish appropriate boundaries. As we are often drawn in to work which relates to our life experiences and individual personal issues, we need to be aware that our personal agendas may spill over into our work with clients. The overlap between personal and professional selves is usually informative, and can energise different contributions.

In supervision, the aim is to help the learner feel more open and resourceful in making these connections for themselves. The route is often through a reflective and critical process, and in helping the trainee to see that they bring more of themselves to interactions at work than they may at first appreciate. Each individual needs to take responsibility for their own part in the supervisory process, and be ready to recognise the learning opportunities as they arise. Adult learners face a complex problem when attending supervision, as they may experience their ignorance and lack of skills. If they are able to develop a secure relationship with their supervisor, an appropriate relationship of dependency emerges between the two which may then protect them from the consequences of their own uncertainties and vulnerabilities. Instead of needing to be in control and become an expert in decision-making, supervisees benefit in the longer term from being open in revealing and clarifying some of the helplessness and disillusion they experience in their work. Understanding personal vulnerabilities can lead to increased understanding of the vulnerabilities of others, particularly of children. Denial of difficulties may mean that supervisees later become overwhelmed by a sense of their own helplessness, leading to rage or frustration. It is important to identify unadmitted feelings so that they are not turned back against the work, the supervisor or the institution.

One of the recurring aspects of concern in supervision is how to recognise and manage stress and 'burn-out'. Awareness of the different manifestations of stress has increased as professionals find themselves trying to function in complex, uncertain environments. In the current climate in education, there are very real threats to professional identity, which are not simply rooted in people's internal preoccupations and anxieties. In the education context, the constant turnarounds of policy and implementation of new initiatives has led to high levels of stress among headteachers, school staff, and other professional groups. Many employers now provide programmes and workshops on how to manage stress, and much has been written on the topic (Palmer 1995). Stress programmes are an important preventative mechanism for maintaining staff morale in the whole organisation, as well as contributing to the health and well-being of staff at an individual level.

The Integration of Learning

In many settings, the weekly supervision slot is a forum for integrating and synthesising different roles and functions. On training courses which are institution-based, and in work settings, some of the connections between different areas of work can be explored, with the supervisee taking some of the responsibility for helping with the integration of learning and experience. On the training course in which I am involved, the supervisory setting is a forum for bringing together some of the disparate styles of knowledge and learning. As the training seeks to instil an intertwining of the practice of skills and techniques in assessment and in-depth work with individual children and families, as well as instructional approaches involved in research and theoretical learning, supervision is necessary to bring together disparate aspects of the work. This prepares trainees to apply specialised knowledge and to develop a wider perspective from which to expand their professional practice.

This approach acknowledges that theory and practice elements need to be wedded together from the outset, and provides a supportive function rather than assuming that the learning is incidental and resides with the trainee. It helps the trainee to develop and nurture their own internal resources for the task, and to develop the confidence to be able increasingly to draw upon this framework in a range of situations. Instead of looking for answers and approaching situations in a routine and stereotyped way, trainees develop ways of finding answers and an understanding of how people bring affects into the process of collaborating at work with others. Supervision helps individuals to increase their capacity for self-management so they can work in a variety of roles by acting upon their environment, rather than by adapting to environmental pressures.

It is important that some staff groups in the educational setting preserve such approaches, which aim to combine a child-centred approach with the capacity to develop broadly-based styles of intervention. Greater accountability to parents in the education setting implies a need to be able to develop practices which reflect concern and understanding for clients in a diverse social context. The qualities required of the reflective professional in education are a high level of flexibility, a capacity to work with uncertainty while retaining the ability to think creatively about future needs and requirements, and the capacity to maintain a breadth of role and vision while interpreting these tasks.

Conclusions

In this chapter, I have tried to draw together some of the many strands involved in supervisory practices in the educational setting. The capacity to stand back and reflect on practice is one of the most important ingredients in developing a professional role. The model of supervision described here helps the practitioner to attend to many levels of the institutional and client-related tasks. Supervision is a formative part of initial training experiences for those trainees who experience the benefits of being inducted in to a professional role in the helping professions. The model of being listened to and having one's anxieties contained is then a basis for being able to replicate this with clients. When staff benefit from supervision, they are able to transfer some of the processes involved to their work at different levels of the educational system. This can then have a greater containing influence in the way tasks are defined at an administrative level, at the whole school level, and at the level of children's behaviour in the classroom.

It is suggested that supervision brings together a greater association between knowledge, skills, values, beliefs, and personal professional understanding. As a model of continuing professional development, supervision can counterbalance some of the more rigidly-imposed tasks and roles which staff need to take up.

We have also seen how the supervisory relationship can help to prepare staff for understanding the changing institutional context, by helping them to attend to the messages conveyed by underlying institutional processes, and integrating these messages within their work. How these are managed affects the organisation's capacity to adapt to a changing environment, and provides the potential for flexibility and development in the future. The survival of services beyond a narrow statutory role is also determined by the psychological health, resilience and capacity for emotional understanding of the individual staff members. The supervisory relationship is able to offer individuals a way of sustaining good practice by helping them to learn from experience and to become less wasteful of their considerable range of knowledge and expertise. Training institutions may have a vital role to play in offering programmes for supervision, so that these practices may become more widely available in the helping professions in the educational setting.

CHAPTER 2

Working with Institutions

Anton Obholzer

Introduction

This chapter sets out some ideas about institutional and group processes. I am not claiming that they should be used to the exclusion of other models; I do hope that they will make a contribution, particularly at times of finding oneself caught up in morale-sapping and infuriating group and institutional processes.

To enable debate and dialogue in this area, it is important to introduce and define two key concepts: institution and primary task. By institution I mean a social configuration that has been arranged to perform a specific social task. This usually means a group or grouping of individuals carrying out roles to service the task. It often also includes premises, a constitution and a variety of other social and legal paraphernalia. Anything from a dahlia-growers club to a nation can qualify as an institution, but for the purposes of this chapter, institution will refer to an organisation in the people field, for example a school, a children's home, a social services department, a clinic, etc. Of late, the term institution has acquired a pejorative quality; this, in my view, is unjustified and is due to confusion between the concept of institution and the process of institutionalisation – a process that is to a degree inevitable, whatever the host body is called.

In order for the institution to carry out its intended social function, its office bearers need to be clear what the primary task of the institution is – that is, the task that the organisation needs to carry out in order to meet its social function. The primary task can obviously change, both over the short term and the longer term, but in order for the institution to be in a position to monitor its results, and thus also its survival, there does need to be ongoing work on defining the primary task.

We thus have institutions to service a variety of societal needs: hospitals to deal with illness, prisons to deal with social deviancy, probation and social services, the church, schools, etc. The primary task of an educational institution would thus be to provide for the education of its members in areas as defined by the task of the school: for example, primary education, or higher, or remedial etc. This of course begs the question of what is meant by education, a point that we shall return to later.

The perceived wisdom is that such institutions are the best way of structuring and organising our work, are most cost effective, supportive of talent, and so forth. I agree with these views, but they do not explain why so much of what goes on in our lives, whether it is at world or governmental level, or on the level of our workplace, is so insane, time-wasting and destructive of our resources. If we look at nuclear issues, environmental issues, third world debt, etc., it is clear that many of the institutions to whom we have delegated management of this planet and its resources do it badly, yet we allow them to continue with hardly a murmur.

The alternative view, therefore, is that we need global structures in order to abrogate our responsibility ('we don't know, let the experts decide!'), even though it is clear that they are making a mess of things. We can then rest in our beds because 'they' can be blamed. Technically, this is known as splitting and projective identification; it means, disown the problem and see it in somebody else. We thus need institutions to foster an illusion that the world is a logical, well-managed place, and that, as long as we play our part as citizens, everything will be all right. The evidence clearly points the opposite way, but that would be disturbing – our response is make-believe, and for that we need structures to operate on our behalf.

The Primary Task and the Process of Transition

One of the key issues relating to the primary task is, who defines the primary task? In a school for example, would it be up to the teachers, the governors, the council, the government, or society? All would claim the right to determine it, all would be subject to a variety of conscious and unconscious forces: personal, group and political.

In looking at these issues, it is essential to understand what the underlying processes and innate difficulties which arise from the nature of the work are; for only if we attend to those issues is there the possibility of reaching an understanding of the primary task that is based on the need of the pupils, clients, patients, consumers, etc., rather than on our own unacknowledged wishes, misperceived as consumer need.

On Specific Institutional Defences

In general, large institutions, for example nations, hold us together by giving us a sense that we know where we belong, that we are better than others, and so forth. Race and sex are also used in this way to counteract a sense of individual isolation and loss. But apart from a general fear of, as Bick (1987) puts it, 'being lost in space' and the institutions to service that fear, there are specific institutions that we need to address and to ward off more specific anxieties. The National Health Service (NHS) is one of these defensive institutions. In unconscious, emotional terms it would be much more aptly named the National Keep Death at Bay Service. All societies have structures, codes and rituals to deal with death, as they have office bearers, be they witch doctors, shamans or health workers. All of them have appropriate 'magic' to keep death at bay. Some of the treatments work, many don't, but we don't want the Service interfered with, lest we come face to face with our fears.

Some of us will have had the experience of having lost our parents. When that happens, we become much more aware of our own mortality – it is as if our parents were a shield between us and death. I believe the same shield effect is served for us by the NHS, and that this in part is the reason why there is resistance to the government's proposals for change.

If the health service stands for a Defence against Death, what does the education service stand for in these terms? All societies have an 'education service' in the broadest sense. It is the system or service that the society has in order to teach its citizens to use the tools they need to survive. In some societies that would be learning to throw a boomerang, in others to shoot with a bow and arrow, in ours it is learning to read and write. From an unconscious point of view the education service is therefore intended as a device to shield us from the risk of going under in our society. By definition it is also therefore an institution that is supposed to cope with (whether by encouragement or denial) competition and rivalry. In this regard the debate about which nation has the best education system is in fact a debate about who will survive and who will end up against the wall.

I started by outlining that we need institutions into which we can project 'unwanted' or 'difficult to cope with' aspects of ourselves. One such quality might be a sense of responsibility for bringing up our children and being responsible for their learning the skills needed to survive in society. Put this way, it can obviously seem a fearsome responsibility.

If we can put that whole responsibility on 'them', the office bearers of the system, that of course lets us off the hook. For the office bearers this is a double-edged sword. On the one hand, they welcome the power that comes with the job, on the other hand the responsibility is fearsome, particularly as the expectations cannot be met.

Just as consultants in the health service are often too busy to talk to patients to tell them bad news – bad news also from their own point of view in as much as it points up their fallibility – so also in the field of education.

Education systems are also geared to deal with other denied, and therefore difficult, aspects of adult–child and adolescent transactions. Envy in adults of their children's qualities and opportunities is often denied by adults, and instead dealt with by the creation of educational systems that can be hard on the children and not obviously beneficial to the learning process. The 'making a man of him' type of systems are an example of this.

Adults quite often have difficulty with dealing with their own, often unresolved, child parts, of which their children are frequently a powerful and disturbing reminder. Similarly, race and ethnicity issues, disability, the state of being a refugee, and others, often occur in the educational system and need to be addressed when the self-same problems are 'swept under the carpet' in society at large.

Anxieties Arising From the Work

This concept relates to the particular anxieties arising from the work, and how they affect the conduct of all in the institution. The idea is a simple one related to hazards inherent in certain industries. Mad as a hatter, for example, comes from the fact that mercury was used in the production of felt for the making of hats, and that the mercury fumes had toxic effects with mental symptoms. Similarly, miners lung, tennis elbow, etc. refer to hazards associated with certain activities.

It is therefore no great leap to assume that workers in the helping and educating professions might develop symptoms as a result of work hazards. You will all have read about and have experienced stress in the workplace. Staff burn-out too is a familiar concept, indeed, one that with luck and harnessing can lead to a change of profession.

But what are the factors causing stress, and why does it help to know about them? Without knowing the factors, it is not possible to put into place systems that could deal with the stress, nor is it possible to recognise counterproductive systems that have arisen in an unplanned and unconscious way to deal with the stress.

The best known writers in this field are Elliott Jaques who was Professor at Brunel University, and Isobel Menzies-Lyth (1988a) who applied these ideas to a study of nursing. She was called in to do this study because there was an ongoing heavy loss of student nurses from training programmes. Her study set out to find the causes of this. She found that those in authority presented the system of nurse training as a logical one determined by the clinical needs of patients and the training needs of student nurses. But the more she studied the system, the more she found it riddled with inconsistencies and illogicalities. Eventually, she formed an alternative hypothesis, namely that the system was structured as a defence against the anxieties arising from the work.

Close contact with seriously ill patients evoked the most primitive anxieties. Breaking the contact with patients into tasks, for example, taking temperature, giving drugs, meant that nurses had part-contact with many people, but no closeness with anyone. It was therefore more bearable for them (although it led to people being described as parts – the fracture on the left, the liver in ward G2, etc.). The end result of this system, which had been unconsciously determined by the defensive needs of the staff, was a system that depersonalised patients and staff, that did not locate or enable the underlying anxieties to be addressed, and therefore led to substantial staff demoralisation and turnover.

Could a similar process be at play in the education field? An example comes to mind. Many years ago, I worked as a consultant in a school for the physically disabled. The general atmosphere was one of denial. The Head welcomed me with 'in this school we treat all children as normal'. While at some level an admirable statement, at another it encapsulated the denial of the problems and hampered all attempts to deal with them. The teachers were particularly demoralised. After a time, I understood that they had been trained and operated on the belief that, if they did their best and their pupils more or less cooperated, then the end result would be most pupils making their way into society with the skills needed to succeed.

The reality, however, was quite different. Very few children managed the transition into the outside world; many went straight from school into sheltered work and accommodation, others – those suffering from degenerative diseases – died. The teachers' unspoken, but clear, expectation of helping fledglings out of the nest was not met. Their way of dealing with this was on the one hand absenteeism, depression, illness, demoralisation, and on the other a changing of the task from school to day-centre with an ever increasing age range.

In how many ordinary schools are the expectations and ideals that one has as a trainee in the field of education met? How many children fulfil their own and our expectations? One way of reducing the pain arising from this disappointment is to alter the primary task. A primary task of achieving basic skills in education is thus subtly modified to, for example, 'life skills'. I am not suggesting that 'life skills' are not important; I am suggesting that a move to something more achievable is sometimes determined by the difficulty in reaching the stated goals. And in subtly changing the goals, we then lose the opportunity of assessing whether goals as set are realistic and how our approach to them needs to be altered. In other words, our falling into unconscious defensive manoeuvres interferes with our capacity to review he task and alter the system accordingly. From an insider's point of view this process is often very difficult to detect.

Groups and institutions accept newcomers and mould them to their institutional ways of doing things. This includes moulding them to their particular version of institutional defences. After a time the newcomer is told something like, 'you're really fitting in well, it feels as if you've always been one of us'. Whilst intended as a compliment, it actually means, 'welcome, you're now as institutionalised as the rest of us'. This, in turn, means that the individual has to a large degree lost their capacity to be detached and to see things from an outside perspective.

Outsiders such as educational psychologists therefore have a much better chance of having a detached perspective. They are part of, yet not part of the system; standing on the boundary, as it were. My favourite definition of consultancy is 'licensed stupidity'. Being on the boundary, and not of the system, means the outsiders can ask a lot of questions without supposedly already knowing the answers. They are thus in an excellent position to work at the question of whether the organisation is essentially working on-task or off-task. By on-task, I mean it having clear goals and ways of assessing results, against the baseline of the primary task; by off-task I mean in the grip of unconscious defensive processes as outlined above.

Towards a More 'On-Task' Institutional Functioning

Certain structures and approaches make for on-task work by a process of minimizing defensive patterns on the part of the staff.

The following are essential:

1. Clarity of task.

2. Clarity of organisational structure.

3. Clarity of time boundaries.

4. A staff venue to locate and work on the innate emotional difficulties arising from the work.

5. An opportunity for ideas arising from (4) above to be transformed into institutional policy.

If the above criteria are met, there is a good chance of the institution working on and remaining on-task. Even then, good leadership is required for there to be a process of a functioning whole, of a sense of 'us' incorporating all staff and all pupils. In the absence of such leadership, the risk is of having an organisation with clear provinces, but no overall identity with which to identify.

An organisation in which there is little or no clarity of task, authority boundary, and no clear venue, is one in which no key issues can be located or addressed. Having this sort of structure is of course often intended for that very purpose, and it is seen as the lesser of two evils – rather carry on struggling in the morass than see daylight with all the problems it brings. For ultimately daylight shows that the educational system has been delegated the whole task of preparing the nation, and possibly collectively the world, for a future that is impossible to foresee. So, from that point of view falling into never-ending staff squabbles seems preferable – although as shown it is this avoidance of key issues that leads to staff burn-out.

Group Processes in Institutions

The usual approach to looking at institutional problems is to see them in terms of personalities. Thus, all institutions have an 'impossible' person on their pay roll. The nature and degree of the 'impossible' behaviour may vary from institution to institution, but not the presence of this phenomenon. The commonly held view is that the person is 'difficult', 'ill', 'disturbed' – the adjective varies depending on the institution. What does not vary is the belief that that person is responsible. With it, goes the belief that if only that person would resign, leave, retire, get sacked, then the situation would be fine and the institution would revert to 'normal' behaviour. This view is very attractive and therefore hard to resist and tempting to act upon. The only problem with the theory is that it does not fit the facts. It is a common observation that no sooner has one 'difficult' person left, than another one appears – either by an outsider being hired or by an insider 'volunteering' for the task.

In thinking about this phenomenon at the Tavistock Clinic, we found group concepts helpful in understanding and managing the situation. Instead of X having a problem personality, it becomes at an unconscious level something like the following: 'Wanted, volunteer required to voice the difficult, disowned, anti-task elements of the staff. Only candidates with suitably difficult person- alities should apply'. In this version, the difficult person represents an aspect of all staff. Viewed from this perspective, it means that the problem has to be tackled on a group and institutional level as related to the work. This way, some headway can be made – what's more, the 'difficult' person can be helped out of the role by other members of staff 'withdrawing', as it were, their projections. It therefore moves psychologically and institutionally speaking from 'It's not us, it's him, isn't it shocking how he is behaving', to 'We all have ambivalent feelings which we need to own, and those that relate to our work in the institution are particularly relevant for us to take up at work'.

Very often, the very nature of the work of the institution determines the type and style of the problem that the 'difficult' person on the staff group is asked to enact. Thus, a fight in a staff group of an adolescent unit between, say, two members of staff about authority, one being 'laid back' one being 'authori- tarian' might very well at an unconscious level re-enact the struggles within the adolescent psyche, the adolescent and the adolescent cohort about learning to manage themselves, coping with authority, finding their own authority within themselves, and so forth.

One hopes that an intervention along these lines would draw all members of staff back into role and enable them to resume work on the primary task of the institution. By contrast, an intervention focusing solely on the difficulties of the two members of staff, in my view, would only produce an (unsuccessful) therapy group or a road show for a vicarious audience. There is an additional factor that needs to be considered here. As mentioned earlier in this chapter, my view is that the tasks we are set or set ourselves in the caring and educational professions are difficult and frustrating ones. Freud (1925) in the foreword to Aichhorn's book on adolescence wrote, 'At an early stage I had accepted the bon mot which lays down that there are three impossible professions, educating, healing and governing'.

Given this reality, it is not unexpected that we should try and turn away from our work into something less exhausting. At times, this turns out to be endless meetings and administrative tasks. They may be awful, but they are regarded as more bearable than the alternative – work at the emotional coalface.

Group processes in institutions are, however, not confined to intra-group stresses as described above, but also manifest themselves as inter-group processes. These might refer to different sites, or different age groups, or different levels of competence. Often they are also outlets for racism and sexism that is then acted out by intergroup tensions rather than dealt with as an overall institutional, and thus societal, problem.

An example would thus be of using, say, a group of racist youths in a school as the focus of racism that needs to be dealt with, and in the process disowning less obvious racist practices elsewhere in the school.

Application to our Everyday Work

How can this system be usefully applied to your everyday work? I think it applies at three levels.

At its most basic, it is a code of understanding which helps us to reduce the work related stress pressures on us: understanding that one is treated the way one is on account of one's role, on account of crossing the boundary, being an outsider, having unrealistic powers projected into one, and so forth, and that this is all part of standard human institutional behaviour. Understanding along these lines helps to clarify that the way you are treated is not personal, that it is *not* an attack on you as an individual. Being at the receiving end of these processes is still uncomfortable, but it is better than feeling and reacting as if one were personally responsible/attacked.

In other words, it is a counterpart of the learning that psychotherapy trainees have to take on board – that when a patient makes it clear they hate you or think you're marvellous, it is probably *not* you; they are re-enacting their accustomed way of relating to people with you – the transference. So, at its primary level such understanding helps to protect you in role. At a further level it helps you to understand institutional behaviour and referrals in context, and enables you to think about what behaviour might represent on behalf of an institution. The following example illustrates some of these processes:

Case Example

An educational psychologist kept getting regular referrals from a comprehensive school of boys who were accused of bullying. All the referrals were sound enough, and all could be dealt with along traditional lines. What was noticeable, however, was what a steady stream of bullies were referred and how few, proportionally speaking, other referrals there were from this school.

A consultation with an outside consultant raised the possibility that these referrals might be saying something, not only about the children but about the system as such. It might be put as an unconscious message saying, 'we have a problem of bullying – and therefore of authority in this school'. In this instance, the most flawed in this regard, and therefore vulnerable members (the referred boys) were used to deliver this message.

Understanding that those referred might not only have a personal problem, but might also be representing something on behalf of the institution, means they might be dealt with differently. It also means that work with the institution to take back its projections and deal with the problem at institutional level becomes at least as important a part of the work as assessing and processing the referrals.

'This boy is a thief and needs treatment or placement' thus becomes, 'This boy has problems with thieving. He represents the tip of the iceberg of this problem in the school – a problem that in varying degrees affects all members of the institution, pupils and staff alike. Could you please help.'

At the third level, the understanding gives one the opportunity to intervene at an organisational level. Thus, at this stage the boy may or may not be seen, but the focus is as much on working with the staff as with the pupils. The assumption underlying this stance is that the referrals are made because they represent an institutional 'blind spot' that the staff cannot deal with. Helping them with the blind spot means that they themselves can to an increasing degree deal with the issues. Which brings me to complete the story of the stream of bullies from the comprehensive:

Further work showed that there was a severe management problem, with the headmaster being perceived as a bully, and in reality managing the school by a technique of bullying. Once this came out into the open, such issues were, with the help of general and role consultancy, discussed in the staff group, with a resultant dramatic reduction in referrals for bullying.

Conclusion

Change and resistance to change

The education field as such is beset by many proposals for change, as are many other institutions in the public sector. Some thought ought therefore to be given to the anxieties and resistances arising from this process of change.

One way of looking at and summarising this chapter so far is to say that all the systems we have in place – institutions as such, educational institutions, the way we work, etc. – are all ways of protecting ourselves from the most primitive anxiety: that of being lost, alone, not knowing. In this regard, someone once defined a theory as a system for containing anxiety.

If it is true that our working practices are bulwarks against anxiety, then any change of working practice must be a breach in our defences and release an enormous amount of stress and anxiety.

This is the first thing that needs to be recognised – that it is *normal* to have anxiety associated with change, even if the change is agreed by all.

It follows that those who say that change can be without stress are not only wrong, but harmfully wrong, because in denying anxiety they do not allow for the development of systems to cope with the stress of change.

We all know that personal bereavement is stressful, that is causes depression and anger and, on average, lasts about eighteen months before some sort of acceptance of the situation occurs.

Yet, change in working practice too is a form of bereavement. We need to lose our old way of doing things and accept the new way – the new professional identity.

Many of the present day changes that educational institutions are expected to deal with embody such elements of change of identity, and therefore trigger anxiety, resistance and bereavement. An example would be the change of identity arising from the league tables of school performance. The schools losing out would be caught in a spiralling process of mourning their previous identity, coupled with a self-perpetuating large group process in its referral network that would be very hard to break without a substantial input of resources and personnel consultancy.

CHAPTER 3

An Organisational Response to Survival

Roger Booker

Introduction

The central dilemma addressed in this chapter is how to ensure as far as possible the survival of one's own organisation when it is embedded in a larger organisational context which is contracting and transforming in response to massive external financial and legislative pressures. This is the case for all public sector organisations at present, and for some there is an additional subtext to deny them a future role altogether (which is the present context for local education authority (LEA) psychological services). By survival I mean not merely maintaining the size of the service but also its role and the values that are inherent to fulfilling this and which give meaning to the individual staff who work within it.

What is clear is that any system caught up in such a context will not escape significant change itself. Survival will be contingent upon the system accommodating and anticipating the turbulence of its external environment. Constraints will be imposed which will be inescapable, however imaginative and flexible the organisation becomes. The goal is to find ways of minimising the negative impact of these constraints, transforming them where possible into positive areas of development and creating niches where the organisation's expertise and skills are uniquely valued.

Perhaps the first thing to say is that there is no *guarantee* of survival. The literature on public service management may point to many examples of good practice out of which survival strategies emerge. It remains the case, however, that many organisations have disappeared as much because they are 'unaffordable' as because they have not had the requisite organisational and management skills at their disposal. Child guidance units in many local authorities are a case in point. 'Affordability' is of course a value-laden concept which reflects priorities as well as budgets. Nevertheless, it is doubtful that many of these services would have survived, whatever strategies they had adopted. For a long time many professionals have believed that they were untouchable; their service was one in which they had such a positive investment that it was inconceivable to them that this would not be understood and shared by those outside who manage the resources. It is not until this fallacy is confronted in reality that ideas really shift. For those services that have had the space, imagination and initiative to adapt, survival has been possible, albeit in a somewhat different form. It will almost certainly have been at the cost of shedding a variety of attitudes concerned with what the *professionals* feel is right for them and their clients, in favour of a balance that asserts the rights of the fundholders and clients to determine more the service received.

At present, the bottom line for most local authorities is not just whether a service is statutory or not but what is the minimum statutory service that can be provided without inviting legal redress or other consequences, the cost of which outweighs the savings made by further reductions. Thus, a local education authority might wish to be seen to meet the needs of its schools so as to prevent the opting out for grant maintained status of significant numbers of them and the consequent removal of a disproportionate share of the LEA budget. It will therefore ensure that the needs of headteachers are very carefully attended to. It will similarly maintain staffing within its special educational needs section to ensure that statutory assessments are completed sufficiently quickly to avoid parental action through the Ombudsman, the cost of which could be the annual salary of an administrator. (Such sections are an example of a niche being created through external circumstances which can lead to growth while all around is in retrenchment.)

From my own perspective, the expertise and skills of psychological services in the educational context have some distinct advantages. Their professional discipline renders them unique within an LEA. What is important is for them to act in a way that demonstrates this professional uniqueness: producing a service that cannot be matched by other, cheaper groups, such as special needs support teams. They have a further advantage in being written in to education legislation in such a way as to make it in the interests of the LEA to employ them rather than to buy in equivalent expertise. The task for psychological services in the medium term is to survive beyond some minimum level that restricts them to providing the LEA with statutory advice based upon single event summative assessment. Such a retrenchment would remove all opportunities for ongoing consultative and developmental work with schools and parents where many of the psychologist's most valued skills are deployed and developed. It will be noted, however, that this aspiration comes primarily from the professional and not the client; for it to happen, the client will have to be convinced that there is sufficient added value to pay for it.

Survival or otherwise can therefore be dependent upon external factors over which the organisation has little control: the legislative framework, the statutory bottom line and the penalties of non compliance; also any residual political imperatives that might have survived the budget setting process. The first task in developing a strategy is to determine what these factors are and identify the parameters within which the option for survival operates. The size of this potential space will in part determine the strategy one adopts. In the following sections the underlying assumption is that there *is* enough space to warrant considerable investment in analysis and strategy development. These proposals may, for some, be water under the bridge and reflect current practice; others may feel that what is described is in place but implicitly rather than explicitly. To those in the first group I would say: splendid, fill in any gaps, evaluate what you are doing and look for what we might both have omitted. To those in the second group I would advise caution, since I never cease to be surprised by the differences that emerge during explicit discussion of issues when before there had been an illusion of congruence.

I am writing from the perspective of a service manager and from the belief that the informed and proactive behaviour of service management is an essential ingredient for organisational survival. The other essential is the consent and commitment of staff. Professional service management, particularly in the helping professions, is a new discipline and many managers are proceeding on an ad hoc basis with little of a clear framework within which to act. The following section examines three strands of a conceptual framework for management which seems to me a basis for informed action rather than ad hoc reaction.

The first strand is that of keeping in touch with the language and concepts of the profession and not being overtaken by a disjunctive management ethos. This is essential if the manager is to keep closely in touch with the professional experience of staff while dealing with the non professional world who will wish to evaluate his service using criteria which do not fit readily alongside the language of the profession – psychology, in my case. He will be facilitated in this by finding a conceptual framework that is able to embrace both in a non trivial way. The second strand involves the definition of organisational role and boundaries as a means of focusing action and containing the anxieties of staff and clients when beset with constant change. The third strand addresses the needs of clients and of identifying the key clients who will most promote survival. Following this I shall consider the needs of staff in such circumstances and the management of the internal world of the service. Then I shall look at accountability and the vexed question of quality, objectives setting and performance indicators; this brings us to communication with the external environment, returning to the discussion of language and concepts started in the next section. The final comments will be concerned with the plight of the service manger in these difficult times!

A Framework for Management

Keeping hold of the professional within oneself

An immediate problem for the manager of a professional service is how to integrate the various concepts and language of 'management theory' with those of her profession, of the wider context of which her service is a part, and of the client groups and other stakeholders. Most professionals are confronted daily with the need to integrate 'their' concepts with those of clients and stakeholders. The language of management adds a further dimension. How, for example, can we accommodate in a single framework 'external' concepts such as performance indicators, objectives, strategic plans and market testing with 'internal' concepts such as anxiety, projection, self-esteem and understanding? There often seems an imperative to adopt an 'either/or' stance towards this, to treat the languages as so separate that one has to move in and out of them with no sense of continuity or mapping of one on to the other. I wonder how much this is an attitude of mind rather than an inherent conceptual difficulty. It is certainly the case that it has been possible to reconcile internal and external in conventional psychological practice when working with the external consequences of internal states. For example, self-esteem, anxiety or understanding are frequently evaluated in terms of observable behaviour. Psychologists in education have led the way in encouraging teachers to seek evidence of understanding and change in pupils through the external evidence of performances.

The aspect of this which seems to be most difficult is the *simultaneous holding of the internal and the external.* There is a strong tendency to become, according to temperament and opportunity, predominantly focused on one or the other. This creates a frame of mind whereby it becomes very difficult to work with the other. Constant engagement in case work and exposure to stress and anxiety in clients leads to an inevitable and (not always) appropriate concern with the internal and qualitative. Constant exposure to budgets, staffing quotas, service objectives and strategic plans leads to an inevitable and (not always) appropriate preoccupation with the external and quantitative. In the same way that practitioners have had to struggle to maintain a balance between the internal and the external, so do managers of services have to maintain an identical balance. It is, however, applied at different levels. For management the internal refers not only to the psychological constructs that the service might employ but also the contents of the system that is the service. It also refers to the internal constructs that will be used by the external world; these are mostly cognitive and rational – such as image, reputation, valuing – and essential to keep track of (which is not to deny the possibility of non-rational projections and attributions onto a service from the outside, of which more later). External refers to the nature of the professional constructs in use, the world outside the service and the constructs in use there.

In a later section I shall discuss the extent to which it is possible to externalise the internal, 'immeasurable' aspects of professional service work and meet, to a degree, the demand for quantitative as well as qualitative data presented so forcefully by the accountability culture within which we now operate. Here I want to emphasise the mirror image of this: representing those external constructs alongside the professional ones that will predominate inside the service.

If the manager is to avoid the trap of either/or thinking she has to maintain close touch with her professional self – to keep alive the internalised psychologist, social worker, therapist etc. There are two levels at which it is essential to work in close proximity to this. First, in relation to the interactions of staff with clients that are the essence of the service – its 'moments of truth' (Norman 1984) second; in relation to the interactions between staff that constitute the culture of the service. A manager makes sense of these interactions through the exercise of similar skills to those used as a practitioner. Indeed, if she does not do this, staff are likely to perceive a disjunction between their own constructs and those of management, with a consequent strain on the system. Interactions between management and staff have to be homologous to those between staff and clients (Reed and Palmer 1972). The manager retains a firm grasp of the professional within herself. In the case of my own discipline, on becoming a manager the 'main grade' professional ceases to be psychologist working in an educational context and becomes an educationalist with a professional experience in psychology (Reed 1987). Similar assumptions of process, autonomy, learning and development operate. These assumptions can clash with those held by management outside the service which too often expect instant change, deny process and emphasise control.

Defining roles and boundaries

I have described elsewhere (Booker 1991a) a possible framework deriving from the Grubb Institute (1988) that enables psychological service managers to retain an idea of themselves as psychologists and educationalists, holding central the values that are fundamental to service identity and culture. While also attending to hard-edged performance issues this *purposive* model views an organisation as an open system in interaction with its environment, some key needs of which it has to satisfy in order to release the resources for its continuance to be guaranteed. An indespensible task for management is to establish what these key needs are and to formulate them as service outputs in a way that is understood both by external line management and by members of the service. A systems framework embodies concepts of boundary and role and construes management as a regulatory function at the system boundary rather than as a controller of individuals. In theory it liberates individuals to create their own boundaries and roles in the context of a system whose own are well defined. It allows for a psychological conception of role which is an idea in the mind of the individual rather than a repertoire of duties or behaviours. It similarly views the organisation as an idea in the minds of those who are part of it rather than the totality of its buildings, physical processes, staff and resources.

The task for management is to ensure that there is sufficient clarity and structure for individuals to engage in this creative process of defining their own roles and boundaries; and also that there is sufficient identification with the aim of the service for them to be energised. This leads to the well documented practice of deriving an aim statement or mission through which the key outputs of the service can be identified alongside the internal processes or core tasks that are required to produce them. Despite the extensive rhetoric surrounding aim statements there are, in my experience, many services that do not have them; neither do they have an explicit account of the key processes that the service engages in to ensure its outputs are addressing the aim. This can only lead to uncertainty and heightened anxiety when so much around is unpredictable.

A good aim statement is an example of the positive value of constraints because it defines the outputs and processes of the organisation and by implication determines what it does *not* do. This can be of immense value to professionals under pressure to respond to escalating demands, in large part created by the turbulence around. In my own case, service line management in the LEA was concerned that schools as institutions should have priority as clients. Headteachers were seen as principal stakeholders in the newly created Authority.

In consequence the aim statement of the Greenwich Education Psychological Service (GEPS) focuses on developing the skills of teachers in meeting the special educational needs of pupils. We make it clear that we do not offer a direct service to pupils, parents or other professionals. Our service to schools is defined through a service level agreement which embodies a time contract as well as broad expectations of quality and redress. Through this staff are able to set their own boundaries and direct their energies more positively in the knowledge that management will support them should these be challenged. These system boundaries act as a container of uncertainty, not just for staff but also for clients because they affirm structure and continuity. Saying no can be held in the context of saying yes to other things. Most significantly, these decisions are seen as not arbitrary but consequent upon wider policy that is not, however, immutable.

The possibility of policy change is an essential element to structure when there is so much external change. Meaningful adaptation to this must take place. However, if individuals are to feel contained by the organisational structure this adaptation itself has to be perceived as controlled. This implies not just an input to decision-making by clients and staff but a recognised *process* for deciding and implementing change. This is essentially the main concern of strategic planning (Bryson 1988) which assumes constant external change and attempts to manage this through a cyclic definition of strategic issues out of which emerge objectives for a defined period (GEPS 1993). It is in this process that the double loop learning described by Argyris (1990) can most readily occur.

Such end products are highly rational and external; however, the processes by which they are produced should be far from it! It is these that allow the non-rational to be exercised and to fuel positively the rational outcome rather than being suppressed and undermining it (consciously or unconsciously) after decisions have been taken. Creating the structures for this takes up staff time if the necessary participation is to be achieved. It is often difficult for outsiders to see this, particularly managers in top-down decision-making heirarchies. Service management has a difficult task in balancing out the need to create this time while demonstrating efficiency in service delivery. Furthermore, any measure of success in achieving it carries the risk of eliciting envy and negative projections from those who have to survive without it. In the case of psychological services this applies particularly to schools where experience of unremitting change has led to widespread feelings of persecution and negative self-worth.

Identifying and serving the client

I have outlined a model that requires management to identify the key needs of the 'context' which it can meet so as to release the resources it needs to survive. This can be a complicated issue since the context is itself a set of inter-related systems, and defining one of these as the key client has an immediate impact on the others. In the case of psychological services in education the key stakeholder is the council who funds the service. In Greenwich the council defined two primary client groups, headteachers and itself in the form of the Education Department. There is a common ultimate client – the child in school or about to go to school. These two primary clients are not of equal value to the Psychological Service since only one is the fundholder – the council. Furthermore, the arena for work (special educational needs) is one of the very few where the council has legal responsibilities which override those of individual headteachers. The Service has to go about meeting the needs of these two clients in such a way as to acknowledge the greater power of the council (through the Education Department) as paymaster and decision maker.

When there is more than one primary client and they are interdependent in the way that schools and the LEA are, it is inevitable that there will be occasions when their respective demands of the service will be in conflict. The key element of strategy here is to operate so that these areas of conflict are reduced to a minimum; and when inevitable to state clearly a position that acknowledges where the greater power lies. A typical example would relate to how time is used. If the LEA needs psychological advice within a statutorily defined time it will wish this to take priority over alternative work that the school may value more highly. In this situation it is important for the Service to have clarified the limits to its independence, given the LEA's role as paymaster. It is difficult to carry professional credibility if the Service is perceived as a tool of the LEA. Given the central role of resourcing in the meeting of special educational needs, one way to achieve greater independence is to make the needs of pupils a focus, rather than the provision to meet them; in this way decisions about resourcing are placed clearly with either the school or the LEA and not with the Psychological Service. Operating as a gatekeeper to resources may do much to elicit demand from schools; however it is a superficial demand which is vulnerable to resources being cut. Furthermore it acts against the interests of the other primary client which may wish to preserve resources. It is therefore in the interests of the Service to sidestep the resources issue as much as possible and focus on other areas which also happen to be those that the Service values most of itself: enabling, supporting, and clarifying needs and intervention strategies within an existing resource arrangement.

These three strands of keeping in touch with one's own professional base, defining roles and boundaries through strategic planning and identifying key clients and working to satisfy their needs to release the resources for survival are the principal elements of a management framework which balances the inner and the outer, places an emphasis on purpose and identifies the management role as essentially regulatory and supportive of staff who have to deliver to the client. The following section considers two ways in which this support to staff can best be delivered.

The Needs of Staff

There is a good case to be made that the development of a service culture where 'customer care' is the predominant theme has led to a neglect of the needs of service providers in the continual struggle for greater efficiency and quality. This is not to deny the legitimacy of this struggle, but to state that there is a limit to which management can become locked into concerns with external outputs and lose track of internal processes – within individuals and within the organisation as an interacting whole. The inevitable consequence of not attending to this is dissociation by staff in the form of lack of commitment and imagination or, in extreme instances, of opting out, prolonged illness or overt rejection of the aims of the service. Two critical ingredients to forestall this are effective communication systems within the service and the provision of opportunities for development.

Communication

Communication is too frequently regarded as an issue of information transmission, usually in one direction – top-down. When so much is changing it is essential for people to know where they stand and management has a prime responsibility to ensure that they do know this. However, it also means listening, not just to facts from the point of service delivery but also to feelings. For these

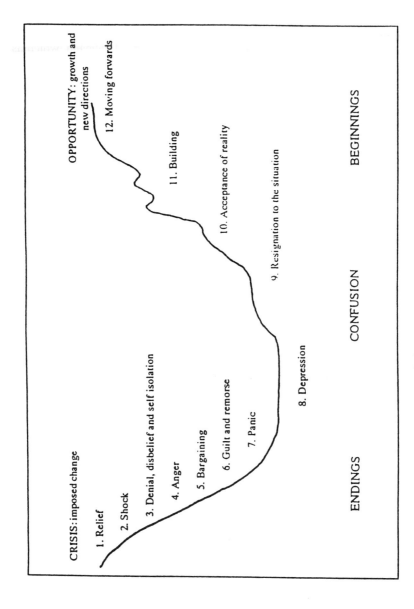

Figure 3.1 Stages of transition in response to imposed change

to be communicated effectively management must provide a forum in which there is reasonable security to do it and where there are clear signals that this kind of communication is valued, even when it is negative or not what management might wish to hear. If survival is going to mean adaptation, staff will have to change – tasks, routines, attitudes. Whilst good information is necessary it is not sufficient for this to be managed effectively.

The range of feelings that beset people when they have to adapt to change have been identified by Barger (1992) who has postulated a cycle of 12 possible stages in transition from a hypothetical moment of crisis when change is about to be imposed towards the stage at which opportunities are perceived for growth. These are illustrated below.

The first part of the cycle involves a preoccupation with endings; this is followed by a phase of confusion. Out of this confusion emerges a sense of new beginnings and opportunities for growth. There may be an initial crisis if the change has not been anticipated. A sequence of feelings unfolds involving resistance to the change in the status quo, attempts to limit its impact, and reference back to the time before the change and actions which may or may not have been taken to influence it. This initial sequence is followed by panic, depression and resignation during which it is difficult for the individual to maintain a consistent focus; such confusion is followed by an acceptance of reality, building on positive energies and moving forwards to take on the new reality. Our own experience of life changes over which we have had little control may provide a personal evaluation of this cycle.

In reality the relative prominence of these 12 stages will vary according to the individual and organisational context. If change can be anticipated before a response is required, the depth of this emotional cycle may be reduced. Staff – and managers – will be empowered by the opportunity to take preventative action or to adapt to the anticipated change.There will be wide individual differences across staff in traversing this cycle. They will depend on external factors such as role and position which are variably affected but also on internal factors such as personality type which predispose individuals to manage change in different ways.

So, in addition to the management of reflected-up feeling that is a necessary part of delivering a service to clients under stress there is the additional reservoir of feeling that develops as a consequence of change. The differences between individuals lead inevitably to conflict and it is necessary, but difficult, for the service to view this as a creative force. For management, it will often represent a challenge to a particular perception of events and hold up rapid decision-making or policy development. As in the understanding of negative evaluations from outside the service it is important to try and grasp the richer systemic picture and not to succumb to the temptation of avoiding the conflict or repressing it through authoritarian responses. A variety of possible causes present themselves. Is this a consequence of poor communication? Are the views of one or two individuals representing the whole group or should they be regarded as idiosyncratic? Does it signal insufficient opportunity to think through an issue or is time being wasted on a service 'theme' which never gets resolved? Is it a mirroring of an external dynamic which we are not recognising? Is it in some way mirroring a conflict within management as a group or in the individual who heads the service? A visible attempt to make sense of conflict in this way and to provide opportunity for resolution before clear decision-making maximises the likelihood of staff identification with the decisions that are taken.

The other strand to communication is that of feedback to staff on performance. Most professionals receive only intermittent feedback from clients. It is in the nature of the relationship that this is not perceived as necessary, often because the professional is regarded as having power, expertise and authority and in consequence not in need of it. There is therefore a task for management to provide positive feedback to staff on as many aspects of their work as possible. This can be very difficult to institutionalise when management themselves are beset with other pressures. One way is through formal management review processes where time is specifically earmarked for mutual feedback about work. Essentially management has to enable staff to feel good about themselves despite the pressures and this is best done by being continually alert to the possibilities of praise or congratulation. This leads to a culture of valuing the diversity of individual responses and style rather than letting the differences between individuals promote splitting and negative projections which make resolution of conflict impossible.

Professional development

Providing opportunities for development is a way of valuing staff as well as providing the service with key skills. Adaptation for survival invariably brings formal requirements of skill development as new needs are met in clients or the balance of activity shifts. All too often organisational survival is accompanied by a cutting or removal of the professional development budget so it is helpful to consider this from as broad a perspective as possible and in particular to view it in terms of internal events as well as external training (Booker 1991b). From this perspective it includes:

- delivering a professional service
- individual supervision – peer, management or external
- group supervision – peer or external supervisor
- development/support group
- internal training events
- external training events
- reading, writing, contemplation

- other life experience.

Looked at in this way the most scarce resource becomes not money but time. Group supervision can allow the diversity of approach and experience across staff to work for the service and maximises the learning that is inherent in practice itself. For this to happen there must be sufficient sense of being contained by the group, for 'failure' to be understood as a necessary precondition for learning and for rivalry to be held in abeyance. Even assuming all of the good practice described in the previous paragraphs this may not be sustainable across a whole staff group and alternative small groupings might emerge. The model of learning implied by supervision is important, namely that we learn inordinately from our own experience and through processes that take place over time. This is in radical opposition to the model underpinning much external training which emphasises bolted-on skills acquired over short training periods.

There is a continual task of monitoring the balance between the wishes and needs of individuals for particular professional development opportunities and the needs of the service in its fight for resources and survival. However much the wish to allow individuals to develop in the directions of their choice there will be frequent instances where the service need has to take priority. This can be sustained to the extent that management has been able to set out an agenda for development which both attends to the demands of the external environment but avoids what Gustafson and Cooper (1990) describe as 'the foolishness of transformative invasions'. By this they mean changes which disregard the past and abandon tradition wholesale instead of appraising it and establishing which structures, skills and aspects of culture are obsolescent and which have continuing value.

Being Accountable

Accountability is an essential prerequisite for survival and this section looks at it from a three angles. First, the conflict between quality and quantity; second, the consequences of being accountable to clients who are themselves organised into a powerful system; third, negotiating definitions of quality service.

Quantitative and qualitative descriptions of performance

The previous section discussed ways of management enabling staff, providing positive feedback and facilitating development. Together with ensuring adequate resources and clear boundaries these are all examples of management's downwards accountability to staff. In turn, staff are upwardly accountable to management in fullfilling the service's objectives, this being reflected out to external line management. This process is absolutely central to the survival and prospering of the service, alongside the feedback provided by clients.

External line management is not (generally) going to be concerned with the minutiae of service delivery. They are going to want indicators of value for money and quality which allow them to make an effective evaluation, on their terms, of how well the service is meeting the needs management has of it. In wanting this they are merely reflecting central government policy (most clearly expressed by the Audit Commission). It is essential that service management is able to produce a variety of quantitative performance indicators which are seen to represent 'real' service and not as being easily manipulable in an impression management exercise. Examples of the former might be:

- 'number of three-hour school visit sessions delivered in one year'
- 'number of children on whom statutory advice was written in one year'
- 'percentage of staff time taken up with face to face service delivery'
- 'rate of pick up of new referrals to the service'.

An example of a manipulable performance indicator might be 'number of psychological interviews conducted in one term'. This is problematic because it is difficult to define 'psychological interview' operationally.

When quantitative measures are called for there is frequently an implied assumption that bigger is better (unless the measure represents a negative event such as number of complaints received). There is no control of quality: does a slow take-up of referrals by a member of staff indicate inefficiency or a higher quality of service that takes more time to deliver? While there is no totally satisfactory way of resolving such issues it is possible to introduce monitoring systems that provide internal auditing data against which individuals can compare themselves. In the context of some review process where work is discussed in detail it is quite possible to identify a service norm and the acceptable range of variation from it. This kind of data is useful for negotiating a 'standard' against which to work. Performance targets do not then appear unbounded and forever extendable; instead they refer to a standard which has been negotiated to reflect an appropriate balance between quantity and quality. The important point is to create space for the kind of thinking that addresses these issues positively, without inappropriate cynicism, thereby signalling to a potentially suspicious external management that you are taking on board their priorities. Nothing could be more destructive than to appear to resist these demands and hide behind protestations of professional work being 'unquantifiable'.

The capacity to provide the necessary data is itself a measure of effectiveness which an external line manager is likely to take seriously. Presenting estimates of performance grabbed out of thin air is no longer a viable strategy when such a variety of indicators are demanded. In the end, however, no amount of quantitative data will adequately convey the content and process of a service, however well standards have been negotiated. It is essential to convey this when the principal output resides in the interactions between individuals rather than some tangible product. The rhetoric of performance indicators needs to be challenged when they are deemed to provide the whole story. We must insist that they sit alongside descriptive accounts of the work being done – preferably from clients as well as service providers.

Arenas of accountability

In the local authority context accountability is ultimately to elected members through line management. In the health service it will be to a less publicly accountable management structure. By definition they are located on boundaries where pressures are intense, a locus of resolution for competing interests. Decisions there will be influenced by a variety of inputs from other stakeholders in addition to those of the service itself. It is therefore essential that the service is in sufficient dialogue with these stakeholders to be aware of and, it is hoped, to influence the pressures they bring to bear. This engagement needs to be carefully judged, however, since dialogue which is perceived to be special pleading can easily backfire, particularly in the political arena.

These stakeholders will frequently be organised into their own separate systems (for example, of headteachers and other professional groupings, parents, patients and other client groups, political factions etc.) and it is essential to take account of the dynamics of these systems and the way that messages about the service are interpreted. This is the real challenge to all service staff and to the quality of support provided by management. It is particularly so when the primary client group is such a system – headteachers in my case. Apart from this group's formal meeting structures there is a grapevine that conveys negativity about external services far more readily than compliments. In this it is no different to any other grapevine. The problem for many professional services is that some negativity in the client relationship is an essential ingredient of quality, an indication of change. It is not a fast food service where the unequivocal satisfaction of the customer can reasonably be demanded at every stage of the transaction.

Managing negativity in a consultative relationship with an institution at a time of rapid change is an art and not a science. For a psychologist in particular it demands a high degree of professional skill. The exercise of consultation carries with it an expectation of negative projections resulting from the elements of the process that involve confrontation and disconfirmation. The issue of saying 'no' has been mentioned already in the context of roles and boundaries. Whilst this may be respected at a rational level, the anger at the imposition of constraint will still be there; as will the anger and frustration that may be consequent upon the processes necessary for the psychologist to come to a judgement which takes into account all of aspects of a situation.

As an individual external to an organisation, the visiting professional may also be a focus for quite unrelated feelings deriving from what he represents rather than what he is. For example, the client may be quite unable to disentangle the perception of 'psychologist' from 'a functionary of an education department which shows complete incompetence when it comes to providing a reliable budgetary statement for the school'. Alternatively he may become the object of envy as being someone who can simply walk away from the mess. He may get sucked into internal games of which it will be difficult to make sense (Palazzoli 1986). To the extent that this happens over and above the positive valuing of the service through its enabling, clarifying and expediting roles there is going to exist a degree of ambivalence. Service evaluation has to take this into account when judging the negative comments that it receives. How much can these be understood as a consequence of the dynamic described above and how much do they represent a shortfall in service quality that has to be addressed? What is certain is that it will involve both and will only be understood properly by stepping back and putting together the picture of the system in its total context. This understanding then has to inform a particular service response that attends closely to the amount of negative feeling in the client. It is here that the issue of service survival comes into play. It will not be seen as a positive force unless the client's negativity is acknowledged and addressed, notwithstanding the particular perceptions the service might have as to its origins. In my experience, this can lead to tricky decisions if the needs of pupils, the ultimate clients, appear to be overlooked.

Consider the case of an angry parent complaining that their child has been waiting for nine months to see the psychologist and that no contact was made during the term just finished despite assurances from the headteacher. The headteacher feels that the psychologist is slow in picking up new work. The psychologist feels that the school expects little of his involvement except the rubber stamping of resource applications. The anger of the parents is fuelled by their pain at living with their child's failure. The anger of the school is fuelled by its perception of the LEA cutting off resources and its own inability to address a range of difficulties. A service management response has to address the pick up rate of the psychologist by comparing data for the school with the service norm; it has also to explore with the head of the school how it might address more effectively the needs of its pupils without resort to external resources. The latter has to be achieved in a way that is ultimately perceived as affirmative and helpful rather than undermining of present practice.

How do we manage this situation in the client group of headteachers? Unless this happens, however well it might have been resolved with the headteacher concerned, aspects of the problem will be communicated within this group where it will resonate with other experiences and, in a large group setting, can easily become a focus of more general frustrations, just as it does within the original institution. The service then could end up as being scapegoated for a range of deficiencies, many of which have little to do with it.

One partial way of addressing this is to have a formal 'liaison' group for representatives of primary clients which meets regularly with service management. It becomes a forum for concerns as well as consultation about future developments. If some continuity of membership is achieved this can become a key arena of accountability because issues can be explored in depth and a common version of reality developed which can be fed back to the wider client group. In such a forum the implications of limited resourcing can be shared; expectations of service throughput and use of time clarified; hostile feelings can also be explored. With luck, as a consequence of this, the service will have its own advocates in the client group who will be able to modulate the more extreme positions that might otherwise emerge. This will succeed to the extent that the representatives are not regarded as having 'gone native' and lost their grasp of the central concerns of the client group. It is therefore in the interests of the service that they be respected and established members of that group.

This kind of accountability is premised on a more general stance of openness to scrutiny and a constant reiteration of the aim of quality and effectiveness substantiated with tangible outcomes so that it is not perceived as mere rhetoric. A continual balancing of the qualitative with the quantitative can lead to a mutual interplay in which the combination is greater than the sum of the parts. This is possible because of the interpersonal nature of the accountability relationship, and the small group dynamic allows the exploration of individual differences within the client group as well as common needs.

Quality

Service survival will be enhanced by the perception that it offers not just value for money but 'quality', that much overused term.

So, where does quality lie? Who defines it? How do we improve it? The answer to the first is 'somewhere in the midst of the interaction between the professional and the client' – that process that may not have a substantive output. It may be a shift in perception, a reformulation, a sense of relief at sharing pain, at relieving some guilt or discharging some anger. This is not to deny the other tangible outcomes (such as changes in behaviour, resource inputs, treatment programmes) but to emphasise that quality is a judgement that has to come from others at least as much as from within the service – the clients being the ultimate arbiters. It is no good having an excellent service that no one can afford or wants to take up.

The answer to the second question is therefore the primary client, one hopes, in collaboration with the professional. The external definition is led by the client since it is his needs, as formulated by him, that the service is trying to address. There will of course be an internal (to the service) definition of quality which attends to the external but supplements it with the skills and processes that are believed by the professionals to be necessary to achieving it (in a recent development exercise my service produced the following examples, among others: communication skills, specific knowledge base, clarity of thinking, taking chance opportunities, locating responsibilities, and good timing). In addition to the difference between internal and external versions of what produces a commonly desired result there is also the tension that can exist between the professional's view and the client's view of what is desirable. This is especially likely when there is an 'ultimate' client whom both are supposed to be serving. In such multi-client contexts quality might be considered to lie also in the process of continually reviewing and redefining it in collaboration with primary clients. In this way dimensions for improvement can be negotiated and realistic objectives set. This takes us back to the kind of client group dialogue described above.

The Head of Service

This account proposes that heads of professional services have a firm grasp on their internal professional self; have led a group process that defines aims and strategy; have developed a culture that is responsive to change; have implemented a system for supporting staff in their service delivery; have integrated the language of management with that of their professional peers, their clients and their line managers; and, finally, have developed systems of accountability to and interactions with the external context that addresses its expressed needs.

How does the head of service manage the stress and strain of being on the boundary, responding to the very different issues that emerge from within and without? The answer has to be, with great difficulty. The legitimate demands of staff for support in their professional work and decision-making are, in a sense, comfortable and familiar – known territory. The demands of the external context are very different and frequently made without the accompanying assumption that external line management has a duty to support action as well as demand it. Integrative skills are stretched by long debates about the accuracy of budget lines, the complexity of maternity leave conditions, the employability of the temporary telephonist, the leaking roof and the building towelling contract. Yet these are all integral to the resourcing of the service and can fundamentally impair its functioning if not addressed. In the struggle for survival and the fight for budgets it is just these issues that take over.

Developing models of collaboration rather than competition in such a climate is an uphill struggle. The service manager has a fundamental duty to herself and to the service to find an arena for consultation and support which is detached from day to day systems. It is only there that the opportunity will arise to attend to the feelings that are taken in without evaluation, the judgements that are made on the hoof without time to develop the wider perspective that has been promulgated here. The most convenient and readily accessible forum is a peer group where experiences overlap. This is also cheaper (if not free!). The possibility also arises for joint funding of an external consultant who can monitor the dangers of 'group think', something which an individual service may not be able to justify.

If that is done, the overall task becomes do-able and models of practice are on display which potentially inform the external environment in its own, possibly less informed, struggles with change. Most important, there is a chance of holding on to and promoting the values that are threatened when decisions are made through budgetary expediency alone.

CHAPTER 4

Schools, Groups and the Primary Task

Elizabeth Kennedy

Introduction

The aim of this chapter is to look at group functioning in schools, drawing from a range of systemic and psychodynamic thinking. A great deal has been written about schools as organisations, but there are relatively few discussions which examine the nature of the relationships between structures, processes, groups and individuals from an unconscious as well as a conscious point of view. The vast majority of us work in and with groups. Every day we are subjected to the challenges and excitement of the forces operating in groups at all levels of the system in which we work. In schools, teachers work with class groups, together with groups of colleagues within the larger institutional group. In turn, the individual organisation sits within the wider cluster of the local education authority (LEA), regional and national structures. Developing a conceptual framework that can help make sense of the relationships within and between these levels presents an enormous challenge.

It is not the intention of this chapter to look at developing insights into individual needs, fears, fantasies and motivations in relation to teaching and learning. (For such an account, see Wittenberg, Henry and Osborne 1983.) Neither will a theoretical overview of research into groups be attempted, as the research is extensive and varied, and is covered well elsewhere. Rather, a selective account will be presented which focuses upon exploring particular unconscious processes in groups. This receives surprisingly scant coverage in the education literature, as the unconscious is not widely explored in day-to-day management and understanding of classroom groups.

Theoretical Underpinnings

A psychologist working in and with schools can draw from a number of sources in order to make sense of his or her experiences. In *systemic thinking*, the notion of interdependence between individual behaviour and contextual influences is clearly explored. The work of Trist *et al.* in the 1950s highlighted the inter-relatedness of working structures and processes and groups and individuals in an organisation (the coal mining industry). The notion of the socio-technical organisation, particularly in the 'human services', is helpful in alerting us to the need for schools to maintain a balance between their 'technical aspects' and their 'relational' aspects. Alongside the conceptual changes represented by the developments in systemic thinking were calls for changes in practice. Critics of the individual intrapsychic approach to assessment and intervention, the model of individual psychopathology with its attendant stigmatising/labelling, were also influenced by economic and practical considerations. The need to move from direct work with clients to a form of indirect service delivery was therefore compelling from both a theoretical and pragmatic point of view, and the practice of consultation has developed apace (see Dowling and Osborne 1994).

> ...the systematic approach requires one to think simultaneously in terms of three clients; immediate or *contact* clients with whom one is interacting in the here and now; *primary* clients who are the real targets of change (and who pay for the change efforts); and *ultimate* clients, who are the stakeholders that must be considered even though one might not ever interact with them directly. (Schein 1990, p.57, emphasis added)

Psychologists working consultatively in schools will work on behalf of all these clients as 'expert' or 'technical' consultants (sharing knowledge about child development, learning theories, reading development, etc.), as 'diagnostic' consultants (the 'doctor–patient' model) and as 'process' consultants (see Chapter 6 of this volume).

An understanding of unconscious forces and their expression within and between individuals and groups is an invaluable tool for the psychologist. Within a *psychodynamic model*, relationships are considered through acknowledging both the conscious and unconscious components, as well as attempting to connect current emotions and behaviours with the influences of earlier experiences. The psychoanalyst Wilfred Bion has contributed substantially to our understanding of unconscious processes in groups. Drawing from Freud and Klein's work on individual psychic development, Bion (1961) described the ways in which this 'aggregate of individuals' regress to more primitive ways of functioning, particularly in situations of conflict and anxiety. Group members experience a 'loss of individual distinctiveness' and behave 'as if' the group has an existence apart or distinct from the individuals. Bion called this phenomenon 'basic assumption mentality' and outlined three types of group behaviour from which it was possible to deduce their tacit assumptions – dependency, fight/flight and pairing (baD, baF, baP) (see Chapter 7 of this volume for a detailed account of Bion) as distinct from the task-focused, more sophisticated work group.

> Basic assumption life is not oriented outward toward reality, but inward toward fantasy, which is then impulsively and critically acted out. There

is little pausing to consider or to test consequences, little patience with an inquiring attitude, and great insistence upon feeling. Basic assumption members often are confused, have poor memories, are disorientated about time. They do not really learn and adapt through experience but actually resist change, although they may shift very readily from one basic assumption to another. (Rioch 1975, p.28.)

In contrast 'The work group requires all the concentration, skill and organisation of creative forces that can be mustered.' (Rioch 1975, p.31). The work group is not a cosy place: '…each individual is very much on his own and may have to accomplish his part of the task in a very lonely way…' (p.32).

The concept of *primary* task was described by Rice (1963) in relation to an institution as the task it must perform if it is to survive. Outwardly a simple idea, in practice it is a complex concept, exploration of which can provide useful information about the workings of a group or institution. It is important to realise that primary task is not a fixed, static concept; rather that it is dynamic and changing, and can be understood in different ways by different groups in an organisation. Additionally, primary task will have different conscious and unconscious expressions. Rice's original conception was further refined by Gordon Lawrence (1977).

> The *normative* primary task is the formal or official task, the operationalisation of the fixed aims of the organisation, and is usually defined by the chief stakeholders. The *existential* primary task is the task people within the enterprise believe they are carrying out, the meaning or interpretations they put on their roles and activities. The *phenomenal* primary task is the task that can be inferred from people's behaviour, and of which they may not consciously be aware. Analysis of the primary task in these terms can highlight discrepancies between what an organisation or group says it sets out to do and what is actually happening. (Obholzer and Roberts 1994, p.30)

Schools

Schools as organisations challenge much of the received wisdom about organisational structure, process and development. Yet they represent powerfully society's hopes and fears. On the one hand they are 'one of Society's key devices for adapting to the future' (Handy and Aitken 1986, p.31), but on the other hand, they are the vehicle for the transmission of social values and attitudes and can be seen as a mechanism for maintaining the status quo.

Schools can be characterised by clear structures, differentiated roles and often well defined rules and procedures. But relative to other organisations, schools' 'outcomes' are often vaguely defined and wide ranging, for example, 'fulfilling individual potential'; or narrow and precise, for example exam results.

The problem for schools is one of *coherence.* They have to manage and understand the inherently contradictory functions they have to perform, at the same time maintaining consonance with their primary task. In the grip of powerful opposing societal forces, many of their 'internal' functions (multiple tasks) are also paradoxically 'opposed', for example

- stability versus change
- care versus control
- intellectual versus emotional
- dependence versus independence
- content versus process
- inclusion versus segregation
- teaching versus learning
- individual versus group.

The reality of good school management in this scenario will be the ability to support and understand difference, conflict and contradiction.

Until recently, schools have rarely been in an overtly competitive market place. 'Survival' as a notion, would best have been applied to individual experiences within the education system. Now, however, the fundamental changes in national and local systems have made the issue of survival central to all schools. The concept of primary task has never been more pertinent than now to thinking about schools. In the tough world of local financial management and open enrolment, the dominance of financial considerations is well recognised and well documented. The academic year is no longer the dominant time boundary, it is now overlaid by the financial year, when, for local authority schools, the yearly round of ekeing out ever diminishing budgets makes the Spring term a tense time. Hard choices have to be made, for example increasing class sizes or losing teachers. In this climate it is easy to appreciate how subtle but important shifts in primary task will be evident.

Schools, Bion and Primary Task

It is against this background that linking together systemic and psychodynamic ideas can assist in understanding some of the aspects of schools' functioning. Bion's work on groups considered alongside the concept of primary task is of particular importance in the current climate, as:

> When a group does not seek to know its primary task, both by definition and by feasibility, there is likely to emerge either dismemberment of the group or the emergence of some other primary task unrelated to the one for which it was originally called into being. (Turquet quoted in Obholzer and Roberts 1994, p.31).

Thus when the notion of primary task is no longer clear, is not shared, or is *inherently strained*, then groups will tend to function in basic assumption mode. Whilst not all basic assumptions are anti-task phenomena, they are ubiquitous, and represent powerful determinants of group functioning. Acknowledging these forces directly and recognising them at work, both in the classroom and in the staffroom as well as within and between other groups, is likely to enhance the quality of experience for all concerned. *Schools, as institutions with inherently contradictory tasks are likely to be in the grip of basic assumption mentality for a significant proportion of time* and for 'effective functioning the basic assumptions must be subservient to and used in the service of the work task. They make good servants and poor masters' (Rioch 1975, p.30).

The Paradoxes

Group vs individual

The responsibility of schools is the development of individuals, but this is to be achieved within groups. Maintaining a balance between the needs of individual children and the groupings within which they have to function is a constant tension in schools. In outside educational debate, this issue is expressed through discussion of the relative merits of, for example, child-centred, mixed ability and whole class teaching approaches and can become politicised and polarised.

Relatively little attention has been paid to groups:

> Perhaps…the desire of teachers to be seen working with and for individual children makes them want to play down the role of the group, to treat it more as an administrative necessity or burden. (Handy and Aitken 1986, p.63)

Handy and Aitken wonder if the 'tradition of individualism in teaching is too strong', or whether 'group work is considered too expensive', or 'that the potentialities of the group are not well understood' (p.64). But it seems likely that a major factor is the powerful and primitive potentiality of groups. Although potentially a positive resource, groups can also be intimidating, ineffective and sometimes destructive.

To be effective as a vehicle for learning, emotional needs and social/group processes must be mapped in a coherent and yet flexible way, as these forces can serve as powerful inhibitors or facilitators. In this analysis, the role of the teacher is extremely complex. In his book *Emotional Growth and Learning*, Paul Greenhalgh (1994) quotes Whitaker as suggesting that

> …a group leader, as part of the work of reflection, has the following tasks: to develop, refine and expand an understanding of each person in the group; to keep in touch with the dynamics of the group as a whole and as it develops over time; to keep in touch with one's own

feelings and to note one's own behaviour and its consequences; and to perceive connections between the group and individual dynamics. (p.213)

The benefits of having a sense of what is going on in a group, of being able to stay in role, of anticipating difficulties and anxieties and their likely forms of expression are vital in all human services. What makes schools a particularly challenging arena is that the workplace is characterised by large groups with very varied needs, skills and experiences, where the largest group (the children) are not there by consent.

In recent years, a greater emphasis in teacher training has rightly been placed on developing an understanding of groups. The focus of these programmes however, has been pragmatic, action and solution focused, working with observable behaviour. In contrast, a psychodynamic approach explores the unconscious as well as the conscious forces at work in groups and looks towards the benefits arising from increased *understanding* for both teachers and pupils.

A case example might help illustrate these points.

Case Example

An infant teacher consulted me about a girl in her Year 2 class. A warm and caring person, this teacher had been teaching in Reception at the school for many years and knew most of the families in the community. Her concerns were about the development of a girl in her class who had been sexually abused while of nursery age. The girl was loud, demanding, challenging and exhibiting some sexualised behaviour. The teacher was sympathetic and understanding and was helped by knowing that the girl and her family were receiving ongoing therapeutic support. The concern she brought related to signs in the girl of precocious puberty, developing breasts and body hair. The teacher was very anxious about how the girl might deal with premature menstruation 'after all she had been through'. Through discussion, however, it became more and more apparent that the girl represented something rather unwholesome, and intimidating. The teacher described how sometimes the girl's behaviour made her 'see red', and how she behaved just like a difficult teenager. As we talked, the problem seemed less to do with the girl herself, and much more what she had come to represent to the teacher and the group.

Observation in class confirmed that in contrast to her 'mothering' style (doing everything for them, cuddling/caressing) with the other children, the teacher allowed herself to be dominated, almost bullied, by the girl's demands. What had been framed as an individual's problem felt more like a whole group difficulty in dealing with the consequences of a loss of authority and purpose in their teacher which was reflected in unsettled behaviour in many of the other children. Intervention focused on helping the teacher to see how the girl functioned as a repository for unwanted feelings for both the other pupils and the teacher. Their angry rebellion against being 'babied' contrasted with their fears about the most difficult aspects of growing up. Viewing this as a group phenomenon, related to their impending transfer to the Junior school, allowed the teacher to step back and work with their fears and excitements directly.

Stability vs change

Any organisation needs stability in order to be able to function. But by their very nature, schools are inherently unstable – the majority population is not there by consent; the essential tasks are changed development, that is, learning; and schools have constantly changing groups. The desired change (learning) is 'internal' but for this to be brought about efficiently and successfully, a balance must be maintained between 'inside' and 'outside' considerations. The task of schools is to create a structure stable enough and strong enough to provide a sense of security, while simultaneously actively promoting change in children. Change and development in one group, however, are inseparable from changes in roles, relationships, values and attitudes in other groups. The expression of collective purpose(s) through structures and procedures to support this purpose is the ideal. But in schools, purposes are contradictory both within and between groups. The implication of linking group dynamics and multiple and paradoxical primary tasks, is that schools as organisations fly in the face of received wisdom that a shared consensus is essential for the health and successful working of a stable institution. Within schools, by definition, the teaching groups exclusively hold the clear sense of purpose and direction. This can only be 'taken on trust' by the pupils, as they do not have sufficient intellectual, emotional or social maturity to do so. This problem will always be central to schools because educational objectives are selected independently of the existence of the pupils who have to achieve them.

To this complex cocktail needs to be added the turbulence created within and around schools from continuous government interference and legislation. Basic organisational constructs, task apart, such as boundaries and lines of accountability have been recently challenged. The Grubb Institute's 'School Generated Management' identified that schools operate a principle of 'downwards accountability' in stark contrast to the business model imposed on them by recent legislation where accountability is upwards to the shareholders. Relationships are no longer clear and locally determined and now schools are more explicitly required to widen their accountability even broader beyond the children, parents, governors, local community, parish or diocese, local education authority, council, to OFSTED, the Funding Agency for Schools and the DFE.

Bion's (1961) basic assumption formulation also described the sophisticated uses of basic assumption mentality. Different professional groups may adopt a different sophisticated basic assumption mentality in the service of their primary task: for instance, the army as an example of mobilising fight/flight, and hospitals as an example of dependency. Schools are often seen in this formulation as being characterised by basic assumption pairing, but it might be more helpful to see a predominance of different assumptions across phases. In many ways it is easy to accept that the predominant assumption operating in a sophisticated manner in primary schools is dependency, with pairing (and I would suggest fight/flight) becoming more evident at the top end of the junior school and in secondary schools. Difficulties in carrying out the task(s) can lead to a more primitive way of behaving

> ...where the capacity for the sophisticated use of basic assumption activity has degenerated, and the professional's action and thought become dominated by its observant forms. Each then produces a particular group culture. Aberrant 'baD' gives rise to a *culture of subordination* where authority derives entirely from position in the hierarchy, requiring unquestioning obedience. Aberrant 'baP' produces a *culture of collusion,* supporting pairs of members in avoiding truth rather than seeking it. There is attention to the group's mission, but not to the means of achieving it. Aberrant 'baF' results in a *culture of paranoia and aggressive competitiveness,* where the group is preoccupied not only by an external enemy but also by 'the enemy within'. Rules and regulations proliferate to control both the internal and external 'bad objects'. [See Chapter 5 of this volume]. Here it is the means which are explicit and the ends which are vague. (Stokes 1994, p.25–6)

Using this framework, it is possible to see how schools are often subjugated to aberrant basic assumption functioning.

Secondary schools have traditionally adopted a structure in which change is the predominant feature. Although supposedly a response to the need for subject specialisms backed by the public examination system, it is also tempting to view secondary organisation as an (ill-conceived) defensive structure to deal with adolescent challenge. The conditions in which pupils work are '...designed to produce confused identities, anomie and powerlessness.' (Handy and Aitkent 1986, p.44) – a recipe, one might think, for aberrant group functioning.

An inner city secondary school with which I used to work encapsulated some of the issues outlined in this section. It drew from a relatively deprived catchment area and had a high pupil turnover within each year. The school's local reputation was poor and, despite a stable and dedicated staff, the roll was steadily falling. What had been an uncomfortable and distressing situation, became an acutely threatening one with the advent of local management of schools (LMS). The budget steadily decreased and eventually staff were made redundant. An unfavourable inspection added public humiliation to the problems. The headteacher retired and the incoming headteacher was charged with 'turning the school around'. What happened were a series of changes which, on reflection, felt like the aberrant behaviour Jon Stokes describes.

A school development plan was drawn up by the head using explicit performance management language. A meetings cycle was devised on a monthly rotation which was so onerous that a 'recovery week' had to be scheduled for staff to draw breath. Management was restructured and the new structure was a slimmer, more hierarchical grouping. Communications became more formalised and prescriptive and senior management were felt to be increasingly remote.

Simultaneously, in the pupil group, fighting between two ethnic groups escalated into violent incidents involving the police on and off the school premises. The number of exclusions rocketed.

Parallel to these events was an increase in the union activity within the school and a hardening into militancy amongst some of the staff.

From outside it appeared that all levels of the institution were in the grip of 'baF'. Parents, governors, the LEA, all became 'external enemies' and vast reserves of energy were used up in arguments with these groups at their point of contact. Against a background of change and demoralisation, management defended themselves against the pain of their decisions by withdrawing, leaving the staff and pupils to fight amongst themselves. Autocracy replaced collective discussion and the numbers of individual 'casualties' was high. This school had lost sight of its vulnerable, dependent and needy aspects. In battle with the outside world and with civil war within, the only way it could survive was by the head addressing the educative task in a conscious way.

'It is worth noting that the word 'educate' comes from the Latin educere, meaning 'to lead out', which suggests that this process has traditionally had something very important to do with leadership and followership.' (Rioch 1975, p.160) Leading and assuming the authority and responsibility for a group is a demanding and complex task. The leaders must be dependable but not foster inappropriate dependency, must be authoritative but not allow the abdication of responsibility by group members. 'The power and strength of the leader are based on the weakness and helplessness of the follower.' (Rioch 1975, p.161) Whilst clarity of authority structure is essential, the more inflexible authoritarian interpretation adopted by this school was anti-task and destructive.

Teaching vs learning

I hope that this chapter has emphasised that neither teaching nor learning can be considered independently of the personal relationships in which they take place. That there is no teaching without learning is self-evident, but convenient sometimes to ignore. Learning is determined by a particular form of psychological 'contract' established between pupil and teacher. This contract sees the teacher as 'facilitator' and 'manager' as well as 'expert' and 'doctor' (after Schein 1990). Facilitating and managing require an understanding of, and sensitivity to individual needs, strengths and concerns, as well as to group processes.

Schein's models of organisational consultancy (see Chapter 6 of this volume) can inform thinking about the schools. The teacher as 'expert' is purveyor of knowledge and skills. For much of the time in schools, such a model is entirely appropriate, but for the child to benefit from that knowledge, it is not a matter of straightforward exposure or transmission. Without sufficient trust, children will conceal lack of understanding, knowledge or skill, will resist risking public exposure by trying something new and will sometimes denigrate either teacher or task rather than acknowledge 'failure'.

To learn, children need to be curious, willing to take risks and able to name what they do not know. They will only do this in a group setting in which they feel secure and valued and where they can identify with the purpose.

The teacher can be construed as 'doctor' (Schein's doctor–patient model) when help is seen to be effected through a 'diagnostic' process, identifying strengths and weaknesses. Once again, trust is a necessary pre-condition as the power imbalance inherent in this sort of relationship is sufficient to lend itself to abuse. The teacher as 'process consultant' however, starts from a position based upon

> a mutual inquiry process that not only creates a shared sense of responsibility for figuring out what is wrong and how to fix it, but also enables helpers to pass on some of their own diagnostic and intervention skills. Helpers must help their clients to learn how to learn. (Schein 1990, p.60)

Schein suggests that this latter approach is the essential starting point for joint problem-solving work.

Schein's framework can be seen to describe a cycle through which children pass during their education. Primary schools seem better able to manage the teacher as process consultant than do secondary schools, until the sixth form when this role relationship returns. It is not inconceivable that these different styles are related to both the ages and stages of the children, as well as to the increasing constraints and demands imposed by public examinations. A focus on results, whilst necessary for survival, might create a climate of attending to *external* factors rather than understanding, managing and nurturing *internal* resources. Neglect of the sentient aspects of teaching, an overfocus on 'task' rather than 'maintenance', is likely to jeopardise pupils' learning.

One of the central tasks for the teacher to understand and manage is *competition* in the group. Competition is a daily reality of school life between *individuals* (the speed with which younger children especially move to get to the front of the line), *groups* (team games, the 'House' system), between *institutions* (league tables) and between wider *agencies* (LEAs and the Funding Agency for Schools).

In the current political and economic context, government policies have consistently and consciously promoted competition as an 'alternative' (and 'better') force to the notion of collective responsibility. Within the public sector, large monoliths have increasingly been fragmented into smaller units such as free standing business units. Professionals' employment bases and contracts reflect a market forces ethos, which has encouraged groups to highlight their differences, specialisms, uniqueness. But whilst these undoubtedly impinge upon teaching practice in the classroom, they are fundamentally at variance, not just within the group structure of schools, but also with their task to equip *all* children with the tools to live independently.

'...the education service is intended to shield us from the risk of going under. It is also, therefore, an institution that is supposed to cope with – whether by encouragement or denial – competition and rivalry.' (Obholzer and Roberts 1994, p.172). In addition, schools are predicated on assumptions about child development which are embodied in both the structure and the process of the institution. Development is seen in linear terms, a progression through stages, a pyramid in which early experiences underpin later ones. Such expectations can serve a less benign purpose, however, by inhibiting or prohibiting learning (her or she is 'not ready' to learn this), by denying individual differences in approach or stage, and by ignoring the complexities of cyclical growth.

Case Example

A newly established prep school made itself attractive to parents in a very competitive environment by admitting children without subjecting them to an entrance exam.

A teacher of the nine-year-olds complained about a boy in his class. The boy was described as 'lazy, unmotivated and unreachable'. The teacher wondered whether the boy was capable enough to keep up with the rest of the class. The boy's story was dominated by self-doubt and a very negative image of himself as a learner. He was quick to describe the number and frequency of 'order marks' that he was given for poor and incomplete class and homework. He was resigned to the series of detentions that were the result of accumulated order marks. He described the work as boring and had no particular likes. He was extremely attentive to certain aspects of task presentation (the need for one-inch margins, date on the right-hand side, question numbers within the margin) which appeared to represent more significance than the content of the task(s). He attributed his 'failures' to his 'stupidity' and the 'success' of his friends to their superior ability. He conveyed a sense of helplessness and despair.

His parents, similarly, were impotent and despairing. They had consistently attempted to support their son and his teachers, but this had resulted in increasing numbers of clashes over homework. They too began to doubt their son's ability and found themselves aligned with the teacher in his frustrations.

In the cut throat private-school world of dominance by results, that is, external forces, the school denied individual differences, and slavishly adhered to an externally determined linear curriculum. Whole class teaching was maintained in spite of small classes. Competition between individuals was fostered and publicly endorsed and a clear system of sanctions was quickly established. Failure to achieve was attributed to individual shortcomings, with parents held responsible for the child's failings.

To an outside observer, this school was manifestly failing to connect teaching to learning. By denying the sentient aspects of the institution, the management were exempted from any sense of pain and guilt for the poor performance of their pupils. By maintaining their 'open door' policy without regard for accommodating the consequent broad range of children, they were able to deny responsibility for failing a number of children and their parents.

Content vs process

An effective school promotes the social and emotional development of its pupils as much as their intellectual prowess. As originally conceived, the National Curriculum left little time for the personal and social aspects of education with the emphasis on the acquisition of knowledge and skills. The National Curriculum has served to emphasise the rational content basis of teaching and has tended to obscure the need to attend equally to *process*. In 1979, Kolb formulated three key points in thinking about learning:

1. We learn best when personally involved in the learning experience.

2. Knowledge of any kind has more significance when we learn it through our own initiative, insight or discovery.

3. Learning is best when we are committed to aims that we have been involved in setting, when our participation with others is valued and when there is a supportive framework in which to learn (from Jacques 1984, p.xi).

In other words, for learning to take place, the relationship between emotional and intellectual functioning needs to be understood and managed. The work of any group must therefore be to attend simultaneously to the process of learning as well as content.

In addition to some of the factors already explored, there are certain other variables that will directly affect the process of learning in a group. Research on group functioning has highlighted *group size* as of great significance: '...it is common knowledge that any group numbering more than about twelve individuals is ineffective as a work group, incapable of useful debate and effective decision-making.' (Obholzer and Roberts 1994, p.169). If this is equally so in child groups, then teachers need to develop particular skills in understanding and managing conscious and unconscious processes if they are to provide a forum for enhancing learning. According to Jacques (1984), the main effect of large group size is that it is more difficult to 'mobilise the intellect' because of the powerful emotional forces at work; in contrast, the smaller the group, the easier it is for individuals to think, but the harder it is for them to feel. Obholzer and Roberts (1994) highlight three other variables affecting group functioning: clarity of the task, time boundaries and authority structures (p.170). Perhaps it is to offset the difficulties evident in large groups that schools have developed very clear responses to these three variables.

We live in an educational world where now the task is very clearly prescribed: there are Attainment Targets and Programmes of Study and performance is measured against well defined objectives Standard Attainment Tasks (SATs), as are the time boundaries (for example, timetable) and the authority structures (for example, governors). And yet there is little evidence of the rise in standards that the recent legislative changes set out to achieve.

Recent legislation focuses on content rather than process. In its more rigid form of expression, this emphasis is inherently antithetical to learning and individual development. In the class group where process is ignored or denied (perhaps the 'talk and chalk' model), the task is very structured, responses are 'drilled', and the form of recording is prescribed in detail. The class group will experience a predictable, if unstimulating, regime. But will they learn? Not according to either Kolb or Bion. Neither will they continue to accept the passive and dependent role that they have been assigned. Any teacher who has had the misfortune to take a class after a colleague with the style described will testify to the hostility such suppression can engender – hostility that may be manifest in rivalry between children just as much as challenge to adult authority.

In Bion's later writings, he describes the nature of the relationship between thinking and feeling. '...Bion is bold or foolhardy enough to claim that all human thought and endeavour, whatever the field, originates in the transformation of emotional experience' (Armstrong 1992, p.267). Using this conceptual framework implies that it is not sufficient to acknowledge the emotional in order to facilitate the intellectual. For Bion, we depend on our emotional experiences to be able to function intellectually, and therefore the emotional aspects of teaching and learning must be given the primacy they deserve.

Care vs control and dependence vs independence

Maintaining a healthy balance between these elements is fundamental to teaching and learning. Broad educational aims of fostering individual independence and autonomy can conflict with the perceived need to keep a group of children dependent and passive in order to 'manage' them. Care and control are essential aspects of successful schooling but can be felt to be contradictory.

Care and dependence are often confused and are felt to be more acceptable when present in teaching young children. Control is more likely to be challenged by the assertion of independent thinking and behaviour. When this becomes intolerable, more rule-bound, inflexible and autocratic styles can develop. In schools where this is the dominant regime (such as prep school mentioned above), conformity is valued above individuality. Collective values and ideals are emphasised, differences are deplored and denigrated, and individuals who exemplify group ideals are the most highly valued. In this scenario, 'autocracy can seem a tempting alternative to anarchy' (Handy and Aitken 1986, p.40), but is antithetical to the rounded development of the individuals making up the group. Only a balance across these different dimensions will allow a group to function creatively.

The opposite can, however, prove to be equally unsatisfactory to the mental health of the participants.

Case Example

A large mixed comprehensive school developed what it called a 'caring ethos'. An explicit and purposeful commitment was made by senior management to a policy which aimed to enhance the educational opportunities of all pupils. In practice, this resulted in an individualised focus becoming dominant in the school. The staff were known for their sensitivity to, understanding of, and work on behalf of the individual pupils. Relations between staff and pupils were flexible and informal, all on first name terms. Many pupils were identified as having special needs and were given academic or pastoral support. And yet in reality, the day-to-day experience of this school environment was chaotic and unsafe. By emphasising care and concern for individuals, control of the larger group was avoided and denied. Staff and pupil differences were minimised by using first names, and adult authority was denied. Pupils and teachers were paired in a collusive relationship from which parents (and others) were excluded. Little respect was shown around the building to either adults or other pupils. Boundaries such as time, appropriate language, and behaviour, were all consistently challenged.

This school was immersed in the aberrant basic assumption states that Jon Stokes (1994) describes. Its failure to struggle to maintain the balance between competing forces of care, control, dependency and independence had a benign intent. The resulting 'anarchy' was stressful and unhelpful to both adults and children alike.

Conclusions

Schools are organisations where an understanding of group dynamics, especially unconscious processes, are relatively unexplored. A powerful vehicle for change, schools are also the mechanism for promoting and maintaining existing values and attitudes – this central dilemma pervades all aspects of schools' organisation. In many ways, the primary tasks of schools are paradoxical, even contradictory. Under these conditions, schools are in the grip of powerfully opposed forces which are, not always rational or conscious.

Sweeping legislative changes resulting in radical restructuring have been imposed on the public sector. Schools have been at the forefront of these changes which are seen to reflect a questioning about fundamental attitudes to education. The teaching profession has been the repository of many ambivalent feelings generated by the changes, with stress and self-doubt accompanying challenge and excitement. In this climate, schools have had to become more outward looking, more responsive to the changing external environment. The balance between the primary task of survival in relation to the outside world and the demands of the internal context has been difficult to maintain. The difficulties in prioritising the multiple, even contradictory tasks can at times lead to defensive basic assumption activity and anti-task behaviour. The task of maintaining an open and responsive system, stable yet permeable to change, consistent yet flexible, has become harder. Difficulties in defining the primary task will lead to staff behaving 'as if' they are clear about their roles and boundaries, when in fact they are caught up in unconscious group and institutional processes.

It is the contention of this chapter that the capacity of a school to work effectively with the groups of children within it and with the groups of other 'stakeholders' (for example, parents) is enhanced by an awareness of unconscious processes. Learning is a task for *all* members of the institution, not just the majority child group. Staff need to maintain a healthy curiosity, a questioning attitude about how the organisation is functioning. In contrast, a more rigid, inflexible, defensive, functioning is characterised by an adherence to traditional practices, habitual procedures and customary ways of responding. It is the task of schools to walk a tightrope, recognising that discomfort and struggle are central to their existence and evidence of active learning. Being open to acknowledging and understanding unconscious processes does not have to be equated with a within-individual deficit model of thinking. Knowing that unconscious forces are ubiquitous, powerful, and accessible to examination, can be liberating. Accepting that we can function defensively in role as well as creatively enables us to mobilise our reflective selves in the service of the professional task.

CHAPTER 5

Work with Adolescents
The Uses of Boundaries, Rules and Sanctions in Institutions for Adolescents

Jane Ellwood

Staff work with adolescents in a variety of educational settings, providing an important context outside home in which young people develop their changing identities. The tasks of adolescence involve laying down the foundations of adult life, particularly in the areas of personal, sexual and work identities. Obholzer (1992) has described these processes as follows: 'This developmental work will not only draw on the strengths acquired in childhood, but will at the same time again reveal the weaknesses and flaws of earlier development – and also present them for review and reworking' (p.2). Schools and colleges often assist in this process of development by mirroring some of the important psycho-social transitions which young people make during these stages in their lives. Changes from primary to secondary schools, to sixth form, college, leaving home, going to work or university, all provide a space for reflecting on issues surrounding the departure of childhood and opportunities for development which are involved. Many schools recognise the importance of building rites of passage which help to mark and contain these transitions. Tutor groups, school committees, school–work links and award-giving ceremonies all help to acknowledge the increasing independence of students as they move away from childhood.

Teachers and parents will also be aware of the questioning and testing out of societal structures and values which is characteristic of adolescent development. This is also manifest in the testing of adult authority in home and school. Teenagers need to be able to challenge and take risks to derive a sense of themselves as individuals and, in doing so, can often rejuvenate their relationships with adults. They also turn to their peer groups to help them establish a separate identity. These processes of rejecting what parents stand for and having a peer group to support one have implications for institutions working with adolescents. They often reflect adolescent conflicts, and later in this chapter I hope to show how these processes can be re-enacted in the relationships made between adolescents and staff. I will also illustrate the importance of setting rules and boundaries in institutions for adolescents. These serve an important developmental function as a framework against which, or within which, their adult identities can be tested out and formed.

Adolescence and the Social Context

Young people are often particularly aware and concerned about social, cultural and environmental issues, and sometimes take the role of social critics. It is relevant here to consider the current societal and political context in which this chapter is written, as it is likely to impinge on several aspects of young people's lives and to be a framework for thinking about some of the realities they experience. The Introduction has outlined some of the wider political changes which have occurred while the current generation of adolescents have been growing up. This generation have experienced only one political party with particular ideologies as governing during their lives. This may be a significant influence on the political, social and moral perspectives they adopt in the longer term, as well as on their attitudes towards change. Young people often provide a refreshing and creative perspective on wider social issues and schools can help them to articulate their views in constructive ways as part of the general tasks of education and preparation for life. Szur (1991) has commented on the dual nature of this process, which can also be presented as a struggle between different generations; the government is never up to its task, and is always working on outmoded assumptions, whilst the 'governors' within the family are also viewed in this way. At the same time, adults tend to project their hopes for the future onto young teenage shoulders, which can 'confuse, alienate or overwhelm the sense of individual identity' (p.153).

Adolescence is also partly about finding one's own authority, and learning to relate to authority figures. This is a confusing process which can be clarified by structures within the school which provide a clear definition of staff members' professional roles. It is also important to demarcate boundaries between the roles of different staff, and to set out clearly the authority and management structures, with areas of responsibility outlined. If staff themselves are clear about these issues, this is likely to enhance the young person's capacity to learn from experience about authority and structure.

Copley (1993) has observed how the ways in which school staff view themselves and respond to society's changing expectations of their roles, including how their professionalism and status are accepted by society, must convey itself to the adolescents with whom they work. Successive legislation (1986, 1988, 1993) has attenuated the authority of schools, both as institutions and by the over-determination of the professional roles within them. Schools are now accountable to a diverse range of outside bodies on matters ranging from staff appointments to curriculum, where the autonomy of professional teaching staff has been removed. As well as being required to implement a national curriculum, the headteacher now needs to seek the consent of school governors in determining the content of lessons, including the National Curriculum, religion and sex education. Young people are thus able to perceive the weakening of authority structures and the accompanying abdication of responsibilities inherent in the legislation, as the following example illustrates:

Case Example

A recent report in the press (1994) was of a school being publicly disciplined for the content of its sex education programme for 11-year-olds. On further scrutiny, it became clear that changing relationships between heads and governors (in the 1986 Act) which were intended to introduce greater accountability had in fact reversed the process. It was not possible to establish who was responsible in this instance for the lesson in question – the class teacher, school nurse, head teacher, governors, local education authority (LEA) or the government. Teachers subsequently found their authority threatened by children in the classroom, who ridiculed this diversification of the claim of responsibility.

Young people have also recently threatened to take their teachers to court, to make them lose their jobs, or have threatened to bring parent governors in on the basis of their acquaintance with the legislation. The lack of clear lines of responsibility and confusion over where the real power lies in schools is likely to affect particularly those youngsters whose home backgrounds are lacking in stability. They are now less likely to find securities and structures which can convey a sense of belonging within the school.

Young people have been particularly vulnerable to some of the combined effects of recent legislation in several different ways. It is helpful to consider some of the tasks of adolescence, and what is required to help them fulfil these tasks. Some of the principal dimensions of the adolescent tasks of growing up involve the gradual acquisition of autonomy, independence and responsibility. Teenagers gradually acquire these qualities by a gradual process of testing out boundaries with parents and teachers, who need to be able to provide models for identification which teenagers can push and rebel healthily against, while feeling that their aggressive impulses can be contained without retaliation. In the family setting, this is usually experienced as a bewildering and unsettling process which is testing of parental resources on many levels. While both parties may project their own unresolved parent–child conflicts on to the other, adults may react by over-protecting teenagers, becoming too permissive, or perhaps emotionally distancing themselves when their own sense of restriction is evoked. Trials and pitfalls of this nature may be an inevitable part of family life, but can become exacerbated by health problems, unemployment, lack of local provisions and resources, poverty and inner-city living.

It is not that adolescents are bored by rules and treat them with the weary resignation of adults faced with more parking, litter or smoking restrictions. Indeed adolescents are fascinated and challenged by rules. This behaviour is all the more noteworthy when contrasted with that of a small child. The young child moves in a world totally defined by her or his parents, who are usually seen as the sole begetters of his or her happiness or unhappiness. The parents are the ones the young child turns to for answers and the parents' power is not there to be questioned. The young child may occasionally, according to needs and personality, venture outside that safe world defined by their parents, but these are short, exciting and usually secret, even marauding, trips into what is felt by the young child to be alien territory – 'grown-up land'.

When the child approaches adolescence their relationship with the outside world begins to change, it widens and develops. This goes hand in hand with the diminishing of the parental pull. As the young child becomes adolescent a balancing relationship develops – that is, the pull of the 'real' world outside the family versus the parental pull. In order to break the ties that bound the child, the adolescent sometimes develops an antagonistic and hostile attitude to what they see the parent standing for – what they want to get away from . It is an easier, if less mature, way of moving away from someone than via reasoning and exploration. The seductive pull of childhood, of being totally dependent, is balanced against the excitement of independence and sexuality. The struggle is not only with parents but also with parent substitutes such as teachers or residential social workers. Thus the more intense the struggle the more we may assume intense, unresolved dependency needs, which have to be fiercely struggled against. Those who work with adolescents will inevitably find themselves concerned with issues of control, containment and the interdependency of the individual in relation to the family unit or the broader social group.

Vulnerable Adolescents

The particular vulnerabilities of young people can be thought about on several different levels. At a meta-level, government policies have meant restricted opportunities for some young people which are likely to have a formative impact on the future shape of their lives, and to be keenly felt at this stage in their development. These involve limited employment prospects and uncertainty for the future in an increasingly technological world; removal of funding at different levels of the education system, student loans and poverty; training schemes without the incentive of jobs; and removal of benefits to prevent young people leaving home.

Although some young people can negotiate these challenges more success-fully than others, many adolescents are likely to feel that society has let them down on the levels of education, jobs and also of housing. There are now many disenfranchised young people living on the streets, and they constitute a new profile of homelessness. In reality, many of these youngsters may have suffered physical and sexual abuse, or fled from intolerable situations in their own families or step-families. They are also likely to be young people who have been living in care and are now forced to live on the streets as local authorities deny their responsibilities towards assisting them as 'children in need' within the Children Act (1989).

Although adolescence is regarded as a process of upheaval for all young people, some individuals and groups are especially 'at risk' during this stage of their development. Teenagers who have lacked the experience of good primary care as children, or who never experienced life in an intact family, will find this time in their development anxiety-provoking. This is a period of life when disillusionment and reality-testing are at their height, and many teenagers are likely to enact their experiences of frustration and confusion in the form of an open rebellion, violence, truancy and delinquency. Winnicott (1956) has provided a helpful framework for understanding some of the parallels between adolescent and earlier processes of development in infancy. It is helpful if staff can reflect on challenges which are presented to them, as episodes of disruptive behaviour can also be understood as primitive forms of communication which may illuminate the young person's perspective.

Adolescence is experienced differently by girls and this is frequently disguised when young people are considered as a whole group. Gilligan's (1982, 1990) important research has detailed how the personal concerns and discourses of teenage girls become increasingly internalised and subjective during adolescence. They are able to refer to an internal world which represents an increasingly rich source of values, insights, feelings and preoccupations, and to share their views and beliefs with close friends. Their strengths in relating to subjective areas of understanding later equips them better for participatory styles of work, as they are more able to attend to internal group processes and relationships rather than focusing solely on task outcomes. However, the socially constructed strengths which teenage girls achieve is often at a great cost to their full participation in school life. Lees (1986) has documented the several areas in which girls still 'lose out' as they need to reconcile several conflicting areas of aspiration, career development, relationships with boys, and pressures towards marriage.

As girls frequently insulate themselves from some of these conflicting pressures, there is a tendency for their particular vulnerabilities to be overlooked in the education system. Research has consistently shown that a single gender distinction is important for girls, as the presence of boys in class groupings frequently leads to sexual harassment and also tends to deflect the teacher's time and attention away from girls; thereby affecting the formal learning process. The implications of these findings are that in thinking about specialised provisions for adolescent girls, it is helpful to consider their needs separately at the planning stages. One of the main themes of this chapter is consider how special conditions and provisions can be made to help vulnerable adolescents negotiate some of the developmental tasks and transitions of this stage.

As a child psychotherapist, I will be focusing particularly on specialised residential therapeutic settings, but I hope that my remarks will be general to all institutions dealing with adolescents. In an earlier paper, I have discussed the relevance of therapeutic ideas to group work for boys in a comprehensive school setting (Ellwood and Oke 1987). I hope that readers and staff in different settings will find these perspectives relevant to their work and that they will help to enhance their understanding of the relationships involved. The settings which I refer to involve both boys and girls, and developing a focus specifically about girls, as I refer to above, would need to be considered in a separate paper.

Specialised Provisions for Young People

Adolescents are usually referred to residential institutions when it is thought that they require the combined benefits of therapeutic containment and placement outside the home and community. Such placements form a necessary part of a continuum of provision which needs to be resourced to meet the broad range of needs of this client group. Teachers and other staff will be aware of the requirement for different forms of intervention for this age group. This is likely to include school counselling, off-site units, family therapy (Carter and McGoldrick 1989), adolescent walk-in clinics (Dartington 1995), group therapy (Copley 1993) or residential placements in boarding schools. The emphasis on these traditional forms of treatment for young people has been helping them find different ways of thinking about, structuring, and learning from experiences which have been too painful to tolerate.

Unfortunately, the last decade has seen a gradual dismantling of some of these provisions for young people and their families. Cuts in resources have affected the infrastructures between education, social services and health, limiting the capacities of these agencies to work together to provide the joint expertise which is an essential part of service delivery for young people. Local authorities are now frequently unable to fulfil their responsibilities within the legislative framework which exists to meet young people's needs (1981, 1989, 1993) due to diminishing resources.

As fiscal considerations assume priority in considerations of specialised provision, many young people are now being denied opportunities for special boarding school placements. Such placements used to fulfil an important preventative function in offsetting some of the crises anticipated during adolescence and later life. Paradoxically, the demise of some of those services and provisions which were psychologically based has been accompanied by a call for greater clamp-downs, tighter security and more punitive measures directed towards young people. The harsh enforcement of rules and coercive measures are of dubious efficacy with teenagers, although they may seem to be effective on a short-term basis when used as a threat.

Thinking About Rules, Boundaries and Sanctions

I am now going to consider the whole question of the meaning and importance of rules to adolescents. The next section surveys the seeming triviality of rules, citing some research carried out by the Children's Legal Centre (1993). Under this umbrella I survey some of the functions of rules, highlighting the developmental need for a framework within which, or outside which, adolescents' adult identities can be tested out and formed. I then go on to discuss the difficulties in maintaining rules and boundaries effectively for both schools and residential institutions and finally I look at the importance of staff in the work of maintaining boundaries.

The functions of rules

One of the first difficulties which is faced is a confusion over the function of rules and how they relate to punishments. Bruggen and O'Brian (1986) summarise succinctly the relationship between crime and punishment, highlighting the rather special purpose that crime (or rule breaking) can have in adolescence.

> We see punishment as the wilful infliction of physical or emotional harm on another person who is seen to have done something morally wrong. We see penalty as a price paid for infringing a regulation. We see sanctions as a curtailment or limit on the availability of a resource. Our view is that it is important in adolescence to challenge authority which administers punishment, penalty and sanctions. It is one of the ways that adolescents test their environment, their structure and you. We suggest that you value the exercise and their need to engage you in it. It is a ritual with rules and tactics. Please do not worry what it is about. (p.16)

'Rules' seems such a childish word. Rules are usually worked out by grown-ups as a way of subduing their reluctant population of adolescents. The very word 'rule' seems to embody, for me at least, a short-term and petty way of responding to a situation, whereas the word 'laws' seems to represent a much grander and wider concept. Perhaps part of the difference in perception between rules and laws arises from the idea that laws have grown up and developed over time, are enshrined in the Bible, by the legal system and by Parliament and have been arrived at by a generally agreed consensus; whereas the word 'rules' exudes the kind of pettiness, arbitrariness and unpredictability which is often characteristic of adolescent behaviour itself. In 1993 the Children's Legal Centre surveyed the measures of control used in residential psychiatric units in England and Wales. Sixty questionnaires were sent out and 22 were returned completed. These 22 showed wide disparities: some had rules outlawing 'chewing gum and bubble gum on the Unit'; another stated that 'residents not allowed on day trips with love bites or evidence of self-harm'; another had rules to do with tidying up the minibus after trips out; and another had something mysteriously called 'a footwear fine'. The function of these idiosyncratic rules seems to be to interfere in and control fairly trivial aspects of the adolescents' life.

Rules, by their willingness to deal with extremely petty issues, readily lend themselves to be challenged and broken. It is hard to take them seriously. As Bruggen and O'Brian (1986) point out, the existence of such petty rules and their breaking is a form of adolescent ritual. Of course adolescent styles of dress tend to attract rules both in schools and residential institutions – even in families. Perhaps the function of these possibly intrusive rules is more to do with adults needing to bolster their power in the face of such adolescent challenges than with any real concern for the safety of the adolescents and the institutions they inhabit. In other words, rules are more to do with the adults' needs than with the adolescents'. Such rules will almost inevitably become bones of contention, highlighting as they do the adult's inability to separate a healthy developmental challenge to adult authority, which needs to be dealt with spontaneously and firmly, from a challenge that has at its root destruction or even serious self-harm. To evoke rules for such apparently trivial aspects of day-to-day life indicates almost panic or an inability in staff to inhabit their own authority. Sometimes rules might be arrived at because of pressure from a parent body, a managerial authority or from the state. For example, rules about smoking might have to be enforced by staff who are smokers themselves, because of health service regulations, and such rules can lead to running dog fights centering around the unfairness of rules that adults themselves break.

We have seen two possibilities concerning the function of rules: that they serve to bolster the uncertain power of adults, and/or that they are imposed from on high on both staff and adolescents, and as such relate the wish of outside authorities to clamp down on the supposed excesses of adolescent units. Another function of rules which I will briefly mention is to maintain and enhance the reputation of an institution; thus there are rules about uniform and behaviour while in uniform. This type of rule is usually more visible and appropriate in schools (and also of course pertains to adult institutions like the Army) than in residential establishments. Such rules are often regarded benignly by staff and students and treated as fair game for infringement. Only occasionally does bitterness creep in when an adolescent's whole identity appears to hang on whether they can wear an earring to school or not.

The developmental function of rules

A fourth and most important function of rules in an adolescent institution is to provide a containing structure that the adolescent needs both to rebel against and to develop within. This addresses the fluctuations already mentioned as typical of adolescents; one moment sensible, attentive, responsible, at another rebellious and hostile, and at yet another childlike and clinging. Rules need to have within them the possibility of flexibility and humanity to help the adolescent cope with these bewildering changes. If rules are perceived by the adolescent as harsh, immutable and therefore unjust he or she will feel justified in law-breaking and will feel almost driven into it; however if rules are perceived as weak and easily manipulated, adolescents will treat them and the adults who attempt to enforce them with increasing contempt.

If the rules in an adolescent institution seem to consist of a mass of petty restrictions that even staff sometimes forget about, it is hard for the adolescent to retain any respect for these rules or for the adults who enforce them. Such rules serve only to perpetuate the adolescent's own confusion about his or her identity, what s/he wants to achieve in life, whether s/he loves or hates their parents. For adults, laws tend to define what it right and wrong in their society; for adolescents, rules tend to define safe and appropriate boundaries within which the adolescent will be allowed to construct his or her own life. Right and wrong are not so much the questions in matters such as sexuality, smoking or drinking or driving as the appropriateness and safety of that activity at that age.

So far we have attempted to differentiate between the purpose of rules for adolescents and of laws for adults in that for adolescents the rules have a developmental task, and a task with regard to the safety and health of the young person; thus right or wrong is not the overt driving force. We have looked at how young people use rules in the pursuance of their developmental tasks.

The maintenance of rules: differences between school and residential homes

How are rules best maintained? Clearly this task falls to the staff, whether teachers or residential workers. Rules are devised in answer to the real exigencies and dangers of a situation, or – perhaps rather more as a result of recent legislation – in response to directives from higher authorities. The aims of a school are different to the aims of a residential establishment; that is, schools aim to educate; residential institutions to provide a stable living situation and possibly therapeutic work.

Earlier in the chapter, the challenge to teacher's authority inherent in the legislation and the effect of this on young people was discussed. In residential establishments, more notably those run by the health service, it is simpler to establish a clear line of authority and responsibility. Nursing has been and to some extent still is run on hierarchical lines, a bit like the Army, whereas in teaching and the social services, this kind of pressure is less in evidence. However, as in schools in the past, authority and power can be misused and there are still instances of children and adolescents being abused in residential institutions. The main point I wish to make is that a clear chain of authority is essential if rules are to be normally maintained and the adults whose duty it is to enforce those rules where necessary must be respected.

When boundaries go: an example from a residential home

I would like to give an example of how a group of residential staff dealt creatively with the total breakdown of rules in a residential institution for adolescents. When I began to work with this institution, the atmosphere seemed to be, on the surface, very *laissez-faire*: no doors were locked, everything was negotiable, no clear rules seemed to exist. Exceptions to this seemed to depend on outside factors. For example, meals were provided at an exact time from outside and night staff arrived an exact time fixed by administration; thus young people had to be in their rooms at that time. Staff would allow young people to take keys and unlock doors. The philosophy seemed to be that these young people had been misunderstood and staff needed to do all they could to protect them from the harsh impingement of rules, boundaries and fixed times and to be totally caring, which seemed to mean no rules. However, within this *laissez-faire* environment, all of a sudden, draconian rules would be enforced and a child could suddenly be excluded and sent away for such a thing as a physical attack on a member of staff – that is, scapegoated.

A daily community group lasting one hour would consist of the interrogation of young people by staff who were trying to find out what was going on. Young people would be given 'carrots' for 'grassing'. Behind the superficial friendliness there was a sense of threat and violence which in fact occasionally came to the surface. Staff had been punched and taken prisoner. There was a sub-culture of drugs and petty theft. The Unit seemed to exist at two levels, the superficial friendliness and compliance with staff interspersed with the sub-culture of criminality and sporadic violence. This system existed uneasily for over a year until finally the young people broke into the staff-room during a handover (that is, the briefing of an on-coming staff group on the previous day's events).

This led to the institution being closed down for two weeks during which the staff worked intensively together planning new ways of working. They were assisted in this process by bringing in an outside consultant who helped the staff group to stay in work mode and to remain 'on task'. They managed to avoid scapegoating either the young people or the staff for the breakdown but realised it was a system they were locked into which was at fault. They decided to do away with their 'wishy-washy' and unclear idea of a therapeutic community and to run the institution with clear time boundaries and a clear programme. They introduced the concept of a key worker, whose job it was to develop a close relationship with their young clients. There was recognition of the therapeutic value of clear boundaries and of the encouragement of a close key worker relationship. From these two main changes came an open acknowledgement of the authority of the group workers and a greatly increased recognition of the value of the day to day work relating to the young people springing from the increased recognition of the key worker role. The young people responded to the new sense of containment by relating to staff not as previously as either rather silly, well-meaning people easily manipulated who could occasionally turn into violent dictators – this unpredictability increasing their untrustworthiness – but cautiously and rather painfully developing a sense of dependence on their reliability and professionalism and interest.

This example illustrates some of the factors that lead to failure: a confusion over aims and methods and oscillation between thoughtless 'theraping' and violent reaction leading to a complete lack of real trust. This contrasted with the second phase when the staff no longer tried to set themselves up as the caring adults the young people never had, but accepted their role as professionals, enforced the boundaries and encouraged the development of a close professional relationship between one key worker and a young person.

Triggers for rule breaking

It is widely known in schools and institutions that there are times and areas that are more likely to provoke confrontation than others. The clinical psychologist at another Adolescent Unit did some research into this, which she presented at an audit meeting on rules and boundaries in 1993 (unpublished document). Findings were that peer group rivalry seemed to cause the most problems, followed by crises caused by adolescents experiencing distress in their own families, possibly to do with rejection or the separation of the parents or a death or abuse in some shape or form. Such adolescents may express their distress by a 'don't care' attitude towards rules or may use this as a possible way of drawing attention to their problems which they are unable to put into words directly. The third area of difficulty when boundaries are likely to be pushed was before an anticipated difficult weekend at home with their parents and siblings. This links to the difficulties that schools often experience at the beginning and end of term, when pupils leave an ordered existence, with a stable structure of lessons and meals kept in place, it is hoped, by clear rules and authority, to go home to a sometimes chaotic situation with no clear mealtimes, no clear structure and no clear boundaries. This provokes anxiety. Teachers often see, especially in special schools, that children are able to stick to rules in a structured setting, but it is at breaks and play time that things can go seriously wrong. The fourth trigger that the team noticed in this instance was the return after a difficult weekend when a young person might need to test out the boundaries before settling down.

The Conditions for Institutional Containment

Obholzer (1992) has defined the following conditions as needing to be met if an institution is to be able to carry out its functioning as a unit for the therapeutic rehabilitation of adolescents. His use of the term 'containment' is based on Bion's contribution to the understanding of group and institutional processes. Bion (1962) originally wrote about the container and the contained in relation to the mother–child dyad. He described how the mother took in the child's distress, metabolised it and then responded to the child in such a way as to give the child the experience of being understood and helped to a degree. Applied to institutions, this means that the institution as a whole entity is required to perform this same 'containing' function for the whole group of adolescents. From this point of view, an individual's functioning is therefore perceived as, and treated as an aspect of group, and *not* of individual functioning.

The conditions are as follows:

1. There needs to be clarity of task.

2. There needs to be clarity of structure, of authority, of role and of boundaries.

3. There needs to be adequate training for staff, especially as regards group and institutional processes.

4. There needs to be an awareness of the risk to themselves, to the patients and to the institution, arising from the nature of the work they are doing.

All of these aspects were an essential aspect of the work I have described, but I would also like to suggest that another perspective which was important was the functioning of the staff team. In the situation I have described, it was also important to help staff consider how they themselves were responding to issues of authority and containment within the larger institution.

Some staff felt their ability to enforce rules convincingly was undermined, not least because, more or less unconsciously, they are themselves in an undermined adolescent role in relation to authority within the institution. This problem can be exacerbated where a rule is seen to be imposed from without as a result of, for example, audit processes or administrative demands or from outside bodies such as health authorities, government or parent bodies. The rule is not felt to have arisen from the life and needs of the institution and the member of staff can over-identify with the adolescent and perhaps collude in their breaking of such rules. However, it has to be said, that the effects of increasing centralisation may mean that even mature members of staff who are at ease with their own adolescence will find difficulties in identifying with some rules and will find the path to a healthy discussion of the relevance of such rules hard to follow.

The Staff Group

Adolescence is characterised by ebbs and flows of feeling, ups and downs, fluctuating between adulthood and childhood, and adolescent institutions are affected by the same vagaries – they inevitably have their ups and downs and ebbs and flows. Nevertheless the institution needs to maintain an ongoing way of thinking about itself. This ability to hold on to and think about the fluctuations and, often, chaos of adolescent life is often focused on the leader of such an institution, whether called headteacher, charge nurse, consultant psychiatrist, social worker or director. If this capacity for thought is lacking, the institution will react, or perhaps I should say over-react and even panic, to behaviour and events with immediate, stick-on solutions.

The leadership role in such an institution depends on the leader's ability to maintain a professional stance and is aided or undermined by his or her relationships with the long-stay staff group and by their relationships with (outside) management. Difficulties within the staff team can often be assumed when, for example, the staff team splits, with half the team looking to a leader who is hoping for change and growth and the other half of the team undermining processes of change and looking to the past. Splitting leads to inconsistency. Fear of change can be intensified when the staff group feel unsafe, whether because of outside changes in the nature of the job or the future of their establishment or because the staff team itself is not safe; there is not, for example, a shared culture and value system within the staff group. If staff do not feel safe in their own group it is difficult for the adolescent to feel safe with the staff. In extreme cases staff members can avoid the staff group and prefer the company of the young people, thus successfully undermining the staff group as a whole.

I would say that the effective authority of an institution follows to a large extent from the maturity or otherwise of the relationships that the staff are prepared to negotiate with the young people. Thus the willingness and ability of staff to look at themselves and their own motives is vital.

The effects that adults have on adolescents when the adults are, for example, consistently late for meetings, dress in an outrageous way or attend unpredictably some meetings and not others, or in other ways fail to maintain the norms and duties of their adult role, cannot be underestimated. Such behaviours undermine the structure of an institution and make it less safe. It turns the adults into naughty children who are themselves breaking the rules, whilst expecting the adolescents to maintain standards of punctuality, dress and attendance at meetings. Such lapses are especially hard to bear for adolescents with their preoccupation with fairness. Adolescent behaviour in adult staff is a worrying sign and can result in a worker stirring up the adolescent to such an extent that the adolescent may break rules, become violent or sexually act out. Work with adolescents is invariably challenging and workers have to be prepared to look at needy adolescent parts of themselves rather than projecting it into the young people they are working with.

Sometimes staff may identify with certain young people who best reflect their own *chronologically* past problems (that is, unresolved issues from adolescence) too strongly and even collude with them. On the other hand, such motivation gives staff the potential for a deeper and more vivid understanding of the difficulties and pains of the adolescent. It is for this reason that the importance of supervision, staff support and training should be recognised, especially in residential establishments, to help staff differentiate themselves from the adolescents with whom they are working so closely and thus to maintain more effectively appropriate boundaries.

The Need for a Thoughtful Space

If the three components of an institution – the staff group, its leader and the individuals in the team – can establish clear lines of authority and management, are able to find the space and time to look at the difficulties in the team with the adolescents and can support and give feedback to the leader, the problems around the periphery of the institution, that is, its rules will be seen in perspective. But without this space for thought and debate, issues around the rules – the boundary of the institution – can become paramount, taking precedence over the work that goes on inside those boundaries. A situation could therefore evolve where the staff could be so immersed in enforcing rules that this *becomes* the work of the institution. This is the kind of institution that might look good on paper but where real thought and the confronting of painful issues does not happen. It is also likely that such an institution has no centre and is all boundaries. Here rules are invariably enforced without thought, and the purpose is one of control rather than containment. The staff member is concerned with the issue of power rather than of authority. Power often means physical power and in this case establishments become concerned about the number of men on the shifts or in the teams and the vulnerability of the women staff.

Thus we can see that there is ample scope for a wide variety of solutions to the problem of rules and boundaries, from the rule-bound institution which leaves no internal space for adolescent development and is preoccupied with issues of control, to the institution where the staff members are acting out their own problems and projecting them on to the unfortunate adolescents in the institution. There is no clear authority structure in such situations, as staff members are not respected, and this can result in institutional chaos and quite often riot.

Final Thoughts

In this chapter, I have illustrated how some of the central themes within the broader social context can be reflected within the lives of young people, affecting their capacities to fulfil some of the developmental tasks of adolescence. I have considered some of the changing approaches to issues of dependency, autonomy, authority, choice and personal responsibility which young people are likely to encounter in their relationships with staff in different settings. Sometimes, legislative and institutional changes can create more problems than they solve, as they often lead to the dismantling of structures which were erected in the first instance to help institutions fulfil their primary tasks.

With so much pressure on schools and residential establishments to produce results – thruput, as we call it in the health service – it becomes harder to justify time spent in thoughtful debate with colleagues. For example, time spent in the staff-room could be frowned on as a waste of time; on the other hand, informal, unpressured conversation in a friendly staff-room could be essential in the formation of a consensus in the staff group as to the meaning and purpose of their work. Whether such time is used or mis-used depends to a large extent on the maturity of the core staff team. Successful rule- and boundary-setting result from clear lines of authority and management structures and the fostering of mature relationships among the staff and professional relationships with the young people.

We have seen in schools how the attenuation of the teacher's power and responsibility has tended to put teachers in a vulnerable and defensive position in relation to their pupils, which does not normally help in the maintenance of effective discipline. Likewise, the Children Act has sometime created authority problems for social workers in residential homes. The young people know that the workers in certain situations are powerless. The wish by government for a magical solution to the problems of adolescence, such as ill-fated 'short sharp shock' regime or the attempt to abolish problem adolescents by the current policy of closing many in-patient and residential establishments and special schools such as Pepper Harrow will not work.

Nevertheless, adolescence is a particularly responsive time in which the adolescent is particularly receptive to the outside world and those members of it that he or she respects. We can all perhaps think back to a particular adult, often a teacher, who influenced us as teenagers and it is for those of us who work with adolescents to concentrate on the quality and thoroughness of out work and await the results.

Maintaining a healthy balance between care and control is fundamental to helping adolescents learn and develop, yet can be difficult to achieve as some of the examples I have drawn on illustrate. I also have shown that learning and development are processes which staff need to engage in as well as young people. Working with vulnerable adolescents is testing of all our resources, and increased understanding of the connections between individual and group dynamics can help staff anticipate and make sense of difficulties as they arise. Reflective understanding can also offset some of the sense of inadequacy and crisis engendered by this age group, and restore a purpose, challenge and feeling of hope for the potential which young people represent.

CHAPTER 6

Consultation and Service Development

Clare Huffington

Introduction

The enormous cultural and structural changes within the public sector have created a need for reflection upon and exploration of the consequences of these changes at local level. Yet it seems there is no time to process them before the next set of changes and associated tasks is upon us. Professionals like teachers, psychologists, counsellors, inspectors, social workers, community workers and the like, who might once have had time to consult one another on far-reaching new ideas and accommodate the new order, can now feel constrained into the strictly prescribed aspects of their role.

Professionals can often feel that the quality of the service they deliver suffers as a result of this lack of thinking and planning of long- as well as short-term consequences of decisions taken; and that they lack a sense of a wider perspective on their task. In this chapter, I hope to examine the potential for working consultatively within the new service structures despite the difficulties and constraints.

Consultation in Context

At this time of widespread changes, many professionals within these systems feel ill-equipped to implement them. Consultation offered to public sector organisations by consultants who work *within* them offers those involved an opportunity to take stock and reflect on the relentless process of change. It also presents the possibility of local, tailor-made solutions to the problems created by applying national policy at a local level. The value of internal consultation of this kind is that these solutions come from 'the ground floor'; they present the possibility of spotting the need for consultancy early on; they facilitate the growth of a broad base of support for change and often the potential for ownership of the change effort by the organisation itself: all these advantages spring from consultation offered by professionals within the organisation. Added to this, it costs less than external consultation, which has become discredited by some expensive mistakes and the frequent difficulties in implementation.

Consultation can also become a vehicle for empowerment, as it can offer involvement and a sense of ownership to all those participating in the process, including management, practitioners and service users. In this sense, offering consultation or working within a consultative framework can be seen as part of the general trend towards quality in public sector services (Ovretveit 1992).

However, having pointed out the obvious advantages of working consultatively, it is as well to bear in mind certain characteristics of organisations in the process of change. Most public sector organisations are under a great deal of stress, with low staff morale and difficulties in adapting effectively to changed circumstances. In many cases, they will be dealing with the most vulnerable members of society. They will unconsciously have developed defence mechanisms to deal with the distress this work engenders and will be unwilling to give them up (Obholzer and Roberts 1994). It is likely that the primary task of the organisation is unclear and that attempts to deal with the difficulty of the task have, in turn, made it *more* rather than less difficult. The person in the organisation requesting your help as a consultant is likely to feel he or she is losing out in some way from the changes afoot and will really be seeking to bind you to the status quo or else request you to change other parts of the organisation but not him or her.

Without going in detail into the process of consultation at this point, which is outside the brief of this chapter, it follows from what has been said that the purpose of consultation is to be able to engage in a collaborative exploration with the consultees about their difficulties, promoting their curiosity in their own condition and to wish to engage in activities that will improve it; the consultation process needs to start from the position the consultees are at, rather than the offer of pre-packaged solutions or radical changes which will be seen as threatening and resisted at all costs.

Definitions of consultation

The working definition that I use goes as follows:

> Consultation is a process involving a person who is invited to help a client with a work-related issue. The client can be an individual, a group or an organisation. The essential issue is one of responsibility for the process, and this may help to clarify the difference between consultation and other activities, such as supervision, counselling, therapy, teaching, advising and management. The responsibility for *fulfilling the task* of the organisation in the consultation process lies with the client, whereas the responsibility for the *consultation process* lies with the consultant.

The consultant uses his or her skills and knowledge about the process of change to enter into a mutual exploration towards an understanding of the meaning of the problem for the organisation as a whole. The consultant's position within the system offers a different perspective from that of the client. From this perspective, the consultant can offer new ideas that may create a new set of meanings in the organisation and allow the problem to be seen in a different way, leading to new behaviours and new relationships. These may allow the organisation to move forward in its development.

What often causes confusion about consultation is *which activities 'count' as consultation* and which do not. I am often asked if the following count: a request for needs assessment of a group of children; designing an operational policy; a survey into parents' views on sex education; establishing 'user groups', writing a proposal for inter agency working; helping a teacher get on better with her nursery nurses; running a training event on child sexual abuse; the list is endless. The point is that *all* these activities and more can be counted as consultation if the responsibility issues as outlined in the definition above are clear; that is, that the person requested to act as consultant is not also responsible for the consequences of the consultation process in a functional role in relation to the tasks concerned. A certain amount of negotiation of the consultation role is almost always needed to achieve this position.

Styles and Models of Consultation

This brings me on to make a distinction between *process and expert consultation*. Consultation covers a range of activities, from those which resemble non-directive counselling (listening, reflecting) all the way through the more directive activities such as report writing, giving recommendations and so forth (see Figure 6.1). One of the skills to develop as a consultant is being able to play up and down the scale according to the request made, the stage of the process, and so on. It may be appropriate at different times to behave as teacher, advisor, facilitator, researcher, trouble shooter, sales person etc. as long as the locus of responsibility is firmly held, alongside a bird's eye view of the primary task of the work to be accomplished as a whole.

It is often confusing to potential consultants that requests made to them outside their strictly prescribed role are often, in fact, usually made to them in terms of their particular 'expert' knowledge. So a psychologist might be asked to set up a service evaluation in a new family centre, or a social worker might be asked to work with a group of foster parents on recognition of abuse in children they care for.

This can be called the 'purchase' model of consultancy (see Figure 6.2). As one can see from Figure 6.2, one often discovers when exploring around the problem that the client may not have correctly diagnosed the problem, so that

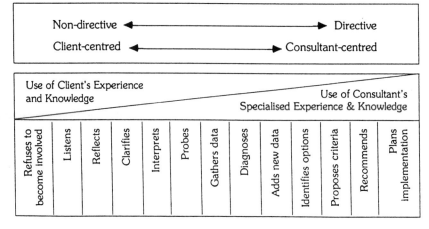

Source: Schmidt and Johnston 1970

Figure 6.1 Continuum of consultation styles

The Purchase Model

This is the most common form of consultancy, usually where a client buys expert services or information, e.g. advice on, and recommendations about, installation of a new computer system. Such a model is very much 'content'-oriented and is most successful if:

- the clients have correctly diagnosed their problems,
- the clients have correctly matched the available specialised expertise with the particular problem to be 'solved'.

The Doctor–Patient Model

Here the clients are aware of the 'symptoms' of their problems, e.g. 'our staff morale is very low', but have not come up with any diagnosis. Instead, they expect their consultants to pinpoint the cause if any problems and prescribe remedies. This model works satisfactorily if:

- the clients have correctly interpreted their symptoms,
- the consultants correctly diagnose the problem and prescribe appropriate solutions.

The Process Consultancy Model

This is the prime consultancy mode of OD. Unlike the previous two models, it is less concerned with the content of a problem, and more with the process by which problems are solved. It focuses on helping clients to form their own diagnoses, based on their proximity to, and hence understanding of, the associated issues. Clients are then helped to generate, select and implement any associated solutions. It is therefore within this model that the consultant may be considered to operate as an Agent of Change (Schein 1987).

Source: Brunning et al. 1990

Figure 6.2 Consultation models

what is presented as a request for a service evaluation, for example, actually requires an assessment of team dynamics and team development work as well, requiring the potential consultant to draw on process as well as expert skills. Of course one *could* deal with such requests as they stand, but what one would often find is that process problems get in the way of achieving the project and that wider perspective on the issue is lost.

For example, when I was asked to undertake a service evaluation in a new family centre, I found confusion about what the service was and how everyone should perform their roles. Whilst the staff were willing and even *wanted* me to go away and devise a service evaluation strategy for them, I could see that it could not be implemented and it would also not solve their basic problem of a need for clarity of their primary task. If I helped them with this, then we could work together devising ways of monitoring how well they were achieving it. Hence, a piece of very different consultation work developed around the initial request.

Sometimes a request will be framed in terms of a 'process' problem, as in the Doctor–Patient Model (see Figure 6.2), but again the client may not have accurately interpreted the difficulties, so again the consultant may need process skills to do this; expert skills may also be required as part of the intervention. For example, a manager within a voluntary organisation asked for team building for a team which he identified as not functioning well within the organisation. However, when I met the team members and team leader, they did not feel that they had any particular difficulties, but alerted me to the general anxiety about a forthcoming merger of their organisation with another organisation. This would have implications for everyone, but particularly for the manager, who would find himself with a new boss, instead of being in charge, and would form part of a second tier of the organisation together with other managers managing the teams. It looked as if my intervention needed to be at this management level; to meet the manager to discuss the impact of the changes on him and the organisation as a whole, perhaps to offer to meet the new management team to help them in their thinking about the new management structure and planning for the larger organisation's future development.

Last, and very rarely, a request will be framed in totally 'process' terms, such as a request from a school about to be amalgamated with another school worded loosely as 'help us to come to terms with and react effectively to this process of change'.

What I am saying here is that the 'process' framework of exploring and trying to understand *the relationships around a problem* which can be presented as a structural/technical issue is the essence of consultative work.

Being able to negotiate a consultation role which addresses both 'expert' and 'process' issues will be essential to future service development in the new purchaser/provider structures: the reorganisation and re-structuring in the public sector is demanding rapid changes in staffing and staff roles. Many tasks

1. Scouting

Change gent decides whether or not to 'enter' the system

2. Entry:

Establishing a relationship with the client as a basis for further involvement.

3. Contracting:

Developing a mutual contract, clarifying expectations and *modus operandi*.

4. Data-Gathering:

Measuring organisational indices and variables.

5. Diagnosis:

Interpreting the data, feeding it back to the client and developing a joint understanding.

6. Planning:

Identifying specific interventions including who will do what, and how it might be evaluated.

7. Intervention:

Carrying out the planned implementations.

8. Evaluation:

Assessing the success of the interventions and the need for further action or withdrawal.

9. Withdrawal:

If no further action by the change agent is required, managing the termination of the OD work, while at the same time leaving the system with an enhanced capacity to manage such change by itself in the future.

Source: Brunning et al. (1990) Diagram reprinted with the permission of Kristof Bien

Figure 6.3 Key stages in consultation

arise from these changes which require both technical/expert knowledge as well as process skills. Some examples, already mentioned above, are: audit and quality projects; creation of user groups; and setting up new work teams.

It should be clear by now that the process of clearly negotiating one's involvement in such tasks is absolutely essential. Figure 6.3 shows that Stage 1 and 2 are all about establishing the ground rules, particularly the responsibility issues. There is a tendency for the consultant to be ascribed responsibility for the outcome of the consultation process unless this is firmly clarified. Missing out these stages and diving in at Stage 3 can scupper the whole process. (See Huffington and Brunning 1994, p.25, for an example of how easily this can go wrong and how in this case it was successfully rescued.)

It is as well to keep in mind these *stages* in the *consultation process*, however informally one is working. In practice, not many consultation requests are made formally and develop into written contracts, even though this might help to clarify responsibility issues as above. Most professionals will be trying to work *consultatively* rather than as consultants within their prescribed roles: that is, they will be attempting to think 'process', think about relationships around a problem even though they have no legitimate consultation role within the organisation.

For example, a manager who has the task of creating flexible working teams from a highly specialised and hierarchically organised staff group can approach this task consultatively. He could decide that rather than immediately imposing new working arrangements, as might be done in some organisations, he will approach this via a staff development study; he will meet each staff member individually to review their career development; strengths and gaps and assess their readiness to fit into new working structures. This may lead to the creation of training packages for those staff with particular gaps in their skills; and possibly to the creation of one or two teams from staff members who feel ready to experiment with the new working style.

External and Internal Consultation

This brings me on to the make a distinction between consultation to individuals, groups or organisations outside the organisation of which the consultant is a member and *internal consultation* which involves consultation to individuals, groups or the whole organisation of which the consultant is also a member. Requests for consultation from one's own organisation are likely to become increasingly common as the effects of public sector changes unroll and organisational difficulties emerge for which external consultants are less and less likely to be employed for financial reasons. For some professionals in the public sector, this kind of work is already integral to their job. For example, a headteacher, responsible for a training budget, would also be responsible for identifying areas of training need within her staff group. The identification of difficulties staff may have in performing their work which may require training input is essentially an internal consultation task.

The advantage of being an internal consultant is the local knowledge, spotting a need for consultation early on and being able to gain support for change which can be carried through to its conclusion. Many external consultants fail at the implementation stage.

The disadvantages of working internally involve some specific dilemmas. The main problem is of the difficulty of developing new ideas for stuck situations. As an internal consultant you are to a certain extent as 'blind' as everyone else to the problems since you too are caught up in a network of relationships with which you need to identify and be included in (Argyris 1973).

It is my contention that the consultant, internal or external, needs to recognise that he or she is part of the system being observed and that this can limit one's potential for bringing about change. This implies that the consultant must have a different enough view from the consultees that change can come about. Sometimes the consultant may need consultation him or herself to maintain a sense of difference, perhaps by regular discussions with a colleague from inside or outside the organisation. It may be that the struggle to maintain a meta-position (a bird's eye view on the whole situation) may be more difficult the closer the consultant is to the problem for which consultation is requested. In Figure 6.4 this would mean a situation in which members of Team 2 approached the consultant, also based in Team 2, for help with a problem in the same team. One is then dealing with conflicting contexts of belonging to a team which means sharing views and having different views which might provoke change. It is my view that consultation to one's own immediate colleagues or team is usually not possible because of the loyalty conflicts which may ensue and also reduce potential for difference. Requests for consultation which arise from within one's own team are probably best refused and dealt with by an external consultant.

However, this is not to say that, having decided not to become involved in a problem as a consultant, it may not still be possible to create a context in which one can work consultatively in one's own functional role, for example, manager. For example, if one was asked to sort out a personality problem within the team of which one was also a member, this might be a piece of work best turned down for the reasons described above. But, as a manager within that team, it might be appropriate to initiate an appraisal scheme which might deal with individual needs development within the team.

It is probably already apparent from what has been said that the role of consultation can become confused with aspects of one's functional role within an organisation. Most public sector workers wear many 'hats' in addition to their basic functional role. For example, a teacher may also work as a counsellor in relation to discussing problems with parents, a manager in relation to specific

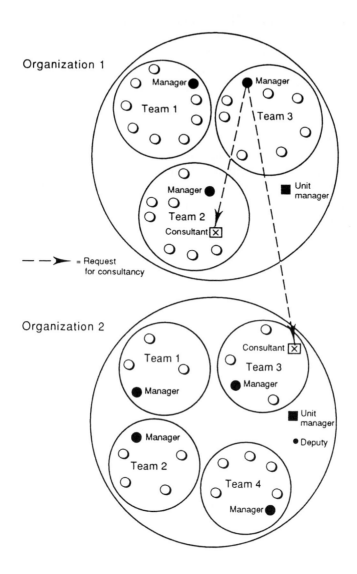

Source: Huffington and Brunning 1994

Figure 6.4 External and internal consultation

organisation/curriculum tasks within the school, a facilitator of group discussions and so forth. It is always important to spell out to those concerned which 'hat' one is wearing at a particular time so that expectations appropriate to one role do not become confused with those appropriate to another. For example, a year head who is counselling a member of staff would need to be clear about the boundaries of confidentiality; whether there would be anything the staff member could say which, with a managerial hat on, the year head might need to pass on to the deputy head. In relation to consultation and other activities, it is the responsibility issues which need to be clearly spelled out so that the person acting as consultant is not deemed to be responsible for some issue, for which in another role he or she might actually be responsible but is not appropriate to the consultation task. This will compromise his or her ability to offer a different or independent view. It is therefore vital that time is spent clarifying the expectations of the consultant in relation to the piece of work concerned from all those who might be involved, particularly spelling out the differences between consultation and teaching, therapy, management and so forth. The legitimacy for taking on the piece of work also needs to be clarified. By this I mean sanction from one's line manager and sanction from other managers responsible for the overall work of the organisation concerned. If this is not obtained, then the work cannot go ahead without risk to its credibility and effectiveness. The consultant may also have to deal with his or her own feelings of entitlement to engage in this kind of work (Ovretveit, Brunning and Huffington 1992).

Service Development

Within the new purchaser/provider culture, public sector professionals have had to grow accustomed to 'packaging' their services and marketing them. They may sometimes feel they make claims for themselves about which they cannot deliver! The pressure initially has been to focus on quantity of work, increasing the output within the basic prescribed role, sacrificing qualitative aspects of the work, into which consultation might fit. However, it has become clear that organisations cannot work effectively without attention to quality issues or 'value-added' features of services. This is where it has become more possible to market consultation services, often within an expert framework. Organisations have begun to see that it is difficult to audit and evaluate services in order to improve them (by setting up quality circles, for example) without the benefit of someone with a slightly different or more distant perspective on the service. Those with particular knowledge of the services involved but at one step removed become valuable to organisations as consultants. From this position, it will become possible to address process issues as well as structural or technical features, since this is what is intended by the notion of 'total quality management' (Ovretveit 1992).

However, before one can market consultation effectively, there are other hurdles to overcome. The most important of these is probably the ambivalence which some professionals may feel towards consulting work. This seems to arise from a value position opposed to the changes in the public sector. Many professionals refuse to help the 'supermarket system' work better: on this view, it may be easier to sit on the fence than to make compromises. For example, some professionals feel that it is important to continue to offer services directly to the consumer rather than move into a meta-role like consultancy, since direct services are shrinking daily.

It is, however, important to recognise that, unless professionals *do* get involved in consultation, they may become cut off from any way of affecting service development which *does* fit with their philosophy. The task of education does not have to be dominated only by considerations of cost. The focus of consultation on the performance of the task which best meets the psychological needs of all concerned – pupils, teachers and schools and local authorities alike (Trist *et al.* 1963) may go some way to ameliorating the dehumanising aspects of the reforms which concern many professionals. It provides a model for addressing partnership issues in education as it is based on the fundamental idea that addressing relationships is at the heart of the effective performance of work tasks.

For example, in attempting to develop a new service for children with special needs (against a background of closing a large special school) meetings with individual parents and children as well as in individual staff were held. These focused on feelings about the loss of the old service and ideas from parents, children and teachers about how a new service could best meet their needs. The new service could then be designed in service of the task according to the wishes of the users and would stand the best possible chance of being effective.

There are obvious practical problems such as robbing time for the basic task of education (teaching and learning), finance, the absence of a clear purchaser, pressure to evaluate and audit. It is my view, however, that some meta-thinking and assertiveness could go some way to dealing with this.

Two of the key organisational conditions necessary for developing consultation are an organisational position and base from which to do the work and an ability to finance it. I would suggest that the creation of organisational conditions paves the way for this work to be the basis of formal contracts. This could be done in the following ways:-

> *Avoiding restrictions*: Professionals need to avoid and oppose conditions which restrict consulting work, such as having contracts only for basic functional tasks and having time tied only to this work and by reframing requests for help so as to open the brief to consultation. For example, a request for help in managing a particular child might, after meeting with a class teacher, be reframed as training input for all staff on managing children with low self-esteem,; or might even address self-esteem as an issue for the staff group as a whole in work discussion groups.

> *Recognising consultation as part of the job*: This includes writing consultation into job descriptions; including accounts of consultation in annual reports, newsletters and brochures; writing consultation into

business plans and contracts; and auditing consultation and developing performance indicators for this work.

Conditions for developing consultation: Working with other professionals or consultants on projects; regular contact with other consultants; offering consultation by *both* responding to requests *and* initiating them; getting work commissioned as far up the management structure as possible; providing progress reports and final evaluations to all management levels; piloting projects and using these as examples of possible future consulting work.

Although it is clear that consultation is an approach which looks primarily at relationships and the processes which need to be created to help people in organisations work more effectively, often it can not be marketed like this. In any case, those requesting consultation usually frame their requests around a technical, structural· or content issue (see section on styles and models of consultation, pp.104–8). It will be important for prospective consultants in the public sector to develop skills in the negotiation phase of the consultation process to open up the brief to include process issues too. They may need to develop 'packages' of consultation around particular key areas of expertise such as stress management and needs assessment, as these will 'sell'. It may be that further training is required in order to be able to do this.

In order to be able to work at higher levels within the organisation, that is, management group level, the consultant who is not at this level in the organisation him or herself may need extra training to provide credibility for consultation such as management training or formal training in consultation including theoretical work on organisations and organisational change.

We cannot leave the area of service development without focusing a little more on the issue of *evaluation*. There are few studies which look at the effects of consultation, yet it will be essential in the audit culture to be able to provide evidence of effectiveness in order to continue to engage in such activities.

In fact, the issue of evaluation, reframed as the formal use of feedback, should not be too problematic for consultants. The use of feedback is essential at all stages of consultation to give meaning to the process as it evolves. The task of evolving outcome measures therefore involves creating formal mechanisms for measuring change within the feedback process. This is essentially a consultative process in itself and at least partly determined by the consultees. Examples of questions that might be asked to begin this process might be as follows:

1. What changes do you expect to see if the consultancy is effective?

    a. At individual level – e.g. pupils, teachers

    b. At group level – e.g. classes, year groups

    c. At system or service level – e.g. whole school

2. How can these changes be operationally defined? How will you see whether it is working or not?

3. How can this be measured and when?
    e.g. Informal discussion
         Interview or questionnaire
         Formal testing, e.g. attendance, pupil achievements.

Training

Many public sector professionals adopt roles outside their basic functional tasks for which they have not been trained. Consultation is one of these roles and, although many people have acquired many of the necessary skills along the way, this is probably not enough to help the potential consultant avoid some of the pitfalls outlined above. There is a need for consultation to be included in the pre-qualification training of many public sector professionals, or, if not, for more post qualification training to be offered. These need to address, among other issues: organisation and organisational development; negotiating the role of consultant including responsibility and legitimacy issues; stages in the consultation process; models and styles of consultation appropriate to the task concerned; internal consultation issues; marketing and costing. Failing this, a minimum requirement for engaging in this work would be consultation for the consultant; that is, that the potential consultant would consult with a colleague about their consultation work, either as a pair or in a group setting of peer consultation and support.

It is my experience from being involved in initiating and running a course in consultation (Huffington, Dowling and Kennedy 1993) that participants report not only a development in consultation skills but a different perspective on all their work, even informing their basic functional roles in new ways.

Conclusions

Far from constraining professionals within their basic functional roles, future service development requires the development of a range of skills, or multi-skilling in order for the changes in the public sector to bring about more effective services. In my view, the development of consultation skills are essential as a framework for operating within the new culture, but not without preparation and forethought, as I hope I have demonstrated in this chapter.

CHAPTER 7

Working with the Workers with the Troubled Child

Eileen Orford

I meet regularly with a group of teachers whose role is to offer support to individual children whose difficulties make for problems both for the child's learning and, more often than not, the child's integration in the classroom.

I have met with this group of teachers for a number of years since I first met them as part of a training event aimed at helping them to move from their previous role as workers in off-site units to that of working with individual children within their school setting.

I was asked to undertake my part in the training event because it was known that I had worked within a comprehensive school as a consultant for some years and that I had developed some ideas about the functioning of schools as organisations, and also about the pressures that arise for teachers and pupils within the classroom.

Psychodynamics in the Classroom

The study of organisations arose not from consideration of institutions within the public sector, but from within industry. Schools, I think, were thought to harbour none of the problems of the factory floor. Such difficulties that arose were laid at the door of the individual pupil – certainly such seemed to be the situation within the literature, both of school stories aimed at the children's market, and also in adult novels. Such a situation was also reflected within schools in which I had worked. Consideration of the functioning of the school as an organisation was far from the minds of most teachers. Yet much can be learned from the consideration of a school as a socio-technical system. This would attempt to view the school from an individual and group point of view, within its context within the wider educational world, as well as from a practical, technical and curricular standpoint.

The School as a System

Systems theory provides concepts that integrate the various perspectives. Defined in the Oxford Dictionary as 'an assemblage of things connected, associated or inter-dependent so as to form a complex unity', each level of organisation can be seen as a system. Most working organisations function as open systems, that is to say, they respond and adapt to a wider social context. Industrially seen, this implies that in producing their product, the manufacturing organisation responds to a demand for it. Open systems exist in a state of constant change. They adapt to demands from outside, and also change in response to the states of affairs within the organisation. Change takes place on the boundaries of the organisation, which is where management has, inevitably, to operate. Management is required to respond to the realities of external demand, to feed these demands into the organisation and to make such arrangements internally as are required to fulfil them optimally.

An organisation comes together to fulfil some purpose, sometimes referred to as a *primary task* or mission. In the manufacturing industry the task is relatively readily defined as the production of a product or a range of products. In other organisations, task definition may not be as clear-cut. What is the mission of a school or university? A task delineated as the education of students might seem to suffice, but other tasks may also seem important; research in the case of the university and the emotional development of the child within the school. The diffusion or lack of concrete definition of primary task may present problems within certain sorts of institution, but I would like to leave this aside at the moment, and to continue consideration of the more general function of institutions.

In organisations of any degree of complexity, management, in response to both internal and external pressures, has to delegate different aspects of its task to sub-systems. Each sub-system will have its own functions and responsibilities – that is to say its own primary task. Within the British school system, there are various common ways in which such sub-functions and tasks are allocated. Responsibility for the curriculum is often distinguished from responsibility for so-called 'pastoral care' – that is, the more general social development of pupils.

There are further divisions into social 'house' groups, into 'year groups' (that is, children at approximately the same age and academic standard) and within the year groups into small class or tutor groups. Each sub-system will have its own task which will vary, therefore, from, for example, the teaching of mathematics throughout the school to the provision of a social context for development for a small class or tutor group. The personnel in these groups may overlap – that is to say, a maths teacher will also have a tutor group. This may provide some complication for the individual teacher, but their task in each group will be different. Teachers need to be aware of their differing roles and tasks depending on which sub-system they are functioning in. If the system as a whole is to function satisfactorily, the tasks of the sub-systems need to be well-defined and the group needs to be able to hold to its task. If the boundaries of a sub-system are too rigid, communication with other sub-systems will be difficult. If the boundary is not well-defined, then the sub-system will find it difficult to hold to its task and will be diverted into consideration of issues other than those relevant to its tasks. Some of the problems in the organisation of sub-systems in British schools may arise from difficulties inherent in membership of too many sub-systems.

The Classroom Group

In the following, I shall draw on the work of Wilfred Bion and, in particular, on his *Experience in Groups* (1961) and also on elaborations of this work by Turquet (1974) and others. In *Experiences in Groups*, Bion drew vivid attention to how the work which groups are ostensibly wishing to carry out is constantly interrupted by anti-task activities. He isolated various processes which he called 'Basic Assumptions', which drew the group from its work – that is to say, what it was assembled to undertake in response to some real demand – and which provided alternative and less realistic objectives. These objectives may become ends in themselves and are therefore liable to displace the primary working task of the group.

Bion's observations arose from phenomena that he saw in professional and therapeutic groups. The phenomena were, he felt, related to the individual's efforts to deal with himself as an identity within the group. The tension within the individual to maintain himself among others – particularly in larger groups – lead him to find ways, rather equivalent to defences within the individual, of coping with the collective.

Bion isolated three such ways, which he called *Basic Assumptions*. First, he noted a *Basic Assumption of dependency,* which is usually referred to as BD. Such a mode of operation depends on the evolution of a leader, who takes responsibility for the group and to whom others subordinate themselves. The second Basic Assumption that he noted was the *fight/flight mode* – usually called BF. The aim in this mode is to find someone or something that requires resistance or movement away from – and that fundamentally requires some negative form of *action*. The third mode of operation is by *pairing*, called BP. In such a group the aim is to create something new, some hope or idea, which will arise through the coming together of two members of the group with whom the rest can identify vicariously.

These Basic Assumptions represent for Bion ways in which groups attempt to manage themselves, and they can operate in a more or less flexible way. If they operate rigidly, the group will pursue the Basic Assumption as an end in itself, and will be diverted from the primary task. In such a case, the BD group will function by the subordination of the will and creativity of the individual to the leader whose maintenance becomes the focus of group activity; the BF function will rigidify into paranoia and aggressive competition; and the BP group will lose touch with the reality of the work it is required to undertake and to take to the pursuit of ideal and unrealistic solutions.

It is also possible, since Basic Assumptions are endemic to all group functions – as defences are to individual functioning – that they can operate in a flexible and sophisticated way. So that, for example, the BD group can encourage participation in learning from an expert, whilst also valuing the experience and individual contributions of members of the group. A BF assumption can foster the development of independence and individual creativity; and the BP assumption can harness individuals in working towards the best possible solutions.

When, however, the Basic Assumptions within a working group are functioning in a relatively primitive way, they may act as a defence against the anxiety that maybe aroused by that work. Isobel Menzies-Lyth (1960) drew attention to this in her paper 'The functioning of social systems as a defence against anxiety'. She studied the functioning of a ward in a hospital from the point of view of the nurses' role in it. In essence, she found a group that functioned in a rigid BD way. The hierarchy in the hospital was a rigid one, with doctors in charge of nurses, and nurses operating within a rigid system in which senior nurses could dictate to junior ones throughout a well-defined authority structure. The actual work of the ward was painful and the nurses were required to work with people made dependent by their sickness and struggling with all the anxieties that can arise in illness and the threat of death. What Menzies-Lyth found was that the system diverted the anxiety of the nurses from their care of their patients and relocated it in their fear of the doctors and the senior nurses. The junior nurse was much more worried that her uniform was correct and that she had pleased her superiors than that she was responding sensitively and warmly to her patients and that she was treating them properly. This piece of work drew striking attention to what can happen to a working group.

I have noted, in the same vein, what can happen in schools where obsessive concern with curriculum can take a teacher from the anxiety of whether the children are really learning. Such defences have been in some schools underwritten by the demands of the National Curriculum, which has reduced the autonomy of individual teachers to adapt what they teach to the needs and interests of a particular classroom group, and in so doing divert their attention from the effectiveness of their work. Where social systems are acting as a rigid defence, it may be that a consultation such as that undertaken by Menzies-Lyth, may be required to, as it were, unhook the system. Knowledge of tendencies such as these, outlined above, can also act as an on-going corrective to the rigidifying of Basic Assumption functioning.

Jon Stokes (1994) in *The Unconscious at Work* draws attention to the way in which different professional groups demonstrate the primacy of different Basic Assumptions. He suggests that this may underlie some of the difficulties that professionals in different roles may have in working together. Teachers and others in education must inevitably work to a considerable extent in the BD mode. The teacher is the expert and has knowledge that the student needs. Some co-operation between teacher as expert and student as dependent is demanded. However, the student's individual approach to his learning needs to be fostered, so that the teacher, at best, must be able to operate flexibly within the BF mode. It is probable that pupils who are difficult in class are unable to co-operate in the BD mode and probably function rather rigidly in a BF way. Too many pupils within a class functioning in a BF way will make for considerable difficulty as a BF leader may emerge in competition with the teacher.

Support teachers need to work in sophisticated BP mode – generating hope and trust in the pupil with whom they are concerned, and with some understanding of the BD atmosphere that will prevail in the classroom. Some sensitive pairing will also be needed with the classroom teacher – but difficulties can arise from the different modes each must employ. Such difficulties will be analogous to those experienced in other multi-disciplinary teams, such as child guidance units, in which the differing tasks of team members pre-empt different modes of functioning within the team group.

The Individual Within the Group

The propensity for any individual to employ one or other mode of functioning within a group will depend on both external and internal factors. Some of the external factors, for example the individual task and role, have already been touched upon, but the internal situation of both child and teacher – which Bion calls their *valency* – will also determine what mode of group functioning is found most congenial. Valency will depend on the individual's experience and history in relationships; on whether that person has found greatest satisfaction in dependent positions, or as one of a couple, or feels most comfortable in asserting him or herself apart from other people. For example, the disruptive and rebellious child functioning in the BF mode more often than not lacks the inner feeling of having a mother who can contain his uncomfortable feelings, and will, as a result, externalise these feelings and provoke and upset people around him.

Combining ideas from Bion and Winnicott, good enough development requires that the good-enough mother of the infant must be able to receive and modify her infant's projections and return them to him in assimilable form. An infant lacking such mothering will be, as it were, left with his bad feelings either uncontained or returned to him unmodified. He will thus be left with an excess of bad feelings, and with the need to find a container for them. Such an infant grown to school age will look for containers within the school situation.

A school setting that does not provide a group of teachers able to pull together and to create a secure container, will, as the child's environment may have done hitherto, be open to splitting and acting out in relation to him. The system thus filled with a child's bad feeling will either be fought by him or he will run away from it. In equivalent ways, valency will be established for the other modes. Putting it rather simplistically, those whose internal worlds throw up issues of control will be drawn to the Basic Group Assumption BD; and those for whom issues of close relationship, perhaps with an idealised object, will be drawn towards the pairing assumption. These valencies will operate within the individual teachers, professionals and student alike.

I should now like to turn to an illustration of work with a support teacher in the classroom. To illustrate these ideas, I have taken an example from the school in which I worked, but which, because I had also worked with the support teacher in question, I could see from the points of view of a number of the protagonists in the situation, and from which it is possible to discuss the operation of various of the Basic Assumptions mentioned above.

Case Example

The action takes place (mainly) in an inner London, school, which serves a very poor area with a huge mix of nationalities. There are large numbers of deprived children from families with many problems. The school has seen many changes over the last 10 years. Indeed, the headmistress to whom I shall refer used to be the head of a prestigious private girls' school until it was amalgamated with a number of other schools, which served the local population. The headmistress remained as head of part of the larger school. Until recently, the school was accustomed to send its difficult children to small, specialised units off-site, for all or part of their school time. The support services are in their first year, and whilst the support teacher I shall mention is quite experienced, her experience is mostly derived in work in those off-site units.

As well as all the past changes, which caused much unrest among staff, the school was in the process of enormous further change of all kinds. Its long-standing educational psychologist had recently retired – a much-loved woman replaced by a young man. Most disturbing of all, to my mind, was the massive administrative change that the school was to suffer. The progressive but expensive and controversial education authority which had been responsible for all London schools was to be disbanded, and the responsibility for education devolved on smaller local authorities. It was not easy to see how this would affect school, but such a change makes for much anxiety.

The situation arose around an 11-year-old boy called Peter. I did not know him personally, but had encountered him, as it were, on paper, as part of a project I was doing with the school. The school was a secondary school and I was looking at the files that are passed on from primary schools about every child coming in to the first year. A certain amount of information is passed on about each child and my intention was to try to estimate the special needs of each child as he or she arrived, and to work with teachers around their special needs. I had spotted Peter as the sort of child likely to demonstrate the fight/flight pattern I have spoken of earlier, and was not surprised to learn that he was in trouble. I learned from a number of reports from the educational psychologist attached to his previous school, and also from application forms for boarding school, that he was the only child of a single mother. Peter and his mother lived with her mother – Peter's grandmother – who is described as 'dominant'. Also in the family were the grandmother's young twin sons – Peter's uncles. These twins had recently left the school that Peter attended and were described as aggressive and difficult. Peter's grandfather was also described as 'aggressive' and it is on record that he had threatened the headmaster. There was no record of this man in the present household.

What was impressive about Peter's file was the number of complaints made about him by his current school. Scores of them fell out of his file. The file also recorded his school history from the age of four. At this age, he was said to part readily from his mother. He was also said to be spiteful and to need firmness. Aged five, he was thought to be capable but to lack concentration – and remorse. A year later his teacher says 'he cannot distinguish rough play from ordinary fun'. At seven a new theme entered – 'he can be kind'. But this was short-lived and the succeeding reports follow the pattern as before. Peter's final report from his primary school says that he tried hard but led others into anti-social behaviour.

Whilst all this tells us nothing of his inner world, we may infer something of his tough experience tempered occasionally by kindness, and we may infer also that he was likely to relate to the group on the basis of a fight/flight assumption.

I first heard of the situation which I wish to examine from the support teacher who, after a seminar, expressed her disgust with the headmistress of Peter's school, who, without consulting her or even informing her, moved Peter to another tutor group. The support teacher felt she would not want to work in the school again.

Following this up a few weeks later, the support teacher was still furious. She had been observing Peter in his group and, I gathered, was feeling that she might help the group to help Peter. She also felt that some of the subject teachers were not dealing with him in class in a way that was likely to meet his needs. This information was, in fact, quite difficult to glean, because the support teacher was so angry with how *she* had been treated. First of all, the head called the educational psychologist without telling her, and now she had *moved* Peter when the support teacher felt he was beginning to settle into the group. What had happened was that Peter had pushed a teacher over, had been sent home, and came back into the new class group. The support teacher added that the educational psychologist was furious too. Educational psychologists frequently share the perspective of the support teacher since they have the same information from the files, and have a fundamentally consultative and 'pairing' perspective with the child.

I next met Peter's former class teacher only a few days after he had been moved to the new group. This was to discuss the shape of the class as a whole, but it was quite difficult to keep Peter out of the discussion, as he had had such a turbulent time in the class. The class teacher was much relieved now Peter had left the class, although she felt his time in the school was likely to be limited unless he was able to settle down. Miss L seemed a sensitive and caring teacher with a group of pupils that seemed quite well-balanced between well-functioning, responsible and social children and those with problems. These problems included a number of children with low academic attainments, two who had only recently come to England and had language difficulties, a few who were rather withdrawn, and another group of turbulent, street-wise, impulse-ridden children, of which Peter was beginning to emerge as a leader. The group who did not manifest difficulties included one or two who had had to take rather premature responsibility in their families of origin, and were sympathetic to the difficulties of others in the class. Miss L had felt worried that the solid core of rather tenuously responsible children would be overwhelmed were Peter to take the lead of the disruptive group. If the responsible group *were* overwhelmed, Miss L was also concerned about the withdrawn and delicate group, which was beginning to blossom as a result of their relationships with the more mature children. Altogether, it was quite a relief to her when Peter left the group. She herself, however, had never had any trouble with him because she believed in structure and organised her classes accordingly, but other teachers had experienced considerable difficulties.

Having spoken with Miss L, I moved on to the headmistress of Peter's part of the school. She was very indignant. First of all, she was indignant with his primary school which, she felt, had allowed Peter to reach secondary age in the state in which he was. She seemed not to have registered the various psychological reports and referrals I had encountered in his file.

In particular, she was indignant with the present situation in the school. She had expected the support teacher to withdraw Peter from the class and work on his difficulties. But she had just observed him. She was furious, also, with the educational psychologist, whom she had asked to test the boy, but who had only offered to observe him also, adding that he was not the sort of psychologist who did tests. She said she was now quite unclear what the support teacher was supposed to do, for, she said the support teacher was now only accepting referrals from the educational psychologist. In particular, she was very angry with the objections that the educational psychologist and the support teacher were expressing about Peter's change of class. The boy had knocked a teacher over and was likely to disrupt his original group. It was better that he had a male teacher. 'I have 25 children to consider not just one naughty boy. He's not getting on well in his group. They [the support ervices] will have to do something.'

This was followed by a string of complaints about a number of children whose individual needs were not being met by the psychological and support services.

It may seem as if this is a rather trivial incident, but in fact, I think it is quite serious. Clearly, the headmistress is disillusioned with the support services and the support services are furious with her treatment of them. It is early in their co-operation, and disillusion at this point may jeopardise their future working together. And this is quite apart from its effect upon Peter.

How should we view what has happened? How are the various groups functioning and how adequately are their primary tasks being carried out?

Clearly, the system around Peter is failing badly. He cannot perform adequately academically, despite some evidence in his history that he is reasonably capable. Moreover, his behaviour is unacceptable both in his class, and in his action in assaulting a teacher. It is true that his primitive functioning both as an individual and within the group in the fight/flight mode is of no help to him, in that it does not help him to fulfil his task in school, of taking in and learning from his teacher. But has the network of adults provided him with a context that might help him to change?

In the fury with each other that seems to pervade the system, it does seem likely that the school will reproduce some of the instability and anger that we may hypothesise has characterised his home life, and contributed significantly to his way of dealing with his world.

It is clear that some of his teachers were able to manage Peter's class better than others – Miss L never had trouble with him; she believes in 'structure', she says, and this fits in well with the need for firmness and that was noted about Peter when he was five. Peter is insecure, and feels better when he feels well held. Without this, Peter has little hope of learning. This also is what the support teacher had noted and was working with when Peter moved class. Presumably, it was why the educational psychologist had wanted to make an observation.

Is there any communication about this common concern? If so, how should action or further communication contained within it be fed into the system? Does it fall in the remit of the educational psychologist, the support teacher, the class teacher or the head? The class teacher seems to be well in touch with the notion that Peter needs firm structures in which to learn, but it seems unlikely that her primary task includes very centrally any remit to convey such information – which might be taken as criticism – to her colleagues. This may be why others in the system have taken it on.

But does it fall within the primary task of the support teacher? Is it more appropriate to the role of the head, or the educational psychologist? Should the head be exercising her management function on the sub-system boundary?

It is clear that the headmistress is functioning appropriately in the BD mode. But internal pressures and external threats to the school force her back into fairly primitive operation in this mode. Her main task is the preservation of the majority of the class, but she loses touch with her concern for the individual (Peter), and in particular, with the professional opinion of the colleagues. Their indignant response to this provokes a fight/flight response on her part, which operates to the exclusion of any flexible use of a pairing mode. Thus, co-operation between different professionals and modes of work is rendered more difficult. It is probable that her main priority has become the maintenance of the system and her authority within it, in the face of the treats to it from within and without. This causes her to lose touch with an aspect of her primary task – the education of the individual within the system – and to perceive and deal with outside agencies as if they were a threat. As in the individual case of Peter, this serves to reinforce her recourse to the fight/flight assumption.

That the support teacher also takes refuge in the fight/flight mode was apparent from her first word to me about the incident – she didn't want to work in the school again and she was fleeing from it. She is new to the role of support teacher in a class, and may therefore be very sensitive to failing to fulfil her primary task. But what is her primary task? The headmistress was critical of her observational role within the class, and certainly she seemed to be as much concerned with group dynamics as with the individual boy. It seems possible that she may be finding her task with the individual boy more difficult than the task to which, as a teacher she is more accustomed – that is to say, work with a BD group.

It is probably particularly difficult to initiate a pairing relationship with Peter, whose fight/flight mode will tend to keep close relationships at bay. It is more than likely that, confronted with the one-to-one situation, Peter will use the teacher as container for his feelings and thereafter need to avoid or attack the object that contains them. It seems that the support teacher did not engage directly with this mode of relationship, and could not, therefore, provide the help that he needed in tackling his problems in reading and writing, or indeed, to give him the experience he lacked of having his projections contained and returned to him more acceptably. Instead, she turned her attention to the group in the class and paired with the class teacher offering advice to *her* for handling him.

I think we can see without too much difficulty how Peter can find himself in the unharmonious situation at school that is analogous to his home situation. It is also very understandable that a new service provided to a system under siege from the extent of its internal problems (in the number of unhappy children) and external pressures (the uncertainty of the changed administrative situation of the school) will run into teething problems.

If the participants could have some understanding of the systems in which they work and of the basic assumptions that underlie their interactions in groups, they might have some possibility of learning from the experience of the early years and building a more flourishing service in the future.

Support Teachers

It was into a situation in this sort of flux that I was precipitated when taking part in the training event for support teachers. I might have contributed to this event something on the lines of the discussion above, but I chose rather to address their anxieties about their new role. What emerged was interesting in relation to their change from the BD to the pairing mode – their primary concerns were with how they were going to be able to relate to their referred pupil, how they would relate to the class teacher of the referred child, and how the class group would relate both to the referred child and also to the individual support teacher. Although I had been assigned only one slot in this training event, the teachers were so grateful for the opportunity to air their anxieties that I was invited to return for a further session. This led to a request to meet regularly in a consultative way with a sub-group of the membership.

Pairing with the Pupil

On the basis of my understanding of the psychodynamics of the classroom, I was very interested to observe and to think about the introduction of a pair into the classroom group, which is, as I have outlined above, essentially concerned with a mode of relating not usually found in the classroom. What would happen in a group in which dependency and fight/flight modes predominate, by the introduction of a working pair.

It was hardly surprising that the support staff, who are of course largely recruited from teaching backgrounds, should choose for the first year of the consultation to concentrate on their work with the individual child.

The support teachers were surprised by the strength of feeling that the children with whom they were working expressed to them, but also by the strength of feeling they experienced in themselves. It was not that these feelings were unaccustomed, but that their evocation by one child and their precision was unusual, and raised all sorts of anxieties in the teachers about their work. How could they cope with these feelings? How could they manage to work with the child for a relatively short time? And what could they possibly do to tackle what seemed like major issues in the classroom (or semi-classroom, as some children were withdrawn) situation. The dilemma for the teachers was exacerbated by the constraints of the National Curriculum.

The first task was to address the nature of the relationship that arose between teacher and pupil to reflect upon the feelings aroused in the teacher and to examine what such feelings might mean for the child. Was the child hostile and defensive with the feeling that the teacher had nothing to offer of value? Was it that, on the contrary, the child seemed over-close and dependent? What, given the child's circumstances, did this suggest about their attitudes to other people? Did it suggest that he kidded himself he knew it all, and therefore that the teacher had nothing to offer him (a frequent state of affairs in children who disrupt classes), thus justifying his avoidance of any relationship? Or was the child so pleased with the relationship that seemed to be on offer that its content was irrelevant, and the learning task equally beside the point? Sometimes the child was able to raise such feelings in the teacher that she was almost unable to pursue her task.

The airing of such feelings proved to be an enormous relief. The realisation that to have such feelings was inevitable and indeed useful as a tool to understand the child's difficulties was a further encouragement to the teachers that there were ways in which their task could be pursued.

Our discussion focused on these feelings, seeing how they fitted in with the child's behaviour in and out of school, using their drawings and anything else that was known about them. Pulling all this together, the group was able to develop hypotheses about the difficulties that underlay the child's learning and behavioural problems, and to address the issues within the educational tasks. We might discuss a book on activity that would enable the difficulties to be thought about at one remove from the child concerned. For example, a child grappling with adjustment to a new family context might be encouraged to write or organise a book that sorted out his or her relationship to the new and the old family, and to express feelings about this situation both to the support teacher, and also, if it seemed appropriate, to share these feelings with other children, who may have had related problems in discussion or in, for example, some dramatic production. Basically, the method was to isolate a key issue and to address the feelings that may have been difficult to recognise and express by curricular means.

The development of a key issue or hypothesis was important from the point of view of the brevity and context of the intervention open to the support teacher, and its uniqueness. It seemed vital to address issues that could not be aired in other parts of the child's life, but also ones that would illuminate their dysfunction in school. What the teacher experiences with the child is critical in this process.

Since teacher and child meet for a relatively short period, the choice of focus must be susceptible to resolution. Equally, the brevity of the contact needs to be kept in mind by the teacher and shared with the child throughout. A number of the difficulties experienced by children in school arise from the sudden departure of important adults, through parental death, divorce, adoption or fostering. The short-term nature of the contact with a support teacher can offer an opportunity to discuss such issues and to provide a more satisfactory model of separation. The teacher will need to have in mind from he word go the brevity of the contact and to discuss the implications of having to say goodbye. In so doing the child can be helped to use to the full what is available, even in the short term, and the capacity to make the most of what is provided is valuable, not only in school, but in all aspects of life. A typical case that was presented to the group of support teachers was that of Sandra. Sandra was a six-year-old girl who was referred to the learning support services due to her apparent inability to learn and her difficulty in interacting in the class room. She was the youngest of three siblings, having two much older brothers. Her parents were devoted to this little girl, who already had quite a career as a child model. They were, however, disconcerted by her apparent difficulty in learning and were anxious to use the facilities of the support services.

Sandra's support teacher had observed her and had found her apparently oblivious of what went on in the class, patting her hair, arranging her clothes and looking at the other children rather than getting involved in the lesson. Her interactions with other children were quite problematic. She had few friends because she became quite aggressive if anyone disarranged her clothes and whenever she could not do what she was supposed to do successfully. After two individual encounters with her, her support teacher was in despair, feeling that she could not make any contact with Sandra or elicit any response from her. She became quite impatient and angry with the little girl, who she felt was entirely superficial.

Discussion with the teachers' group suggested that Sandra felt she could only be successful in things to do with her appearance and that anything more serious was too difficult and had to be kept at bay. It was suggested that the support teacher's experience of impatience and anger might be just what Sandra experienced about anything that required more thoughtful work. If Sandra could find that appearances could be a little less perfect then she might be able to tolerate the pain of learning, which involves making mistakes and doing things in a less than perfect way. A number of suggestions were made that the support teachers might be able to use to work with Sandra: Russian dolls to indicate that there may be more in people than meets the eye; the story of Cinderella, who of all fairy-tale characters shows that a shabby appearance is no bar to success in the long run; work on a book called *Elmer, A Patchwork Elephant* by David Mackee. This is a story about an elephant who hates his appearance which is different from that of other elephants. He tries to change it by rolling in the mud. But it rains and the other elephants show that actually they like him as he is, regardless of his appearance – what you are like is more important than what you look like.

The support teacher felt, herself, much supported in these discussions and in particular, felt much less impatient with Sandra in her next session. She began to see that when modelling came so easily to the child she had turned away from harder effort, in a way as she, the support teacher, had been in danger of turning away from the difficult job of engaging Sandra's interest. She read the patchwork elephant stories to the child, who became interested in this character, and little by little more inclined to take on the difficult business of reading – a 'patchwork' effort that was sometimes successful and sometimes not.

Pairing with the Class Teacher

The other pairing implied in the role of the support teacher is that which will exist with the regular class teacher of the child to be supported. On the whole, the support teachers found that class teachers with a problematic child in their form were only too glad that the support teacher was going to be around. Some, however, felt ashamed or chagrined that they should need help; some felt rather intruded on; others felt uncomfortable, or rivalrous, in being observed. These sorts of feeling were far from the rule, and far more common were the situations in which children themselves used one of the teachers to be in touch with the more benign parts of themselves, while using the other in a different way. From the outset, support teachers were very aware of their relationships with their colleagues, and if it was at all possible, spared no effort to discuss their role, work and their pupil with their opposite number.

However, sometimes more problematic situations arise, such as the one that was described by one support teacher whom I shall call A.

Case Example

She was engaged with a child, Z, with whom she could hardly work because she so hated him and was frightened of him. These feelings were in sharp contrast to those of his class teacher, who was very sympathetic to his predicament as the neglected only son of a young, alcoholic single mother. The teacher could impose few limits to Z's wild and aggressive behaviour, and when he assaulted another child, would actually turn to the understanding of Z before comforting the injured child. The support teacher, by contrast, felt impelled to impose limits on Z's behaviour, found him impossible, and could barely contain her violent feelings towards him. It was for this reason she decided, as a matter of urgency, to bring him to the group for consultation.

As a result of the intervention of the consultation, A made overtures to the teacher, but it did not get very far. Then there was a change. It was time for Z to move to a new class. After much discussion, he did so, and in the process he acquired a new class teacher. She had been an assistant in his old class and was a newly qualified graduate.

After a few days, she confided to A how infuriated she was by Z. In the meantime, A had been finding Z much more tolerable – 'more of child', she said. She and the new class teacher talked about the change in A's feelings and the management of those of the class teacher, and agreed a view of Z as a child with nice and nasty features. His behaviour has changed markedly since then. He has apologised for a piece of violence, at least to the extent of describing it as an accident, and will not dodge the punishment of standing in the corner when naughty, but will accept the discipline of those two grown-ups acting together. This experience of containment by two kind but firm adults must be a seminal one for this little boy.

Pairings with class teachers, it can be seen, need constant maintenance. Where difficulties arise, as in the above example, whilst discussion with the support teacher's peer group may be helpful, there is no substitute for talking with the teacher concerned.

If the children can observe a harmonious relationship between the two adults in their classroom, it can provide them with the example of grown-ups able to get on together, taking different but complementary roles, an example which a proportion may lack in their family homes.

The Wider Context

The interaction between support teacher and class teacher may be affected by provocation from the child that brings the two together. It may equally echo some stress that exists within the outside world. The story of Peter, whose handling in a school under stress from uncertainty consequent upon the disbanding of the Inner London Education Authority (ILEA), is one example of where conflict between school and support teacher might have seemed underwritten by external pressures. Other pressures of a less immediate and obvious kind may affect the support teacher's work and deserve consideration, where problems arise in individual work with a child.

Case Example

A support teacher reported a situation about which she felt very uncomfortable. Indeed, she felt so uncomfortable that she was reluctant to talk about her problem. The problem was that whenever she went to talk about a child to the headteacher, the headteacher locked the door of her office. This actually rather frightened the support teacher. She was working with a boy with marked difficulties in learning and wanted to withdraw him from class to help him with some basic skills. She had dreaded the occasion of asking whether this would be possible.

Discussion suggested that school itself (an inner city primary school) had a rather unusual population. There was a group which had lived in the area for many years whose parents had also attended the school and who were active in the running of it; there was a group of children who lived over the borough boundary; a group of children whose parents worked locally and came to school with parents going to work; and a further group of refugee children. These various groups had not integrated and there was constant discord between the factions and resentment on the part of the parents and children who had long-term commitment to the school. The previous headteacher had retired early due to illness and was known to have found the position difficult, and the current head's attempts to get the school together seemed not to be very successful and to be resented by the strong local parents' group.

Seen in this light, the headteacher's wish to keep discussion of individual children private made a bit more sense, as did the wish on the part of headteacher and class teacher alike not to single out any one child. The support teacher, however, had been determined that she would do what seemed in the best interests of her pupil, and had stood up to the headteacher and insisted on withdrawing the boy. She had been surprised when the headteacher had capitulated in the face of her determination. On discussion in the group, and in the face of the implications of the social situation in the school, the support teacher wondered about the wisdom of her determination and its consequences for the child.

The child was rather disadvantaged and from the indigenous group, an only child of a single mother, whose own disadvantages made it a problem to give him the attention that his difficulties in learning required. It seemed an important message to the school as a whole, for the support teacher to be able to stand up for the individual needs of her pupil, unabashed, and to provide for him the necessary help, regardless of the rather tough ethos of the school. The support teacher felt much supported, herself, by the discussions in the group, and much less frightened by the behaviour of the head. Moreover, the lad whom she had withdrawn to work with began to make some progress. Whilst the school context in which he and the school existed could not readily be changed, its impact on the support teacher's functioning could be modified, to some extent, by an understanding of its nature.

Such an understanding, however, requires the clearance of a space in which to think, and preferably the presence of someone other than those involved in the work – that is to say, a consultant. Such an outsider can observe the processes within the group and also take account of the anxieties aroused in participants without sharing them, and can put them in their place. Thus when supported themselves, teachers can also begin to use the feelings that they experience in their work with their pupils, and in so doing help their students to do likewise. Where feeling can illuminate academic learning, schoolchildren are able to make the most of their educational opportunities, which is, after all, the primary task not just of support teachers but of the educational system as a whole.

Summary

In this chapter, I have tried to show that work with children in difficulty can be facilitated by consideration of their situation both within the classroom and also within their school of origin in its context. Further understanding of such troubled children can be gained from sensitivity to their manner of relating to the individual teacher. Such understanding can, in many cases, be communicated to the child by work within the curriculum. But the understanding of all these levels of interaction which may affect the pupil in the school demands time and space for thought and discussion.

CHAPTER 8

Responding to a Tragedy
Consultation in School

Joyce Iszatt and Enid Colmer

Introduction

The authors of this chapter, an educational psychologist (EP) and a child guidance (CG) social worker, work in a multi-disciplinary child guidance service (CGS), based in a local education authority (LEA).

At the start of a summer half-term holiday the service learnt from the news media that Maria, a 12-year-old pupil attending a local school, had been murdered on her way home.

The violent murder of a young child provokes strong reactions in everyone. When it happens in your own professional patch it raises a dilemma about whether it is appropriate to become actively involved. There are uncomfortable connotations of voyeurism, fuelled by media attention and feelings of disquiet about fantasies of rescue which can serve to inhibit professionals from taking action. However our role within a LEA which is to support parents and schools in the promotion of pupils' educational, emotional and social development and an awareness of a theoretical framework emphasising the importance of preventative help in the aftermath of a trauma (Nader and Pynoos 1991), clarified our responsibility and made it possible for us to offer our services.

Our next dilemma was how to respond effectively. Systems theory informs us that for an intervention to be successful it must be presented in a way which is acceptable to the school. A proactive approach may be considered intrusive and support offered this way could be rejected. On the other hand, a purely reactive response may result in professionals colluding with the status quo, and the needs of staff and pupils could be overlooked. These tensions are exacerbated when common defensive reactions to trauma such as psychic numbing and denial can result in closing ranks, keeping a tight rein and a 'business as usual' stance.

In this chapter we aim to describe how the child guidance service responded to this tragedy. We will give an account of how the school was approached and support offered using a consultative framework. This will be followed by an in-depth description of work carried out with a class of children in the school. Finally we will reflect on some of the issues raised by the intervention.

The Child Guidance Service

The 1989 Children Act and 1993 Education Act both emphasise the importance of multiprofessional, interagency work when considering the needs of children. The child guidance service is uniquely placed within the local authority as it offers a flexible, multi-disciplinary and integrated model of support to schools, families and individual children.

The service is comprised of an educational psychology service and child and family service working together. Each school in the borough is allocated an educational psychologist who visits regularly. As a member of the wider child guidance service, the EP is able to draw on the expertise of colleagues from the range of disciplines within the team to inform his or her work. CG social workers have developed a role in schools which complements the EP's work, offering direct consultation to teachers, parents and pupils, and joint work is practised.

Following this tragic event, the primary task of the service was to provide a continuum of support to staff and pupils which would facilitate the natural grieving process and serve to prevent the emergence of long term problems.

The service alerted the LEA that it was available to respond as a matter of priority. Because of her special relationship with the school, the school EP agreed to contact the headteacher by telephone at her home and to act as primary consultant.

A co-ordinating group was established within the CGS comprised of the school EP, a child guidance social worker, a child and adolescent psychiatrist and another EP. This group provided a forum in which strategies could be formulated and resources co-ordinated flexibly, over time, with in-built opportunities for reflection and shared learning. Other members of the service could be called upon as and when required and the team kept informed of developments.

Crucially, the group provided a framework for mutual support. This was especially important for the school EP who was closest to the event. The intensity of the feelings aroused and their impact on interpersonal relationships and group dynamics could be safely explored in this setting and used to inform our work.

The intervention spanned the second half of the summer term. In all, the group met on five occasions. This included a preparation meeting and review after the school holidays.

The School Consultation

The school context

There is a body of literature which draws attention to the important contribution of systems theory in school consultation work and in the implementation of school-based interventions (Dowling and Osborne 1994). A systemic framework enabled us to consider the pupils' needs and how these might best be met within the context of the whole school, alongside the needs of staff both in their own right and as primary supporters of the pupils. The EP was able to draw on her working knowledge of the school to consider how best to enter the system to strengthen support structures already in place.

The school, Oaklands, is a large comprehensive with a good reputation. As an all girls school there is an added assumption by parents that it will provide a protective environment for more vulnerable pupils. It is also chosen for religious reasons. It is multi-cultural and draws its population from all parts of the borough. Under the leadership of a strong headteacher and stable management team, it functions as an open and caring system. This is reflected in a committed and experienced pastoral staff, working in close association with the special needs department and active participation in the LEA partnership scheme which promotes interschool co-operation.

Maria was a popular Year 7 pupil. Police came to school to interview teachers and pupils the day before the summer half-term holiday because she was missing. Some senior staff knew the extent of the tragedy before the end of the school day but were unable to share this with their colleagues because of the police investigation. Most pupils learnt of the news from the media.

Horrified and in varying degrees of shock, staff needed to work through their own reactions to the tragedy and begin the process of grieving the loss of Maria, whilst helping pupils to do the same.

Entry into the school system

The school EP contacted the headteacher by telephone. The headteacher had already linked into formal and informal support systems within the LEA and met with her management team to plan for the pupils' return to school after the holiday period. The intention was for school to proceed as normally as possible. In her dual role as professional linked to the school and member of the CGS, the EP was able to empathise as a colleague whilst offering support which respected the headteacher's authority. It was arranged that the other EP in the co-ordinating group and the consultant child and adolescent psychiatrist would be available to meet with staff after school on the first day and that the school EP would visit school the following morning.

One teacher who had worked closely with Maria took up the offer to meet with CGS team members. As well as providing support, this meeting highlighted some of the particular concerns of staff working in close contact with

Maria's class. It emphasised the need to consider the school hierarchy and to offer differentiated support.

On the school EP's first visit to school after the tragedy the intense sense of shock, disbelief and horror associated with the event was all-pervasive. Intuitively, the EP took on the stance of befriender as staff with whom she met informally recounted their experiences. She gradually moved into her role as consultant in a more formal way, as and when it seemed appropriate. In all, the school EP, working in collaboration with the child guidance social worker, visited the school six times during the intervention period offering a flexible consultation service to staff. During the course of this process it was arranged for the two other members of the CGS co-ordinating group to meet with staff supporting Maria's class as a group. A follow up to this was also arranged but was cancelled by the school for practical reasons at short notice. Another outcome was the school's request for direct work with Maria's class. This was negotiated through the year head and form tutor who was consulted about whether or not she wanted to join the group and participate in work carried out by the school EP and CG social worker.

The process of consultation

Critical Incident Stress Debriefing is a preventative group technique which emphasises the importance of ventilating feelings within a structure as well as normalisation as a means of mobilising resources in the aftermath of a traumatic event (Mitchell 1983).

We were able to draw on these ideas and other psychological frameworks, including a psychodynamic perspective during the course of our work. The EP had already established a working relationship with school based on a consultation model and so was able to offer support in ways that matched the school culture (Morgan 1986). This in itself helped foster normalisation and acceptance.

By using a consultation framework, the locus of control remains with the client who is enabled to express feelings safely in an atmosphere of mutual respect, where professional boundaries are preserved (Caplan 1970).

The EP, on occasions accompanied by the CG social worker, met with individuals and various interchanging small groups of staff. Some teachers, generally those closest to Maria and her class, requested individual meetings and in several instances follow-up sessions were arranged. Support was provided more indirectly to pastoral staff and management. This was linked to the structure of established EP practice, which involves ongoing liaison, negotiation and forward planning.

Confidentiality and privacy were essential. Staff talked about the impact on both their personal and professional lives. It was important to acknowledge and legitimise the range and intensity of different feelings evoked by the event. This involved listening and sensitively offering frameworks to help staff make sense of their experiences. This process of normalisation helped staff move back into and refocus on their various professional roles. It became possible to help reinforce the teachers' impressive and considerable range of skills and expertise, introducing more formalised support strategies for staff and pupils as appropriate and at a pace which matched the school's needs.

Emerging issues

The various stages of bereavement could be traced during the course of the intervention. These ranged from shock, intense feelings of anger and sadness, to an emerging sense of hope. An ongoing theme involved issues of control.

A traumatic event such as murder can evoke overwhelming fears of loss of control. A basic sense of safety is lost and the world can seem unpredictable and dangerous. The impact of this on teachers, whose role is usually associated with being in control and having answers, can be particularly stressful. It was common for staff to feel anxious about showing their emotions in front of colleagues or pupils and of seeming unprofessional. There were additional pressures on managers because of their high profile and level of responsibility.

By placing their experiences within the context of a normal reaction to a traumatic event and a healthy grieving process, staff regained a sense of competence and professionalism. At the same time they gained insight into the experiences of their pupils.

Several teachers worried about how they would react at registration. One thought she might become emotional, another was worried in case she called out Maria's name by mistake. These reactions were positively reframed as opportunities for the teacher to share with the girls just how difficult it was not to think of Maria who had been such an important member of their class. It was suggested that it might be a relief for the girls to see that their teacher was human and give them permission to express their feelings too. Later one of the teachers described a very moving session with Maria's class. A girl had drawn a picture of Maria on the blackboard and the teacher had used this to open up a discussion about how they all missed her. The girls spontaneously sat near her as though for comfort.

Some staff expressed concerns about the safety of their own children and others were reminded of previous losses in their lives. This provided an opportunity to think about the different kinds of impact the event could have on individual children. Later on the staff were asked how they would tell if a child was distressed and needed help.

The shared experience of a trauma can bring a sense of unity. This feature was very evident at Oaklands where there were many informal staff support systems based on friendship groups or departments and an impressive level of sensitivity. Conversely the anger, fear and uncertainty associated with trauma can be mirrored in the system to trigger conflict, fragmentation and splitting.

In a school with a caring, counselling approach, there may be hidden assumptions that staff will cope and not need support or that those who ask for help and seem less sure are in some way less experienced. We were able to reflect back and positively connote staff's different responses to the tragedy as complementary, with different groups performing important functions at different times on behalf of the whole school. Whilst management focused on maintaining the school routine, on the funeral and formal ways of marking Maria's loss, some were providing informal ways for pupils to express their grief. Others provided structure by focusing on the teaching routine, whilst some, often those closer to the event, performed the important function of holding the uncertainty, grief and raw emotion for the whole school. In this way the pupils had permission to show their feelings within a safe structure.

Group Work with Maria's Class

We will discuss some ideas from the theoretical framework which influenced our intervention, and will follow this with a description of the group work we engaged in with the class.

Theoretical framework

Pynoos and Eth (1985) and Yule (1991) in their recent research work have explored children's reactions following a traumatic experience. This has led them to promote the value of a psychological first aid approach at such times. They argue that helping children to debrief, talk over the event, and reflect on their own reactions to it plays an important part in preventing traumatic reactions developing at a later stage. Nader and Pynoos (1993) have developed some ideas about how this approach might be adapted to school situations. Professionals working with children following a bereavement have emphasised the importance of helping children to talk, play, draw and act out their distress (Black 1993). Recently authors have argued that trauma reactions are distinct from those of bereavement and that it is necessary for these to be worked through as a separate process before grief work can take place, (Harris-Hendriks, Black and Kaplan 1993).

In parallel to these ideas, therapists have advocated the value of group work in the aftermath of traumatic events (Garland 1991). People who share an overwhelming experience also share having a relationship to it, however individual their response may be to the event or to each other. It is argued that in the group situation it becomes possible for mutual learning, support and comfort to take place. In this climate, people are able to share and give each other permission to express feelings, as well as to validate and respect different reactions. Traumatic events, it is suggested, often leave people with a sense of helplessness, loneliness and a need to regain a sense of mastery and coping (Raphael 1983; Goodyer 1990) The group experience enhances a feeling of closeness and unique understanding making it possible to address these common reactions. An agreed number of sessions is offered which implies a normal process of recovery and prevents the inadvertent retention of a fixed personal identity with the event. The emphasis is on normalising, allowing space for the story to be told, in a non-pathologising context.

Working together we (the authors) reflected on these ideas. Whilst this tragic murder had for some, and in differing degrees, been traumatic, we were uncertain about the appropriateness of framing it as 'trauma' in a narrow clinical sense. Nevertheless, this debate provided a useful framework for us to build upon. We were able to bring to this our own experience, both personal and clinical, together with our theoretical belief systems. A systemic perspective enabled us to engage with the school, on different levels, and to place our work with the class in the context of the wider school system. Influenced by social constructionist ideas, we attempted to hold an observer's stance to our own assumptions and expectations. This helped us to stay curious about the girls' reactions and to validate their many different realities. Cecchin *et al.*'s (1993) description of an 'irreverent' stance to any one theory modality proved useful in enabling us both to incorporate visualisation techniques from cognitive therapy, and to integrate a psychodynamic awareness into our work.

The meetings

The CG social worker, protected from the initial emotional impact that had confronted the school EP and less involved with the school dynamics, was in a useful position to take the lead role in the group work.

There were four meetings with the class. The first session took place a few days after the news broke and the children had returned from their half-term holiday. There were approximately two weeks between this and the second and third meetings. The fourth was four weeks later. Extracts from three of these meetings will be presented, followed by a discussion.

THE FIRST MEETING

There was an expectant, nervous hush: all the girls stopped talking as we entered the room. They were all sitting at their desks as if for a lesson. We attempted to create a different and more informal atmosphere. The girls willingly responded to our encouragement to move forward, moving desks, huddling up closely on chairs in the aisles. We questioned the context for them and learnt that this was their scheduled English lesson which, we believe, they were not given an option about attending. We shared their nervousness and uncertainty, absorbing the respectful and reverent atmosphere that seems so often present in proximity to death. We worked together, at times imitating a team approach, with one of us staying in an observer position, allowing space for valued reflections and assisting us to manage the powerful feelings aroused. The conversation flowed easily. We encouraged them to speak out and to name feelings in an effort to dispel some of the mystique around the subject of death. Most of the girls contributed, some looked away, concentrating on a repetitive pulling at their possessions. Most of them reacted, showing with their body language and expressions their agreement or disagreement to statements. A handful stayed silent and impassive.

We asked how they had first heard the news. They described where they were, who was with them, and how left out one had felt having been away and only hearing the news as she arrived in school. We explored with them the effects on relationships at home, validating the different experiences we heard, and the differences in family attitudes to expressing feelings. A girl spoke with wonder as she reflected on how very much she had cried and continued to cry, especially at night. We invited girls to make connections and to reflect on what had, or may in the future, make it possible to begin to cry less.

The girls spoke simply about how much they missed Maria. We soon obtained the impression of her as a lively member of the class who was fun to be with. There was some competition to confirm a privileged position of friendship. They offered their different connections to particular places and times when they thought about her most. One told us about a clapping game which she started before lessons. This, the girl quietly assumed was now taboo for her. They spoke of Maria leading singing sessions in the class and others of their association with Maria with the lockers where they kept their things. They talked about this area, with some comfort, as if her spirit lingered there. We listened to and confirmed these statements, and in circular fashion used them to develop thoughts, inviting comments from class members thus keeping conversation and ideas flowing. Then there were silences.

The class had been on a previously arranged school trip the day before. They spoke openly about their feelings of guilt, having had a good time and not always remembering. Some of the girls believed that she had been there with them in spirit and this had freed them to enjoy the day. As the girls relaxed they expressed their anger, their fury with the murderer, their feelings of vengeance and of the anguish they assumed for Maria's parents.

We engaged the girls in reflecting on the effect this has had on them. The daily pattern of life had changed. Their parents, they said, were being protective towards them and they were unusually pleased about this, unsure and openly scared to venture out themselves. The effect on friendships was of paramount concern. It had brought them closer. A quarrel, intense before the murder, had been made up after it. One spoke of having been left with an outstanding quarrel with Maria. There had been a lot of hugging of each other. Some thought it was good to cry and others were uncomfortable with this. There was a consensus about how difficult it was to do exams and frustration at the teachers expectations that these should be done.

The girls spoke of their thoughts about death and of their ruminations about the murder. Could Maria have got away, could she have escaped, was she terrified, in pain? What was the man like? There were some ideas, some images which would not go away. They spoke about the notoriety, the school on television, the misquoted articles in the paper and the disruption of the police investigations.

THE SECOND MEETING

The children were given the option of attending. Six chose not to join the class. The mood was different this time. There was an angry, frustrated restlessness. This anger was directed outwardly towards other pupils, not belonging to this class, and deemed to be insensitive or intrusive by some of the girls. Other classes did not understand and sought to minimise the effect on them. Did other pupils care? Some of these had used, in their view, the murder, and a fear of going home late, as an excuse for getting out of detentions. We were curious: can girls in the other classes be allowed to grieve or is this something exclusively belonging to this class? Did distress show itself in different ways? How can it be possible for some to be openly upset and for others to show or to feel differently? The children helped each other to think about this, containing and soothing feelings.

They were angry with the teachers, divided about whether teachers should be showing that they were upset too, and whether or not they should be allowing or discouraging a show of emotion. Did the teachers care? Why did the teachers read a formal statement to the school? Were they keeping things hidden from them? What could they, the school, do? We acknowledged their feelings, staying with the distress, whilst allowing and inviting other girls to offer different perspectives, supporting or understanding the teachers' position or making some suggestions towards commemoration.

They were angry with the media and confused about the attention and the notoriety that this brought for them and their school. One girl was overwhelmed that her uncle, who lived in Canada, had heard at such a distance about the murder on the news. It became possible for the girls to shift their anger towards the actual murderer,. and with this they expressed their feelings of vengeance. They spoke of vivid dreams of fury, damaging, hurting, murdering this man. We wondered whether this brought forth fears of retaliation and were told of many frightening, violent fantasies.

They began to think about their memories of Maria. One told us of her hopes for the future. She had planned to be a famous singer. Now this wouldn't happen. We reflected with them about giving up hopes and wishes and how this affected their own thoughts. Connected to this was their worry about how they could hold on to memories and whether it was all right to let these fade. One girl said her mother had talked to her about a girl who had died when she was at school. They marvelled at this, and took some reassurance that they would be able to remember Maria. They began to recall photographs, letters and video recordings that they had. One girl articulated the distress that they all shared when Maria's name on the register was approached.

This session reflected the complex and varied thoughts and feelings aroused and there was a less marked sense of class cohesion. It was as if this comfort in class identity connecting them to events was slipping away. The excitement and heightened emotions seemed assuaged, and a sense of emptiness, of irritation and of frustration seemed to be taking its place. This striking sense of being part of something very important was becoming elusive. How was it possible to move on, to enjoy oneself again, was a theme that thread through the session.

THE THIRD MEETING

This was to have been the last, but some of the girls, supported by the school, requested that we meet again as the funeral had now been arranged. This session focused on how they were going to manage the funeral. Who was to go, the teachers' part in this, their previous experiences, fears and expectations were the main themes.

THE FOURTH MEETING

Our last meeting was the day after the funeral. We were told that a number of girls, close friends of Maria's, had asked to join us and that this had been welcomed by the class

There was some initial disruption and bustle as we settled into a different classroom. The mood abruptly changed. It was very quiet, uncertain and heavy with sadness and expectant tears. Different from before, there was a reluctance to speak. The girls who had not attended the funeral spoke first, trying to manage their feelings of exclusion, of guilt and regret. One described how she had cried and cried and wished she had been there. Some of the girls' parents had stopped them attending and others had decided themselves not to go. There were long silences.

We reflected on the differences in feelings now from those of previous meetings. One girl articulated clearly for the group. 'Now, after the funeral it seems that Maria really is no more.' We wondered whether they had been surprised or had expected these feelings. One girl owned that she had been less upset then she thought. Another spoke about the worst moment for her as seeing the coffin go down. Another that this was seeing her friend crying and being unable to stop her. For another it was seeing her mother cry. The teachers too had visibly been upset and this had enhanced a sense of shared grief. There was a numbed, heavy, yet unsettled silence in the room. We stayed with this for a while.

We commented on the sadness and wondered if they could imagine what this looked like, how they would describe it? One girl responded immediately. 'It's like a big heavy load, like a big solid rock that would stay there for ever.' One by one the girls added their voices in what became a crescendo of comments. It was 'black', 'hard', 'cold', 'thick', 'smooth'. We wondered how could it be changed? 'It will be smashed into little pieces.' 'Cut off its head like the murderer and all the murderers in prison.' 'It should be crunched up like all the badness in the world.' We encouraged other ideas and images. 'It will gradually melt away at the edges.' 'It will dissolve.' 'Become smaller, lighter.' 'Become chipped and cracked.' 'It will rot and fall apart.' 'It could be burnt so that there are only ashes and they will blow away.'

Focusing on this brought an enormous relief. Conversation could flow again. One girl told us that she lived near the cemetery and she used to go to the pond nearby to show her little sister the ducks. She had thought that she could never go back there again. Now she thought that she could, but that it would be different. Another girl explained how irritable she had been with her little sister who had wanted to play doctors and nurses and the patient dies. She couldn't let her do this. Girls spoke about their sensitivity to news items, especially the music before the Police File programme on television. One spoke about her lack of interest in school work and the things she used to do and of feeling depressed. Girls spoke of not sleeping, of their irritability with friends and family, of their anxiety about losing friendships, of their parents complaining that they were answering back. One girl said that she can't get off her horse and just wants to keep riding and riding.

There was talk of a murder trial in the future bringing back these feelings. We talked about remembering and forgetting, about guilt, and of having to let go. We talked with them about our ending and who they would talk with, and how they will speak with each other. We talked about the holidays and whether it was all right to enjoy themselves; about the next academic year, possibly a different phase where they would sometimes remember and sometimes forget too, and what that might be like. A number of girls came up to speak with us as the session ended. One girl came into the class who had not been at our meeting and said 'I didn't go to the funeral because my father died last year and I thought I might be too upset, but I wish I had gone'.

Discussion

This had been an emotional experience for us both. We felt privileged to have been able to engage with, and share, something of these girls' experiences. We wondered whether for some this murder will remain a core memory and perhaps a reference point for them in their development (Raphael 1983). The most significant outcome of our meetings with the class was to provide them with a sense that the way this experience had impacted on them was important. Their own feelings, reactions and its effects could be validated. We hoped that something of the way this was managed may connect to their memory and be useful to them. We learnt a great deal from the girls and were impressed with their ability to express themselves, to listen to each other and to us. The sessions seemed to reflect the process from traumatic shock reactions, through to a discomforting accommodation and on to the progression of grief and its uneven integration.

We had attempted throughout this meeting to convey a genuine neutrality, accepting differences, believing ourselves that people find their own way, the one best for them, of dealing with adversity. We acknowledged that it was both hard to have attended and not to have attended the funeral and offered no preferred view. We attempted to be sensitive to, and were interested in, the girls' different ethnic and religious backgrounds. At times they were able to connect their ideas and attitudes to death to their cultural beliefs. We tried to hold a balance between the expression of yearning and despair and positively connoting, moving through the bereavement process, recovering mastery and self motivation. Alvarez (1993) usefully reminds us that 'it is the negative experiences of life that are the great teachers and the great stimulators' (p.395).

Reflecting on the Intervention

Support to pupils and families

The school kept in touch with Maria's family who had to leave the area to escape media attention. We had not considered if there were other ways of offering support other than through the normal channels but the EP attached to Maria's primary school attended by her brother was alerted.

Oaklands had sent letters home informing parents of the sessions, yet we wondered whether we could have consulted with school about the possibility of holding an open meeting for the girls' parents so that they could share their concerns about their daughters and their own reactions to the event.

Some girls approached us informally about their worries and we wondered whether a 'drop in' surgery in school might have been helpful. Although no formal review was held the school EP continues to be available should concerns emerge.

Support to staff

The form teacher joined the class halfway through the first session. This helped connect her with the work we were doing and provided a link for the pupils following our departure. Apart from this our work with staff was separate. Although there are clearly advantages to this, direct work with staff and pupils together could be considered in the future.

There were some concerns that the second staff group meeting was cancelled at short notice. We wondered whether this group comprised of staff teaching Maria's class may have seemed rather contrived as it was not naturally occurring. On reflection it might have been better to have held an open group. We felt that it was important to have made early contact and to have offered all staff support on their first day back after the holiday. This is backed up by comments from the headteacher who said that she found it helpful just knowing that the service was available.

Feedback from management and other members of staff at Oaklands has been very positive. It is generally felt by all parties that professional relationships between the service and the school have been strengthened.

The child guidance service

A tragedy, especially a violent murder, has a powerful impact on all involved and can be overwhelming. The potent dynamics generated, which can serve both to unite and fragment, reverberate not only through the school and community but also into the professional support agencies. These impinged on us too.

Responding to this event was challenging and we learned a lot during the course of the intervention. Our experience underlined the advantages inherent within a child guidance service where there is an ethos of shared work, mutual support and in-built models of reflective practice. Within this context and through the structure of the co-ordinating group, underlying processes could be recognised and used constructively to inform our work. The multi-professional perspective enabled professionals to work together creatively, drawing on one another's complementary skills and expertise to offer a flexible service.

The school EP considered the support structure to be crucial to her work as primary consultant. It enabled her to utilise her special relationship with school and stay close to the event whilst holding onto a clear theoretical framework so that she could work sensitively, in a way that was acceptable to the school. An opportunity to debrief following her first visit to school was especially valued.

Prompted by this and previous experiences, the service has since produced a set of internal guidelines on responding to a trauma. It has worked in other schools where traumatic incidents have occurred and is in the process of developing this area of work.

The LEA context

There are a range of traumatic events which impact the lives of children in schools, but their very nature mitigates against forward planning (Yule and Gold 1993).

In her feedback, the headteacher of Oaklands school emphasised the importance of having ready access to both formal and informal support structures within the LEA. Examples cited included efficient and effective LEA responses to practicalities such as managing the media; knowing that the child guidance service could be called upon; and, most important, the informal support she received from other headteachers and colleagues from within the borough.

Oaklands is a particularly open and caring school, led by a committed headteacher, based in a supportive LEA structure. However, many schools do not operate a system which recognises or accepts the importance of such preventative work. In a climate of local management and increased competition schools may be even more wary of this work. The local authority has a crucial role in both generating an ethos of mutual support and co-operation and in providing a co-ordinated set of known and trusted services.

In this context, there are many advantages in having a local authority-based child guidance service which is uniquely placed to offer integrated and flexible support to children, parents and schools. Boroughs without this facility need to establish other integrated models of support. In parallel, local authorities need to be proactive in alerting schools to the value of preventative intervention in the aftermath of a trauma and to develop and raise the profile of the support services available.

CHAPTER 9

Reflecting Light and Shade
Psychodynamic Thinking and Educational Psychology in the 1990s

Sue Holt

Introduction

This chapter is concerned with a small, but significant, professional group within education – educational psychologists – and considers their changing and sometimes conflicting roles and tasks. Educational psychologists, like so many professional groups in education, are faced with the challenge of upholding professional standards, addressing issues of accountability and meeting the demands imposed upon them by legislation and employers. This challenge is rooted in a context of educational change, shifts in socio-political constructs concerning the place and purpose of education in a post-industrial society and increasing sophistication in theory and practice within the profession itself. In the face of rampant managerialism on the one hand and an increasing awareness of the differences which exist in the profession at a theoretical and practice level, on the other, it is tempting to retreat to the professional safegrounds of psychometry and bureaucratic imperialism. At such a time it is vital if the profession is to continue growing in its understanding and effectiveness that the difficult issues which beset the profession are debated, thought about and understood at a psychological/process level. Indeed, Argyris and Schon in their classic work *Theory in Practice* (1974) state that 'Learning must be based on the discovery or surfacing of dilemmas' (p.86).

A central quandary which arises from the challenge outlined above is how to balance responsibilities towards children, parents, schools and local education authorities. Furthermore there is a responsibility to act in a way which is compatible with both personal and professional moral and ethical standards.

Beyond Unconscious Practice

During the late 1970s and early 1980s one way that the profession attempted to solve the dilemma of being seen as agents of the 'establishment' rather than agents for change was to remove the focus of their intervention from the individual to the system.

This was a time when the profession was rapidly expanding its skill and knowledge base. However, as is often the case, during the process of change and innovation the search for the new way forward (systems thinking, problem-solving approaches, in-service education) also involved the oversimplification and denigration of established theory. Thus the individual focus was seen as labelling and restrictive, and so too were ideas derived from a psychodynamic standpoint. Thus Gregory (1981) states that '... treatment of individual cases is based upon a medical model of human behaviour. It has resulted in clinical investigation centring on the child and intrapersonal variables, and has rarely included an examination of the environmental variables within the institution in which the child was functioning' (p.47).

In the same volume of collected papers (*Reconstructing Psychological Practice*, 1981) Burden states that the 'systems approach' is underpinned by at least two major premises:

1. That the problems of individuals can only be understood within the context of the systems within which they live and work.

2. That it is more likely to be the system which is in need of change than the individual.

What has become clear over the intervening decade is the fact that brining about change at an individual *or* organisational level is a highly complex task. Unfortunately the fact that psychoanalytic theory has been set in opposition to forward-thinking practice, at its best seen as having nothing to offer and its worst being seen as reactionary and outmoded, means that opportunities for exploring the intra- and interpersonal dynamics of change and organisations have, until recently, been overlooked by educational psychologists and educational researchers.

However, at a recent conference (Reynolds 1994) Reynolds, talking about his work on effective schools, outlined his edifying experiences in trying to help failing schools improve their performance. Despite an international reputation and an unambiguous invitation to assist in organisational change the attempts of his team foundered. According to Reynolds they foundered because of the following factors which he identified from his experience of trying to work with them:

- the schools lacked basic competencies

- the schools used a large number of defence mechanisms to resist change

- the schools projected all problems onto the pupils
- staff denied the need to change
- staff could not face change
- staff had a fear of outsiders
- relationships among staff were pathological.

Many educational psychologists will recognise this profile of the 'hard to work with' school. Despite Reynolds' whole-school focus and his understanding of the ways in which health and effective schools function, his analysis of the problems of real life change focused largely on individual and organisational processes at an intrapersonal and interpersonal dynamic level.

Further illumination on the complexity of the contextual influences on individual children, teachers and indeed educational psychologists is provided by a paper by Miller (1994) where he states that the results of a teacher interview study of successful outcomes following intervention by educational psychologists in referrals of children with emotional and behavioural problems were 'far more closely related to factors such as staff culture, organisational boundaries and interpersonal dynamics than is normally recognised in the literature on behavioural interventions' (p.6).

Miller also has the courage to acknowledge that his own experience in orchestrating interventions for children with behavioural difficulties reveals far more failures than successes with very little generalisation within schools of approaches and techniques used successfully with individual children. Miller invokes notions of boundary maintenance and homeostasis taken from systems theory to explain this phenomenon of little or no change.

Roger Booker, in his chapter in this book on the management of psychological services, sees one of the primary tasks of managers as being to provide a niche in which 'the organisation's expertise and skills are uniquely valued'. It is my belief that the expertise that psychologists can offer within the education system should not and must not rest solely upon our usefulness to our employers in helping allocate scarce resources. There is a need to acknowledge that:

1. The problems that psychologists encounter in their day-to-day work are frequently complex, involving the inter-relationships of both individuals and systems (at the very least schools, families, and LEAs).

2. Difficult and negative emotions are as much a part of human relationships and the learning process as their more acceptable counterparts.

3. Some problems do not have readily available solutions.

4. Some solutions are easily arrived at but not easily taken on board by others (viz Miller 1994).

5. Creating a climate in which difficult issues can be thought about and held onto is an important function of the psychologist.

6. Educational psychologist themselves are part of a bigger system and need to think about this in relation to their own functioning.

7. Educational psychologists need space and time to reflect upon the above to inform their practice, rather than react to each referral or situation as it arises. For me the above is summed up by continuing to ask the question 'What is going on here?' rather than automatically thinking 'I know what to do here'.

In many ways it is most unfortunate that an embryonic trend towards a synthesis of theories from different traditions should begin to impinge upon educational psychology theory and practice at a time when the legislative demands of the job could potentially restrict educational psychologists to 'providing the LEA with statutory advice based upon single event summative assessment' (Booker in this volume).

Different Lenses but the Same Pair of Eyes: Using Psychodynamic Theory within a Systems Framework

As discussed earlier, focus on the individual has often been seen as synonymous with labelling and supporting the system, with psychodynamic theories being seen in the same light. However, a psychodynamic view of individuals and relationships, informed by systems thinking and organisations psychology, can help make sense of the individual and the contexts in which they find themselves.

There is a growing awareness among practitioners that looking at individuals is not, *ipso facto*, pathologising: 'Whilst on the one hand all work done with the school as an institution is not necessarily systemically based, it is equally true on the other hand, that work based on an individual child can still be influenced by a systemic approach and about our own concepts and interests' (Dowling and Osborne 1994); and among researchers that looking at individuals is not the same thing as studying uniqueness, and is therefore of little relevance in terms of increasing understanding and knowledge. Golby (1994) argues forcefully in making the case for case study as a valid form of educational research that:

> To study a case is to observe it closely and render it in some way intelligible. Intelligibility is not principally a matter of looking but, inseparably from looking, a matter of inspecting the lens through which we look. The lenses through which we look are not our optical apparatus alone but the concepts and interests that guide us. Case study is, then, not the study of uniqueness but the study of particularity. (p.7)

Translocating Golby's words to the context of educational psychology, it seems to me that he has succinctly identified the key elements of reflective practice, where we examine closely what we see, and how we and others interpret and react to what we see. In taking this approach it is entirely appropriate, as Thomas (1992) says, to include in our close examination school policy, curriculum and physical environment (an ecological approach) as well as attempting to understand the dynamics of relationships between people and surrounding the child in question.

Psychological Theories which Inform Reflective Practice

It is not the remit of this chapter, nor indeed this book, to explore extensively the theoretical foundations of psychodynamic thinking. However, it is relevant to outline some of the thinking which has significantly informed my thinking and practice as an *educational* psychologist.

The work of John Bowlby (1988) on attachment clearly roots fundamental aspects of human development within the context of relationships, as does the work of Melanie Klein before him. Wilfrid Bion's (1984) work with therapeutic groups offers a way of looking at group behaviour which takes into account individual and group psychology. Winnicott's (1958) notion of holding and Barrett and Trevitt's (1991) elaboration of his concept 'playing space' into 'working space' offer ways in which the educational psychologist can create a reflective space so that those working directly with children and young people can begin to explore ways of helping based upon an individual's functioning and needs, particularly when such an approach is likely to challenge formulaic and systemically determined precepts.

The above can be diagrammatically represented using an adaptation of Bronfenbrenner's ecological system of child development (1979) Bronfenbrenner's model offers a helpful way of thinking about all of the influences on a child's development in the widest sense, and here I have adapted it to include a fifth system – self system. This self system represents the interrelationship between the direct external work of the child, their experience, and their thoughts, feelings and actions.

Case Example

Billy was a rising five who was re-referred to me with a view to helping his adoptive parents manage his challenging and confrontational behaviour and for advice on school placement.

Billy had been know to me when he was two-and-a-half and was in the care of the local authority. At the time of the original referral he was being placed for adoption and advice was sought on his development and needs in terms of family placement. Extended assessment work at the time of re-referral, including direct work with

Table 9.1 Focusing on the self system – difficult and negative emotions in a learning context

System	Definition	Description	Examples relating to Education	Relevant theory
Selfsystem	Child's view of self (conscious and unconscious)	Interrelationship between experience, thoughts, feelings, actions	Child's view of self as a learner	**Bowlby** Inner Working Model
Microsystem	A child's immediate setting	Pattern of roles, activities and interpersonal relationships	Class/school organisation relationships between children and staff	**Bion** Group Theory
Mesosystem	Interrelations between two or more settings in which a developing individual participates	Home and school are prime settings	Home/school policies Relationships between teachers and parents Attitudes and influences towards teaching and parenting	**Bion** Group Theory **Klein** Projective identification **De Vries and Miller** The Neurotic Organisation
Exosystem	One or more settings in which an individual is not active but in which there are events which affect or are effected by her	The processes by which outer settings influence child	Effects on learning of marital relationship, relationship between school and psychologist	**Winnicott** Holding Working Space
Macrosystem	The ways in which lower order systems enshrine culture and subculture	The level at which beliefs, ideology and public policy and impinge	Impact on education of societal views of teachers, children family functions etc. Policy regarding special educational needs	All of above in relation to responses to change.

Put together the above begins to look like a psychodynamic understanding embedded within a systems framework.

Billy, observation in his play group, discussion with other professionals, speech and language therapists, pre-school advisory teachers and social workers and his adoptive parents revealed a complex picture.

Billy's early experiences before coming into care were reasonably well documented and he had suffered a serious degree of physical neglect. He was frequently left by his parents in the care of neighbours or in the care of his five-year-old sister and three-year-old brother. The children were often left without adequate food.

His behaviour and emotional responses in his adoptive home were very suggestive of emotional neglect too. He was often enraged and aggressive and demonstrated a desperate need to be in control of every situation he encountered. He avoided eye contact, resisted physical contact unless he initiated it and then it would be rough and invasive.

The work of John Bowlby (1988) on attachment and attachment disorders is helpful in offering an understanding of how, despite two years of positive nurture and care, Billy seemed to have made so little progress in terms of his social behaviour. In Bowlby's terms, Billy was a boy with a marked attachment disorder, originating in early emotional and physical neglect, compounded by two changes of foster-carer before he was placed for adoption. Billy's internal working model (cognitive snapshot of himself, his caretakers and their relationship to him) was a negative one. He saw himself as impotent, unsafe, and worthless, whilst his lack of trust in previous carers led him to see his adoptive parents as unresponsive, unreliable and possibly rejecting.

Within this context Billy's behavioural responses can be seen as serving three important functions (Delaney 1991):

1. to increase parental interaction, although they are likely to be negative and potentially abusive

2. to keep the parents at an emotional distance; to vent pent-up feelings of anger and frustration which cannot be verbalised

3. to vent pent-up feelings of anger and frustration which cannot be verbalised.

This understanding of Billy had important ramifications for his learning and education. Billy's need to retain control and keep adults at a distance meant that he found it extremely difficult to learn from an adult as this suggested a frightening dependency and lack of control to him. He also needed to be constantly alert and aware so that in any group situation he would be constantly scanning his environment and processing what was going on. Initially this seemed to be poor concentration but was in fact excellent concentration on the wrong thing.

When Billy's mother, who was a teacher, attempted to show him how to do simple counting tasks, matching games or drawing he would refuse to settle, shout that he hated her and would respond to attempts to soothe him by pushing her away. If presented with a new task Billy would rush at it, not waiting for support or instruction. If he did not meet with immediate success he would become very angry, shouting in a deep and aggressive voice, and would sweep everything aside. After this, Billy would retreat into himself, his head buried in his hands.

In short, Billy was unable to learn from experience, because he needed so badly to control the outside world. His approach meant that he frequently met with failure, thus denting any fragile sense of self-worth that his new parents were able to instil in him. Learning for Billy was an intensely painful business and it was important that any formal educational setting was able to recognise and work with this.

In this instance the local education authority were, very helpfully, able to bend their rules concerning school placement and found a place for Billy in a small assessment class. There was resistance to this initially as he was not a traditionally slow learning child. (The purpose of the unit was to see whether, given appropriate input, children could progress educationally to a degree where they would be able to manage in a mainstream class.)

Working with Billy's parents and his teachers, it has been vital to acknowledge the frustration, anger and despair that they have felt in trying to bring about change in his levels of trust, aggression and capacity to learn.

The family, school and psychologist have worked closely together towards a shared understanding of Billy's developmental needs and to plan ways of helping. These have included:

- direct work with Billy on understanding feelings, through stories and books

- respecting but not colluding with his need for control through offering controlled choice of activities where appropriate

- relief from the need to constantly check out what was happening in the group by regular individual work outside the classroom for basic skills work

- the creation of the foundations of cause and effect learning through the application of simple rewards and sanctions at home and at school. This was particularly hard to carry out as rewards appeared to make little difference and Billy's distress and anger used to make his teachers and parents feel like ogres for insisting on compliance.

Focusing on the Microsystem: Not all Problems have Easy Solutions

Case Example

Simon was nine years old and had been referred to the school's psychologist because of difficulties in concentration, problems in relating to his peer group and a range of unsociable/disruptive behaviours in class, such as spitting and dribbling and making noises and rocking in his seat.

Discussion with parents revealed that Simon had joined the school two years ago and after a difficult initial period had seemed to settle. He had particularly enjoyed his previous year at school but this year he was always in trouble and seemed to have no friends at all at school. Simon also complained about being bullied by other children in his class and they had approached school several times about this. Nothing, however, seemed to change.

Simon's parents told the psychologist that Simon had been sexually abused by a babysitter when he was three, and this was partly why they had moved areas and school as this was known about in their previous community and school and seemed to have a detrimental effect on how Simon was seen. The abuse had been investigated and dealt with and Simon and his family had received help. The school had been aware of this.

Observation of Simon in the class on two separate occasions showed a stark and disturbing picture. The class as a whole was not well organised and controlled. Simon usually started the day well, going to his desk and reading a book. However, few other children conformed to this expectation and soon Simon would join in wandering around the room. Simon's teacher rarely gained the children's attention before issuing instructions.

The psychologist noticed that two other children in the class seemed particularly 'stroppy', answering their teacher back in an inappropriate way and refusing to get on with work.

On two separate occasions Simon was hurt by a fellow pupil – once a boy pushed his chair into him, and on the second occasion he was deliberately tripped up in the playground. On the first occasion Simon told his teacher, who briefly reprimanded the child in question and then told Simon off for being out of his seat. On the second, Simon told the meal time assistants who looked at his grazed knee and sent him off. Later Simon was sent inside for spitting at the child who had tripped him up.

In order to make some sense of what is going on in this situation, beyond writing the teacher off as badly organised and uncaring, we need to think about the situation both in individual and group processes.

First, the psychologist discovered that the long-term (previous but one) head of the school had been convicted of child sexual abuse. The parents had not known this, nor had the psychologist. Clearly this was not something that could be talked about. The teacher's reaction to comment being made about Simon's abuse, and previous reactions to it, were met with complete dismissal suggesting that this whole area was something far too difficult to think about. In fact it seems that in this instance the teacher was unable to think about Simon in any feeling way. In discussion she indicated that he more or less deserved the treatment he got from other children because of his behaviour towards them in the past (from two years previously when he first entered the school). In Winnicott's (1986) terms, the teacher could be seen as being unable to contain or hold the painfulness of Simon's early experiences, possibly because of the distressing history of the school. Simon's presence in the class threatened to destabilise the status quo in the class and the school with regard to its history, and the only way to deal with Simon was to see him as the cause of all the problems.

At a group level of analysis, one can also see how this teacher, under stress of a difficult class to manage as well as attempting to shut out painful memories, was becoming more and more submerged by the basic, immediate demands of the group and less and less able to hold onto her adult, organising and teaching function.

De Board (1978) offers a lucid and accessible synopsis of Bion's work in relation to organisations. In brief, Bion (1984) postulated two main kinds of group functioning, the Basic Assumption Group and the Work Group. The Basic Assumption group is characterised by an inability to do any real work as all members will be acting out their wishes and fantasies. One assumption of the Basic Assumption group is that the group is together 'to be sustained by a leader on whom it can depend for nourishment, material and spiritual protection' (Bion 1984). In a primary teaching situation this may be entirely appropriate for the children; however, they require a leader (teacher) who is dependable and realistic. If this is not the case the group is likely to slide into using basic defensive mechanisms such as splitting, denial and idealisation. This seemed to be what was happening in Simon's situation with him rapidly becoming the scapegoat for unexpressed fears and anxieties in the group.

In this extremely difficult situation the family were advised to move Simon as it seemed unlikely that the situation could be changed quickly enough for him. Clearly it was not appropriate to talk with the family in detail about the psychological processes at work but being able to think about the situation in this way helped the psychologist recommend a route that was not one she would usually take.

Focus on the Mesosystem – Making Space to Think about Difficult Issues

Transition times in school life are frequently difficult for children to negotiate as they have to cope with feelings of sadness and loss as well as feelings of excitement and hope about the future. Transitions in terms of developing new policies and ways of doing things can be difficult for staff too, sometimes having unexpected repercussions.

Case Example

The head of a large primary school contacted the schools psychologist by telephone, speaking with some urgency. She had just admitted a five-year-old into the reception class who 'could do nothing' and who was always in trouble in the playground. The girl, Wendy, had previously attended a nursery group at the local Family Centre. The headteacher was asking for immediate help with this little girl or was suggesting that she would exclude her as she needed to be in a special school. Attempts by the psychologist to suggest interim measures (discussing mornings-only attendance or returning home for lunch) were rejected as unmanageable.

The psychologist was puzzled by this referral as she had a good relationship with the head and a good relationship with the Family Centre, and children who may experience problems on entering school were always discussed with the psychologist well before school entry. Wendy had never been mentioned to the psychologist at all.

In talking with the headteacher of the primary school there was a lot of blame in the air. This was focused on the Family Centre for not alerting the school to Wendy's problems, and to a certain extent, on the psychological service for not being able to react instantly and provide resources.

Discussion with the Family Centre indicated that for the first time the school had started making home visits to the families of the new entrants. This meant that the school staff had discontinued their liaison meetings with the Family Centre and relied solely on written information about the children. In discussion with the home–school liaison teacher it emerged that she had been horrified by the fact that Wendy's parents were both virtually illiterate, and distressed by the poverty of the home. This concern and distress had left her feeling hopeless about how to make things right for Wendy, and she had sought extra help. From the Family Centre's perspective, they had seen Wendy's parents cope well with bringing up their daughter under very difficult circumstances and felt that she would manage well at school because she was a well-loved and supported little girl. They were of course used to seeing many families who live in less than ideal circumstances and who struggle with a variety of limitations.

From the psychologist's point of view, it was important to take the school's concerns seriously and some individual work was done with Wendy and strategies to help her learning were worked out with the teacher. At a systemic level the psychologist arranged and chaired a meeting between the two heads to look at some of the issues raised by Wendy and to reinstate direct liaison between the Family Centre and the school. In fact the increased awareness that the school gained about their children and their families through the home visiting led to an increased level of liaison, rather than less, and Wendy was no longer causing concern by the end of the summer term.

Focus on the Exosystem – The Need for the Psychologist to Reflect

Psychologists' relationships with schools are not always easy. When schools are under a lot of internally-generated stress they become particularly hard to work with on a collaborative level. In these circumstances, the psychologist is often seen as the one person who can bring relief from stressful situations, either by removing troublesome children or by sanctioning extra resources.

Case Example

Brightwood school was a large first school (Reception to Year 4) which was very demanding of the psychologist's time. The head felt that, because of problem children and families introduced to their school by a new housing trust estate, they should have more psychological and support service time than other schools. After working in the school for a while the psychologist felt that there were indeed a significant number of children with learning and behavioural difficulties, and she worked hard to assess and plan interventions. She also supported a bid to the local education authority for some extra funding for a special needs post to focus on preventive work and support statemented children in school. The creation of this post did little to alleviate the demand on the psychologist for individual assessments – getting to work at a more consultative level seemed to be impossible, although the head said she was committed to this. It was also becoming obvious that more and more professionals were being pulled into the school to 'help' – health advisors, primary advisors, curriculum advisors, the child abuse team, and the local social services child care team, and so on. The psychologist made specific time with a valued colleague to discuss the school and her input. It was felt that as a response to stress in the management and increasingly fraught relationships within the staff group that the school had somehow lost sight of its boundaries and had become overwhelmed with home-based problems (the special needs teacher spent a great deal of time visiting homes but very little helping colleagues devise in-class strategies to help the children). The need to import more and more professionals into the school was a reflection of this failure to maintain boundaries, as was the increasing number of angry parents who entered the school. In consultation with the advisor for the school the psychologist set up a professional support group for the school which comprised members from the advisory services and social services. Individual children were not discussed but staff concerns and anxieties were picked up, as well as issues concerning the roles of supporting agencies. Increased understanding and communication between the school and other agencies as well as increased communication and awareness between helping agencies was able to lead to a more united and cohesive response to crises.

The Macrosystem – Educational Psychologists are Part of a Bigger System

There is a certain degree of frustration among members of the profession in relation to what could be described as a 'return to basics' in educational psychology focusing on individuals and assessment. Dessent (1980) in his paper on the history of educational psychology services describes how the need for a psychological service in education arose directly out of the implementation of the 1870 Education Act because:

> ... till then the voluntary schools had been able to reject the duller and more troublesome children if they wished ... and the school system had to absorb a large number of children who were to experience learning difficulties in the formal education setting. Interest in this group emerged because they interfered with the "payment by results" method of determining teachers' salaries. (p.61)

Tests of intelligence were established as a 'scientific' way of identifying, assessing and classifying children in the education system who were failing. We can see how strongly this tradition has survived in educational psychology, and increasingly local education authorities (LEAs) look to the educational psychology service to provide 'objective data' (psychometric testing) to help them decide who should need extra support in schools or placement in special provision.

Unfortunately there is no societal consensus about 'how needy is needy' or how much money should be spent on such children. Thus psychometrics are seen as a legitimate way of addressing what is essentially a moral issue. Substitute the 1981 and 1993 Education Act for the 1899 Act and the figure below holds true. The only difference is that standards and expectations have changed in line with society's increased knowledge and sophistication. The process remains the same.

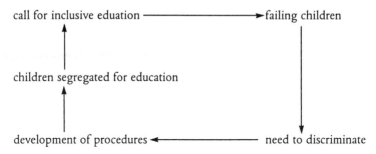

Figure 9.1 Resource allocation to children in need

From a systemic point of view we can choose to punctuate the repeated cycle outlined above at a place where it feels comfortable for us (providing the information that enables LEAs to administer scarce resources) or we can adopt the wide lens view and work towards a greater equality of educational opportunity for all children at the macro level as well as at an individual and lower systems level.

Concluding Comments

In this chapter I have tried to illustrate how taking a psychodynamic view is compatible with systems thinking and relevant to the work of an educational psychologist. A clinical psychology colleague commented on a talk that I gave concerning the marginalisation of vulnerable children in teachers' thinking, that she saw educational psychologists as an oppressed group – oppressed by overwork and bureaucratic demands. The profession must not let itself be muffled into saying nothing about what it sees and hears in the real world, or worse still be stifled to death.

CHAPTER 10

Child Sexual Abuse, Can we Bear it?
Training Perspectives in the Educational Context

Judith Trowell, Carmel Jennings and Su Burrell

The Children Act (1989) carries a number of provisions and implications for the staff groups working in local authorities to take action to protect children. The important emphases of the Act concerning child protection were enshrined in a climate of increasing public and professional awareness about child abuse, following the Cleveland and Rochdale inquiries in the 1980s. Successive legislation through the twentieth century has recognised the right of all children to be protected from cruelty and abuse. This has highlighted the complex and changing relationship between family and state, particularly in the rights of the state to intervene in family life. However, practice in the field of child protection has only recently, in the last 20 or 30 years, been given a central emphasis. Professionals are still struggling with some of the complexities of engaging in this important area of work.

This chapter is written with all practitioners in mind, but particularly for child psychologists and teachers who need to clarify their position in the minefield of confusion which surrounds this important area of work. We acknowledge in this jointly written chapter the challenge to traditional structures of interprofessional collaboration if multi-disciplinary work is to become more effective. We also illustrate the importance of staff understanding not only what they themselves are doing, but also the impact of their actions on the tasks of other professionals and on the general direction of the complex overall intervention.

The inquiry following the death of Maria Colwell (DHSS 1974), introduced fundamental changes in policy and practice for educational practitioners. It emphasised the important key role of schools in dealing with child abuse, but was highly critical of the way the education service was functioning in the areas of awareness, communication and record-keeping. Subsequently, there have been more systematic attempts to introduce guidelines and procedures into the educational network, with specific indication of lines of referral to other agencies who have child protection as a statutory component of their work. During the 1980s the findings of the Cleveland Inquiry drew great media attention to the area of child sexual abuse, and was very much in the minds of the policy makers who drafted the Children Act.

The most significant outcome of the Cleveland Inquiry chaired by Lady Elizabeth Butler Sloss was in the first paragraph of the conclusions: 'We have learned during the Inquiry that sexual abuse occurs in children of all ages including the very young, and boys as well as girls, in all classes of society and frequently within the privacy of the family...' (p.6).

In other words, child sexual abuse exists and we have both to acknowledge it and accept that inevitably children who have been sexually abused will be present in any large group of children. The recognition that most of these children are abused by people they know from within their own family framework has also encouraged a more sensitive approach to the issues involved in this highly complex and emotive area. Helps (1995) has highlighted the need for teachers to be able to explore communication and understanding of abuse in the context of family dynamics.

This chapter is concerned with some of the particular dilemmas faced by teachers in working in the sensitive area of child sexual abuse. One of the conundrums is that while child sexual abuse is now recognised as a major problem in society, which is unlikely to go away, increased recognition of the problem does not help to alleviate it. Working with sexually abused children and their families requires the co-operation of a wide range of professionals with different tasks. The disclosure of child sexual abuse leads to an immediate crisis in the families and the professional networks alike, with an accompanying recognition that the context in which a professional intervention is performed may lead to family breakdown, and precipitate further trauma in the child.

Integrating some of the incompatible concepts from the legal, health, educational, psychological, and therapeutic domains challenges not only our understanding of the phenomenon, but also affects our chances of ensuring the safety of the child. King and Trowell (1992) have discussed the need for significant change in the way legal systems deal with child welfare issues and suggest a separate decision-making body outside the Court structure. Furniss (1991) has also outlined a more integrated approach which spans some of the different conceptual systems involved: 'It has been most useful to examine the different concepts of responsibility, participation, guilt, power and blame in a metasystemic framework of linearity and circularity in order to help distinguish between child protective, legal and therapeutic aspects of child abuse' (p.8).

Denial and other distortions of feelings by abusers, children, families, teachers and other professionals is common in suspected discovery of child sexual abuse. When teachers face the likelihood that a child in their class is being abused, they are likely to feel they are positioned on the edge of an abyss. There are still strong forces and pressures in society which surround these issues with silence and secrecy, reflecting some of the specific problems of dealing with child sexual abuse as a syndrome of secrecy. In the aftermath of the Cleveland and Rochdale inquiries, attempts to be open about the issues led to scapegoating and 'witch-hunting' of some of the individual professionals who were involved.

It is understandable that many professionals, when considering their subjective reactions to the possibility of a child being abused, may decide that the evidence is insubstantial, and turn their minds away. In educational institutions, teachers may recognise the need to create an open climate where it is possible to think about and discuss some of the issues surrounding child abuse. This is an important step in considering some of the different stages of intervention and the possible involvement of teachers in contributing to treatment programmes. There is also a need to be clearer about some of the definitions of child sexual abuse and to acknowledge that there could be a continuum of psychological damage to the child. This is likely to depend upon the extent and the circumstances of the abuse. The emotional implications of child sexual abuse are discussed later in the chapter.

There are currently five definitions of child sexual abuse to which professional staff may refer. Until there is a nationally and internationally agreed definition we are going to have problems in diagnosis and practice. Individuals still need to spend time arriving at an agreed working definition and agencies have to have some agreement if multi-disciplinary work is to proceed on a sound agreed basis. The most commonly used is the the current Department of Health (1991) definition; but this is not used by everyone, and many find it rather too vague. It is important to be clear about what we mean when we talk to each other and the broad sub-groups of non-contact and contact abuse seem to be the simplest division.

Definitions of Child Sexual Abuse

1. Department of Health (1991). Sexual abuse is defined as the involvement of dependent, developmentally immature children and adolescents in sexual activity that they do not fully comprehend and to which they are unable to give informed consent; or sexuality that violates the social taboos of family roles.

2. Baker and Duncan (1985). A child (that is, anyone under 16 years) is sexually abused when another person who is sexually mature involves the child in any activity which the other person expects to lead to their sexual arousal. This might involve intercourse, touching, exposure of the sexual organs, showing pornographic material or talking about sexual things in anerotic way.

3. Incest Survivors Campaign (Feminist). 'The sexual molestation of a child by any person whom that child sees as a figure of trust and

authority. We see the questions of age, blood relationship and taboo as red herrings which obscure the central issue: the irresponsible exploitation of children's ignorance, trust and obedience. Incest is the abuse of power.'

4. Royal College of Psychiatrists (1993). Child sexual abuse has been defined as the involvement of children by older persons in the following types of sexual activities:

   i. exposure (viewing sexual acts, pornography and exhibitionism);

   ii touching of sexual parts (child and adult genitalia and post-pubertal female breasts);

   iii sexual intercourse (oral, anal or vaginal; acute assault and chronic involvement);

   iv other sexual acts (ejaculation of semen on to the child's body, sado-masochistic acts).

5. Mrazek and Mrazek (1981). Sexual abuse is:

   i Exposure (viewing of sexual acts, pornography and exhibitionism);

   ii Molestation (fondling of genitals of children or adults);

   iii Sexual intercourse (oral, vaginal, anal);

   vi Rape (acute or chronic assaultative forced intercourse).

Incidence

The next question is, how extensive is the problem?

Baker and Duncan's (1985) survey in the UK gave a prevalence rate of about 10 per cent. Childline reports about 37 per cent of their calls are from sexually abused boys and girls. Incidence estimates vary, and may be unreliable, as they are often based on retrospective reports, where there may be additional memory factors involved. In a San Franciso study, for example, Baker and Duncan (1985) describe 38 per cent of women as being abused at least once by the age of 18. However, as some definitions of abuse involve a broad spectrum of experiences, the authors acknowledge that not all of these women are likely to have been psychologically disturbed by their experiences.

This, then, is the extent of the problem; but does it need to concern professionals other than social workers? The Social Services Department is indeed the lead agency in child protection but following the implementation of the Children Act (1989) the document 'Working Together' (HQ et al. 1991) was revised. 'Working Together (under the Children Act 1989)' is a guide to arrangements for interagency co-operation for the protection of children from abuse. It is issued jointly by the Home Office, Department of Health, Department of Education and Science and the Welsh Office. This is a highly significant change and means that all state employed professionals have to take responsibility for 'working together'.

Recognition of the likelihood of high levels of frequency of child sexual abuse has several important implications for teachers and other professionals working in the educational context, which will be considered in this chapter. Awareness that child sexual abuse is likely to occur much more frequently than was previously understood means that many staff will find they need to reflect on their own personal attitudes and feelings about the likelihood that a child in their class is being abused.

Other pressures and stresses upon staff can restrict their opportunities to think and reflect upon this area of work in a safe way. The impact of ongoing, rapid change at a legislative and structural level has made it difficult to accommodate new working practices. It is likely that the impact of the Children Act on all the caring profession has been one of awe and fear of the implications, particularly in the present climate of greater demands and fewer resources. This means that teachers may find that defensive working practices are reflected in other areas of the professional networks outside the school.

Education Psychologists (EPs) can be an important resource, but many EPs have had their roles restricted by successive Education Acts (1981, 1993). Peake (1991) has described in some detail how EPs are ideally placed to be a major support to teachers if they are able to take on work in the field of child protection. However, work overload in other areas of statutory and contractual practice can prevent psychologists from undertaking additional responsibilities in this area. Many staff are already under-resourced, and pressures can be reflected in lack of flexibility in thought, over-rigid interpretations in functioning, lack of time for meetings and planned follow-through of concerns, and beliefs that some workers in the professional network are more qualified than others to undertake work of this nature. Another misleading issue is an implied distinction that some groups of personnel in health and educational fields do not have coercive powers in the same way as social workers. This requires further clarification within the context of the interprofessional network.

Roles and Responsibilities: Understanding the Child Protection Network

Some of the roles and responsibilities of staff within the interagency network have been operationalised as local procedures which are determined by the Area Child Protection Committee (ACPC) (*Working Together* HQ *et al.* 1991). Most ACPCs meet two or three times a year, and have developed systems for the active monitoring of fieldwork practices, including oversight of the local child protection register. As the management of children in need of care and protection can be an extremely complex organisational problem, it is important that teachers and other educational professionals have guidelines about how they should work with other agencies. These are now likely to be issued in the form of handbooks, which are determined by the ACPC and then issued by the local authorities to schools.

Working Together describes the requirement of local authorities to produce guidelines for the interprofessional management of suspected child abuse as follows:

> In every local authority area there is a need for a close working relationship between social services departments, the police service, medical practitioners, community health workers, the education service and others who share a common aim to protect children at risk. Co-operation at the individual case level needs to be supported by joint agency and management policies for child protection, consistent with their policies and plans for related service provision. (2.4)

The section on the role of agencies goes on to describe in turn what is required of each agency and the education service. These paragraphs start with

> the education service does not constitute an investigation or intervention agency, but has an important role to play at the recognition and referral stage. Because of their day to day contact with individual children during school terms, teachers and other school staff are particularly well placed to observe outward signs of abuse, changes in behaviour or failure to develop. (4.35–4.40)

There is then an outline of the need, where there is concern, to inform the head teacher or designated teacher so that the local social services or NSPCC or police can be alerted – this applies to all schools from nursery schools to further education colleges, state schools, opted-out schools and independent schools. The need to attend to child protection of which child sexual abuse is a part cannot be avoided.

In order to plan an efficient investigation, to avoid duplication, and to identify the role of each agency, *Working Together* refers to the need for a strategy meeting to be called at an early stage between the statutory agencies. Once the child is the focus of a strategy meeting, the ground has been prepared for the possible further involvement of the social work, police and health professionals. However, it is essential to take this process back a few stages in order to understand the distinctive potential contribution of teachers in facilitating the systematic daily monitoring where there is concern about a child and those of staff who may become involved later and whose role has a statutory component. Class teachers have a particularly important key role, as they are likely to be chosen by children to be the 'trusted person' with whom the child discusses the abuse, or to be the first professional to suspect abuse.

The importance of the role of the trusted person in the communication of child abuse cannot be underestimated, and must be distinguished from the role of all other professionals who undertake specific tasks during the subsequent processes of disclosure and follow-up. The teacher is likely to be an important attachment figure in the world in between home and outside. As the child spends the greater part of his or her day in school, the teacher has an important potential role in containment of the child's feelings and behaviour. For many children, the influence of the school is vital, and may prove to be their main stability, providing the security and organisation that is lacking elsewhere.

Statutory/Non-statutory Aspects of Work with Children who may have been Sexually Abused

The distinction between statutory and non-statutory aspects of work in this area is not a particularly valid or reassuring one. It is confusing as the Children Act (1989) clearly places an onus on all professionals working with children to take responsibility for reporting their suspicions. It also implies that some professionals know better than others how to act, whereas in reality this is an area of work where all staff are likely to feel immobilised by some of the particular anxieties which beset their thinking, planning and decision-making capacities. Kraemer (1988) has described this as a process of 'professional stupidity', arising from the seemingly irreconcilable principles and aims which are embedded in thinking about incest and how to respond to it.

Some of the distinctions between the educational, therapeutic and legal approaches to the work are inoperative in practice, and can best be understood as a split between different professional approaches in each domain. Splitting mechanisms on an inter and intra-agency level are an instance of defensive working practices which occur when anxieties arising from the work reach intolerable levels. They are subsequently likely to be re-enacted within the professional network, which may inflict further psychological damage on the child and family, which can be greater than the abuse itself. For these reasons it is suggested that intervention in instances of suspected child sexual abuse is considered as a continuum of involvement. This would range from suspicions aroused in the teacher or child care staff at one end of the continuum to court proceedings at the other extreme. It also leads us to consider the necessity for joint training initiatives for the different professional groups involved.

As chair of an ACPC, Judith Trowell has been involved in developing multi-disciplinary trainings which involve under-fives staff class teachers, designated teachers and Education Social Workers (ESWs). Many ACPCs now have training sub-committees as recommended in *Working Together*, and local training initiatives can be funded by applications to the Department of Health, via the ACPC. This is the mechanism for developing trainings which will include educational personnel alongside other staff groups and, it is hoped, will facilitate better working relationships with the police, social workers and paediatricians. There is thus a great potential for development in bringing staff together to train effectively in child abuse, and to help them be clearer about their roles and tasks. This also requires innovative energy from the staff groups themselves. In a climate where other resources are being dismantled and taken away, practitioners are likely to feel deskilled and isolated, and it can then be difficult to perceive new resource niches and to use them creatively. This is one of the tensions which stems from recent legislation, and is also explored in Chapters 1, 3 and 6.

Professionals in all disciplines need to be able to move freely between the three different domains and levels of discourse which can be represented in the following figure:

Figure 10.1. Overlapping professional discourses in issues of child protection

Figure 10.1 illustrates the need for understanding the interactions between different professional roles and concerns, and an ability to switch perspectives and imagine different possible outcomes for the child and family at different points along the continuum of intervention. Supervision plays an essential and crucial part in this form of professional learning, and has particular advantages which are discussed in Chapter 1. The supervisory relationship is concerned with respect for the individual practitioner, listening to particular individual needs and responding to them. This produces a model for listening sensitively to the needs of others, including children and parents, and is more likely to equip teachers to work sensitively in this area.

Training can take different forms, but educational practitioners will also need to be able to draw on different theoretical frameworks: attachment theory, learning theory, systems theory and psychoanalytic theory if they are able to think about all the aspects of these cases. Feminist theory (Miller 1990) has contributed to our understanding of the abuse of power which is inherent in these situations. It leads us to examine the relationship between, on the one hand, social policies and the ideologies which generate them, and on the other hand, the specific issues concerning children and families which are presented in schools, clinics, and courts. Bentovim (1992) has presented an integrated concept of a trauma-organised system for making sense of child abuse and family violence and its effect upon development. This framework helps workers to think more coherently about the way events are connected at many different levels, and to plan appropriate interventions.

For education and nursery staff in particular, it is helpful to have a system for recognising signs and indicators that arouse suspicions. It is then easier to proceed if suspicions become serious concerns. The following tables illustrate some of the different physical and psychological indicators of abuse at different stages in the child's development. Although some of these signs can be insignificant if considered in isolation, they may back up a particular hunch or suspicion which a teacher feels in relation to an individual child. It is important to consider the whole context and meaning of the child's behaviour, and to be watchful of one's own feelings and reactions in this area, including the tendency to interpret signs over-zealously. Some of the possible symptoms of sexual abuse may also overlap with other signs of emotional disturbance and be recorded as more general indicators of concern that not all is well with the child.

Table 10.1 Warning signs commonly associated with sexual abuse
(Indicators depend on the development stage of the child)

Development Stage	General Physical Signs	Emotional/Behavioural Effects
Up to 4 years	Failure to thrive Signs of physical abuse or neglect	Developmental delay Sleep disturbances Loss of toilet training Fear of men Insecurity/clinging Withdrawn or frozen child play Inappropriate sexual behaviour or sexualised drawings
4–6 years	Recurrent abdominal pain Faecal soiling/constipation Urinary tract infections Diurnal/nocturnal enuresis	Overstimulated – acting wild Compulsive cleaning Repetitive symbolic destruction of both parents Tantrums Overfriendly Sexual approaches to adults Displays knowledge of adult sexuality in play, speech or drawings Sleep disturbances
7–12 years	Recurrent urinary tract infection Soiling/enuresis Abdominal pains Migraine Emotional asthma Eating disorders	Sleep disturbances School failure Pseudo-mature dress Poor peer relationships Secretiveness Obvious lies Stealing Firesetting Sudden mood changes Emotional lability Eager to please Anxious Assumes maternal role in home Aggression at home Refusal to go home from school Overclose to adults Unexplained suicide attempts

Table 10.1 Warning signs commonly associated with sexual abuse (Indicators depend on the development stage of the child) (continued)

Development Stage	General Physical Signs	Emotional/Behavioural Effects
13 years plus	Frequent attendance at GP for minor complaints Requests for contraceptive advice Hysterical conversion syndromes Anorexia Nervosa Complusive overeating	Poor peer relationships Running away/truancy Conduct disorders Drug/solvent/alcohol abuse Promiscuity Unexplained wealth Self-poisoning Self-mutilation Depression/despair Social inhibition/withdrawal Episodic psychotic states Phobic states and compulsive disorders Assumes maternal role Aggression at home Sexually abuses smaller children

Taken from Shetland Islands Council Education Department Child Abuse Procedures

The Continuum of Intervention

Prevention and training the children in self-protection

Child abuse is most usefully thought about as part of an ongoing personal, social and health education curriculum, rather than as a one-off programme, or in response to a crisis in the school. There are a number of training aids, videos, training packs and other resource materials available for class teachers, some of which are more well developed than others. Readers are referred to the end of the chapter for references to some of the training materials. However, until a person has had child protection training, and feels comfortable with the subject and grasps the issues which the children may raise, it would be unwise to consider implementing the programmes in a piecemeal way.

Educational psychologists are in an important key role at the preventative level, and could take some responsibility for INSET programmes. As they have an expert knowledge of child development, EPs can take into account the conceptual understanding of the children, together with other socio-emotional and contextual factors which may influence children's responses to certain types of material and presentations. The EP has a close liaison and understanding of the individuality of schools and is able to draw on this knowledge to help set

Table 10.2 General Symptoms of child sexual abuse Maher (1987)

Physical Indicators	Behavioural Indicators	Familial Indicators
1. Sexually transmitted disease, especially in young children	1. Unexplained regression in development milestones	1. Jealousy and extreme protection of the child
2. Complaints of pain or itching in the genital, gastrointestinal or urinary area	2. Withdrawn infantile behaviour; preoccupation with fantasy world.	2. Isolation/alienation of child and family members in the community
3. Difficultly in walking or sitting; refusal to assume straddle position because of 4 below.	3. Poor peer relationships; often prefers to be alone or with an adult.	3. Frequent absences from school by the child which is justified by the male caretaker or parent
4. Torn, strained or bloody underclothing	4. Statements indicating that he/she has been sexually assaulted or hints about involvement in sexual activity	4. Frequent absences from home by one of the caretakers/parents
5. Bruises or bleeding in the external genitalia, vaginal, or anal area: unusual lesions around the mouth should also be noted	5. Behaviour of an unusually seductive manner with peers or adults; overly sophisticated knowledge or interest in sexual acts or vocabulary	5. A pattern of rigid, restrictive control by the father over one or more of the female children
6. Unusual odours around genital area	6. Reluctance on the part of the child to go home after school.	6. A father whose behaviour is characterised by frequent drinking and/or a history of abusive, unfeeling treatment of other family members

up more effective support systems for children and staff. EPs can also help set up supportive frameworks for teachers and parents to work together.

In their consultative capacity, they may occupy the position of a 'respected outsider' to schools and help to identify potential obstacles and tensions which could undermine work both within the school, and between the school and other agencies. Consultative styles of work help staff to reflect on the stance they are taking and to guard against tendencies towards over-zealous practices and certainties in pursuing the detection of sexual abuse. We all have a responsibility to examine our own actions in this area of work, and consultation models can help us to do this ourselves before committing ourselves to particular courses of action.

Fotheringham (1988) found in a study of teachers' attitudes that just over half of the teachers in his sample saw prevention as part of their function. Those who did see it as part of their responsibility did not necessarily feel comfortable with the idea of dealing with such a topic in their classrooms. This was linked to anxieties about lack of suitable training and knowledge as well as to the sensitive nature of the topic. Teachers expressed a need for small group support and mutual discussion in helping them to set up training initiatives for children. By sharing the planning of the sessions, it is easier to anticipate and be prepared for the outcomes and issues which children might want to raise. Parents may be involved at the earlier planning stages, and could also be present during some of the training, as their consent is an important issue to be clarified.

It is helpful if feelings can be explored and contained during training initiatives, which are designed to help staff offer support to each other in pairs or small groups. In a safe environment, teachers can be helped to establish greater familiarity and comfort with their own attitudes in this area. This is an important step in overcoming biases which may either give double messages to children, or block their communications. Some preliminary biases in the area of child sexual abuse include disbelief, blaming, and fear that the situation can be exaggerated and escalate out of control. Although some of these feelings may be directed towards parents or other professionals, it is particularly important that the child is believed. Several studies have established that children are unlikely to lie or invent stories of sexual abuse (Maher 1987). Teachers therefore need to be prepared to believe that it has happened, as this can prepare the way for the child establishing trust and receiving treatment.

Suspicions, concerns and discussion

In some of the earlier chapters we have presented ways of taking into account the whole school context when thinking about the individual child. This is particularly important in issues of child sexual abuse as the culture in the school is likely to influence some of the beliefs and assumptions about possible recognition of abuse and how to respond to it. Several other factors can interact with the capacity to think about abuse on a daily basis in the school setting.

These include the incidence of special educational needs in different schools and neighbourhoods and particularly of other forms of behavioural acting-out which can obscure specific issues of abuse.

Recent findings by Wodarski (1993) suggest that children who have been abused are more likely to express behavioural difficulties than comparison children (that is, children who have not been abused), and to find it difficult to learn, regardless of the learning programmes they are presented with. It is likely that many children who are identified as having special educational needs at different levels of the Code of Practice may also have been sexually abused. Difficulties in clarifying the abuse persist, including the reluctance of the majority of children to voice their fears, and the overlap between sexual abuse with other forms of abuse and neglect.

Educational staff are often caught in a dilemma, believing that in order to protect the child it is necessary to maintain contact with the parents rather than to risk further abuse, and possibly jeopordise the working relationships which they may have taken several years to attain. The conceptual frameworks for considering children's needs within the 1981 Act are of a linear nature, and do not enable practitioners to switch to a more multi-dimensional and interactional perspective, as illustrated in Figure 10.1. In the educational context, the procedural frameworks for recognising child sexual abuse are incompatible with the frameworks for considering other aspects of special educational need. The onus is therefore on individual staff who are likely to be educational psychologists or teachers to integrate data from different frameworks. They somehow need to be enabled to overcome the tendencies towards incomplete and inflexible thinking which are implicit in the legislative procedures.

Teachers in inner city schools are likely to experience higher levels of general emotional and behavioural disorders in their classrooms (Elton 1989). This may lead to a gradual accommodation and blunting of sensitivity to some of the more subtle nuances and signs of concern in children's behaviour. This is an inevitable human response to dealing with high levels of stress, and is not to be equated with a lack of concern among staff. Teachers are also attuned to the likelihood that some children may have been watching TV material of a frightening or sexual nature which is being repeated in their play, rather than expressing more direct instances of abuse. This is a confusing area as it can be considered abusive to expose children to material which is beyond the limits of their emotional, sexual and cognitive development.

Again, teachers may understandably feel hesitant about raising concerns of this nature with parents. They may anticipate clashes in expectations and values and unintended obstacles in the different forms of child-rearing based on class, race and cultural factors. The lack of a clear model for how to raise concerns which seem to challenge parental practices can then lead to avoidance of the issues. This is an area of confusion for some practitioners, as the 'partnership' models of involvement with parents which have been developed in some educational and health settings (Davis 1993) are not always compatible with the need to protect children. Lindsey (1994) has clarified this as follows:

> Partnership, together with parental responsibility, as well as the obligation to discover children's wishes, implies that professionals must endeavour to inform fully and involve parents where possible, and children where appropriate, in decision-making. But where partnership threatens the protection of the child, *the child's welfare is paramount.* (p.164)

Where children are enacting overtly sexual behaviour in school, it is essential that this is contained in a safe place where it is possible to think about it in more depth. Teachers may be able to help children understand how they may place themselves at risk by acting out precocious sexualisation in unsafe places such as the street or neighbourhood. This can be approached by the setting of clear boundaries and explorations of why certain behaviours are unacceptable. A further issue is that the impact of the abuse can affect other children in the class. Sometimes the problems are propogated and an overtly sexual culture can spread through the class, which places other children at risk.

Such a crisis can lead professionals to take immediate action and may lead to an unco-ordinated intervention which is an expression of the school or professional crisis. In the preparation process for disclosure staff need to be able to deal with the crisis of the professional network before attempting to think about the second distinct element, which is the crisis of the family. This can be a time of startling realisation, as the person who first names the abuse may feel that they have personally created the abuse as a reality.

Children communicate sexual abuse in several different ways, and it is not always clear to staff whether children are conveying awareness of abuse as a reality or as a fantasy. It is less common for children to disclose directly; instead they often communicate by drawings and essays to test out whether the reality of the abuse is recognised, and whether the adult can be trusted to help. Communicating with children by talking to them and listening is an essential aspect of being with them, yet it can be a particular area of conflict and difficulty where abuse is suspected. The important aspect is to register that the child is troubled, and to find ways of talking to the child over time.

Teachers and psychologists need to register that there are two distinct modes of reaction when a child may be trying to communicate the facts of sexual abuse. In the first mode, we need to be *interpretative* and to establish meanings between events without asking leading questions. During this stage the practitioner can be open-ended and unpressurising, trying to reflect back some of the feelings the child is conveying, such as confusion and fear of breaking a secret. Concerns can be recorded by making full notes of what the child said and how the practitioner responded. This may lead into the second mode, where the child communicates more directly the reality of sexual abuse and the staff's response is likely to become *investigative*. The adult, whether teacher, school meals supervisor or assistant, needs to explain to the child that they have shared something that has to be taken seriously and that they will not left alone with it.

At this stage, the first professional who has realised the likelihood of abuse or listened to a child's disclosure must not immediately think about involving other professionals, as this can lead to a hasty referral. They nevertheless have a mandatory responsibility to share their concerns in a planned way with professionals outside the school. The person to whom the child has spoken is now a 'trusted person' to them and needs to be involved in the next stage of the intervention, in order to respect the child's trust.

It is particularly important for the trusted person to take into account their knowledge of the child's family and to share their concerns with the designated teacher or headteacher in the school. There is also a responsibility to take a meta-view of the whole situation, and to ask the question: 'How do I act in this situation to ensure the child's future safety and treatment in the context of the possible wider multi-professional interventions?' If children are referred too quickly to other experts, such as social workers, psychologists, school medical officers and police they are likely to 'close up' and withdraw their allegations. The trusted person can later accompany the child and help them to relate the abuse in a more official disclosure interview, where the child may need to talk to strangers in a more intimidating setting.

Interagency consultation

Prior to an intervention, it is possible to discuss suspicions and concerns in a problem-solving way within the professional network without identifying the child concerned. This is known as an *Anonymous Diagnostic Interprofessional Consultation* (Furniss 1991) and is positioned to occur before a strategy meeting, where confidentiality is less likely to be maintained. The advantages of consultative meetings are that they help the professionals to clarify some of the specific criteria surrounding the suspicions, and to determine how to increase the chance of successful disclosure by the child and family.

During the meetings, the therapeutic, child protective and legal aspects need to be represented equally so that these different functions are balanced in the goal-oriented planning of the subsequent intervention. It is particularly helpful for social workers and police in child protective capacities to avoid intervening prematurely in ways which may precipitate unpredictable and often catastrophic consequences for the child and family, such as imprisonment and family breakdown. Similarly, it is important to work towards planning a therapeutic intervention and to distinguish this from the need for legal interviewing. Sometimes it is easier to resolve potential conflicts in the professional network in a meeting of this nature than in a strategy meeting or case conference.

The trusted person is more likely to experience the planning process as contained in this consultative approach and to feel that it is more likely to be a predictably better outcome for the child. Alternatively, by referring outwards to a strategy meeting the staff member may feel they have lost control of the process, and are left wondering whether they have done the right thing as they may have betrayed the child. It may also be possible to address some of the conflicts which arise in the professional network, as professionals tend to identify with different family members.

Some of the most frequent conflicts involve staff identification with parents rather than children. Many professionals express pro-parent views in meetings which undermine the child's perspective and emphasise how they would feel if this happened instead of focusing on the child's feelings. This can lead to subtle and mutual undermining by members of the meeting, leading to paralysis and a lack of worthwhile outcomes. Another conflict can be expressed between professionals who want the child to stay in the home situation and receive therapy and those who want to protect the child by removing him or her from home. Recognising that these tensions reflect splitting mechanisms and denial which often mirror the family process makes it easier to prevent them being enacted and can lead to a more task-oriented process of negotiation and co-operation.

Discussion at this stage needs to aim towards clarifying whether there are sufficient concerns to proceed with an investigation. This leads to further assessment by outside agencies, with the likelihood that cases fall into the following categories, which have different implications for treatment programmes:

1. *The clear cut cases.* These have definite signs and the alleged offender agrees and accepts what has happened, or it is proved.

    There is a criminal case and usually in parallel a civil case where the child may be the subject of care proceedings and the offender is prevented from returning or the child is removed. A treatment plan is set up and rehabilitation at some point may be possible – or not.

2. *Probable cases.* These are child sexual abuse cases where we think it highly likely that abuse has occurred. The child may have made a clear declaration and then have withdrawn it, or the indications are strong that child sexual abuse has occurred but it cannot categorically be stated. There may be criminal proceedings which may result in a conviction or may not and there are often civil proceedings where the child is the subject of care proceedings. The child may be removed for a while; the main dilemma is the protection of and the emotional damage to the child. These children may have difficulties but if the case is unproven the caretakers may or may not co-operate with any intervention. These cases are

extremely difficult to manage if the legal path has been tried and fails.

3. *Possible cases.* These are the 'grey area' cases where many people are concerned. Under possible cases one can include those cases as part of divorce proceedings – access or custody disputes where child sexual abuse is brought up. Non-contact sexual abuse is where the child may or may not have been involved but has explicit knowledge which may have been acquired by observation of violent or perverse sexual activity. For example, one little girl of four was referred to the Tavistock and was particularly terrified of taking her knickers down in her nursery. It became clear after interviews with the parents that she had had to watch her separated parents still having violent sexual intercourse. Experiences of this nature can lead to disturbance and although it may be possible to intervene it is often not.

Some children are relieved to talk but many are silenced by fears and threats, terrified of what will happen to themselves, their families or the abuser offender. This can leave experienced professional staff with the dilemma of not being certain whether the abuse really occurred or not. Living with this 'not knowing' can be very difficult and distressing. In some cases where the children or families are offered help for other problems the position may clarify in six months to a year but often it does not. Increasingly in a range of cases where children are placed in alternative placements or taken on for treatment somewhere, child sexual abuse is revealed after a while.

Interventions outside the school

When a firm suspicion of abuse has been clarified, it is mandatory to report this to social services, who have responsibility for setting up a strategy meeting. This will involve some of the following different considerations and outcomes, although the order of these will depend on individual circumstances:

- discussion with the referrer/reporter and a network meeting
- family interview as appropriate
- family history and social history: interviews with parents or caretakers alone and together
- interview with alleged offender
- interviews with children individually and with sibling group
- assessment of the child's developmental status and mental stage
- physical examination – paediatrician/police surgeon
- case conference.

The skills of many disciplines are required to take account of the interactive nature of abuse, with an understanding of how families function and of how to assess the parent–child relationship. At this stage, assessments of both the child and the family situation can involve forensic considerations, as involvement may require that the case is presented in court.

Many professionals, particularly social workers, paediatricians, child psychiatrists and psychologists are spending more and more time in court. Hodges (1994) has found in a national survey that 36 per cent of child educational and clinical psychologists have appeared in court as an expert witness. Training for this is still limited, although essential as evidence suggests presenting oneself in court is an area where many professionals feel ill-equipped. The evidence of the education service staff in court can often be critical, as teachers have ongoing contact with children. Nevertheless it can be difficult for teachers and other school staff who might prefer to stay out of this aspect of child protection. It is often vital in establishing 'the case' for the child and thus essential that this work is recognised as part of the education service task. The adversarial nature of working in courts introduces potential conflicts of interests and styles of work which are discussed in more depth in King and Trowell (1992). One of the dilemmas concerns how to convey some of the findings of a multi-faceted diagnostic assessment in a straightforward and concise way which makes sense in court and will stand up to cross-examination. The court has a need for immediate answers to yes/no questions:

> 'Will these children be at risk if they are returned immediately to the home?' tends, through pressure of time, to slip into broad generalisations. Parents are often then categorised, and evaluated according to simple stereotypes. The complexities, the subtle individual and family differences, tend to be flattened in the legal process. (King and Trowell 1992, p.50)

Communicating with children

It is only recently that it has been recognised that there needs to be particular training to enable professionals to communicate with children. Investigative interviewing techniques which are illustrated below are a case in point. This coincides with a turning point in the thinking of the law which incorporates giving children more rights, and allowing children to seek representation in court, independently of their guardians (Harris Hendriks and Williams 1992). The 1989 Act has encapsulated some of these ideas by setting out a check-list which is headed by 'the ascertainable wishes and feelings of the child concerned (considered in the light of his or her age and understanding)'. However, the Act does not state unequivocally that children's wishes are determinative, as the child's wishes may not be consistent with their welfare needs.

Investigative Interviewing

Planning the interview

Consider the duration and pace of the interview

and BE FLEXIBLE

Take account of development stage, age, attention span and particular intellectual or physical limitations of each child.

- Generally an hour or less – excluding breaks.
- The child's pace – not the adults.
- Be sensitive to cues from the child.
- Interview in the context of the child's usual routine.

The Interview

One interviewer at a time

A special blend of skills is required to interview children effectively for evidential purposes. Be guided by the pre-planning information taking into account race, gender, culture and all developmental information.

An understanding of basic rules of evidence and the elements of criminal offences is also required and the ability and availability to give evidence in court.

- Consider support for the interviewer as well as for the child and carer – a consultant for the interview and support for interview related tasks.
- Decide on lead interviewer – be prepared to swap over, take a break, seek advice in response to pre-arranged signals.
- Consider very carefully the 'pros and cons' of the presence of a trusted adult in the interview room
- Allocate tasks – who is to operate the camera; who is to support the adult with the child.

Pre-planning/Planning the Interview: Assessing Competence

Information collected may have bearing on preliminary decisions about the appropriate STRUCTURE, STYLE, DURATION AND PACE of the interview.

Record all discussions

You must consider

RACE	CULTURE
GENDER	FIRST LANGUAGE
DEVELOPMENTAL STAGE	OTHER CHILDREN

throughout the planning process, as these issues will have a bearing on the:

- choice of the interview
- materials used
- methods of communication – language, type
- timing of interview and breaks
- other action that needs to be taken.

Assess the child's development – in consultation

- chronological age
- physical development
- cognitive development
- language development
- emotional development
- social development
- psychosexual development.

   A child's developmental stage can be influenced by:

- the child's relationship – loving, etc.
- home environment
- presence of abuse
- child's personal history
- child's likely state of mind
- presence of any disability in the child or in the child's family.

Hodges (1994) suggests that a satisfactory definition of when children's wishes will be paramount will be likely to emerge over the years through case law, that is, through individual situations arriving in court and being thrashed out on an individual basis. The specialised nature of such assessments and the emphasis on the child's voice is likely to have a major impact on the work of psychologists, who are well positioned to make professional judgements which take into account children's intellectual, emotional and social development. Hodges found that there has already been an increase in referrals to educational and clinical psychologists for the assessment of a child's ascertainable wishes and feelings, as well as requests for consultation and interagency communication on this topic. Changes in the pattern of workload need to be addressed at the level of the local education authority and the educational psychology service (EPS) in planning service delivery as local authorities have a responsibility for resourcing such assessments. Hodges (1994) has suggested that contracts which clearly define the work proportions would clarify expectations and an increase in the number of psychologists employed by social services would ease the pressure on other aspects of psychologists' contractual work.

Treatment issues

Treatment programmes for the individual child, any siblings and the family can be planned to occur alongside legal interventions, although sometimes the incompatibility of these approaches can mean that the counselling or therapy is jeopordised. Careful planning is required to consider the optimal timing for therapeutic interventions, and to ensure that the child's treatment is safeguarded. Helps (1995) has found in a study of teachers' involvement with children who may have been sexually abused that they were very concerned about the whole area of treatment, yet had little idea about the types of treatment children might be receiving, or even what was available. This was related to anxieties they experienced about their own ways of dealing with these issues and whether their approaches were compatible with those of other professionals.

Treatment is likely to take place in child guidance, child and family centres, mental health clinics and other specialised settings, although there is regional variation in the resourcing which is available.

Brief therapeutic groupwork for children is the most usual form of intervention. Groups are likely to have a psychoeducational focus and involve preschool, primary school or secondary school children for 10 to 15 sessions. The aims are to reduce the sense of isolation, to try to enhance self-esteem and to educate the children in self-protection, sex education and appropriate behaviour. Sometimes sibling groups may be used where children in one family have been abused. Alongside children's groups it helps to have groups for the caretakers – foster parent groups or parent groups with the non-offending parent – as these children are often very difficult to manage.

It is our experience that in a group composed of six children, usually two children may be thought to be so troubled that they need further individual help. Some can use counselling but the most disturbed need skilled individual therapy. The intensive individual work with very disturbed children is slow, painful and very distressing for the child and the therapist; it is very demanding work. The training, supervising and support for the therapists is a massive undertaking.

Family therapy can often be helpful but this is more likely to occur later in the rehabilitation process. Sometimes family sessions to consider the issues if the abuser has been excluded and to help the family develop coping strategies are important (see Bentovim 1992). This is based on the high probability that the abuser was male and the remaining non-abusing parent is female. Offenders are particularly difficult to help, and although there is gloom about how much they can really change, modifying their behaviour is possible. A psychodynamic approach may provide us eventually with sufficient understanding to be able to effect some real change but at present there are still many offenders we cannot help to change fundamentally.

Work with the non-abusing parent, usually the mother, and the abused child is important to re-establish their relationship which was often distant and lacking in trust. Otway and Peake (1993) have described the setting up of a self-help group for mothers of abused children. They describe the process of the group as similar to a grieving process, which enabled and supported the mothers in their capacity to protect their children. They have found that mothers' initial reactions to the likelihood that their child is being abused is not indicative of their ability to support the child, and see this as a much longer-term process which the mothers need help in working through.

In addition, there is the increasing number of adults who are coming forward needing help with the child sexual abuse they experienced as children. They come when they embark on an adult sexual relationship, or when they marry or are pregnant, or have their first baby, or the child reaches the age they were when their abuse started. Suddenly, their past which they had 'wiped out' begins to surface and cause problems even when they can't 'remember' what happened. There is evidence from consultation workshops that when health visitors who were running groups for post-natally depressed mothers began asking about child sexual abuse they were very troubled by how many of the mothers disclosed sexual abuse in their own childhood.

Many people are suggesting we are going to need to rewrite a lot of our text books. How much of paediatrics, child mental health and adult mental health problems are going to be linked ultimately with childhood sexual abuse is unclear. In our experience it begins to seem that problems like learning disability, mood disturbance in children, enuresis, encopresis, attempted suicide, post-natal depression, depression in adults and sexual problems could all have child sexual abuse as a possible cause.

The Emotional Impact of Child Sexual Abuse

Why is child sexual abuse so damaging? Why does it take so much input to effect change? We can only understand these questions and move towards answers if we try to understand what happens in the individual's mind. If we can do that we can understand and then perhaps intervene most effectively. Child sexual abuse is of a different order to any other form of abuse because the linking up of sexuality and aggression – violence results in a very primitive destruction of the child's mind. In sexual abuse there is nearly always some physical abuse; there is the massive emotional abuse – 'soul murder'; and at the same time the child's mind is being raped – as well as its body – because of the sexual element. The body may recover fairly quickly once the abuse has ceased but the mind is left profoundly traumatised. We do not fully understand what has happened but the more we struggle the more damaging sexual abuse is revealed to be.

We know that the impact of child sexual abuse is strongly linked with the severity of the abuse, the duration of the abuse and the degree of coercion. But it is also and perhaps most significantly linked with the child's developmental stage – that is, her or his emotional, intellectual and psychological development. Some children are profoundly damaged by what to us does not seem to be horrendous abuse. Other children who have been through what to us seems to be really horrendous confound us by not being as damaged as we would expect. There may be external mitigating factors – an adult who believes and supports them or someone on the end of a telephone 'helpline'. Sometimes a 'small' intervention like this can enable a child to survive less damaged than one would expect.

For most children sexual abuse is a terrifying impingement that they must struggle with alone. The child has to handle a massive split – at one time the apparently normal, perhaps caring adult, and then the bizarre experience of the intrusion, the secrecy, the threats, the fear, the lack of acknowledgement of what is happening. There is a madness. The offender forces this split, this madness into the child's mind. The secret experiences that are split off become encapsulated. How much of the child's mind is taken over depends on the combination of the state of the child developmentally – as well as the severity, duration and degree of coercion. This becomes an encapsulated piece of experience. This is not a diagnosis but describes as well as we can with inadequate words the bizarre, distorted, twisted experience of the child, that is out of contact with reality, because of the inability to validate the experience. In child sexual abuse the child is forced to believe that what is happening is 'normal'. There is interference in thought process, in thinking, in making links because the abuse cannot be integrated into the rest of the child's experience.

What happens to these children? Their minds are left damaged and distorted by responses to the abuse which occur on an *unconscious* level. The child may switch off, split off their feelings by avoiding further close emotional involvements and close, intimate relationships. The 'refrigerator' child that noone can get through to may appear quite competent and get on fairly well with her school work; some children do very well academically, seeing their intellect as a passport, a way of escape. But many who cope this way are just out of touch and become detached, drifting, isolated, aimless individuals. When provoked beyond their threshold they can erupt into unexpectedly violent or provocative behaviour over which they have little control and no insight. They may go on to wrist-slash or overdose, or prostitute themselves, having little in the way of feelings about anything they do or anything that is done to them.

Other children can switch off, split off their intellect and their learning capacity. They behave as if they are 'stupid', don't know, can't learn; they may be quite warm and friendly individuals or rather flat and apathetic. Increasingly children who do not learn are found to have been abused (Sinason 1992). To not know, not let themselves make sense of anything, not let things add up is a way that is protective, avoids recognition, realisation of what is happening, but at a terrible price. In some schools for children with moderate learning disabilities, children have been found to have been sexually abused – and in some schools for children with severe learning disabilities, child sexual abuse is being increasingly detected (Sinason 1992). This is of two varieties – some children have been so seriously abused they then function at a very low level of intellectual ability; other children, disabled mentally or physically, are secondarily abused and then function at a much lower level than would be expected from their degree of disability.

Many aspects of the reaction to child sexual abuse can be covered by using the term post-traumatic stress disorder (PTSD). This usually applies where there has been a disaster, a major fire, or accident of some sort in which an individual is caught up, which involves life-threatening events and in which others may have died. The individual is left experiencing what are now recognised as a group of difficulties – irritability, high level of emotional arousal, mood swings and emotional lability, 'flashbacks' when the traumatic event is felt to be re-lived and dissociation when areas of experience are outside awareness. These all describe aspects of the abused child's experience but there are other areas of difficulty not covered. The abuse is generally a prolonged experience unless it was a one-off rape and so the child's personality and life has tried to adapt to the abuse and accommodated it. The child is therefore left with difficulties not covered by PTSD: the threats and secrecy surrounding the abuse, the very disturbing body responses – perhaps sexual responsiveness, excitement to pleasure as well as the pain – the choking sensation if there has been oral abuse, beatings, being used in a variety of perverse or sado-masochistic practices, all these things leave the child confused and bewildered about themselves, their feelings, and their bodies.

Emotional Impact on the Workers and their Institutions

Anyone working with cases of child sexual abuse needs to have to come to terms with their own sexuality and their own sexual orientation. The worker needs to be comfortable, at ease with themselves. If not, then these cases will be overwhelming. Finkelhor (1979) did a survey of professionals in this field and found that 55.7 per cent of females and 26.3 per cent of males had experienced some form of sexual abuse; 24.75 per cent of females and 12.75 per cent of males had experienced child sexual abuse involving physical contact, that is, masturbation, mutual masturbation, oral, anal or genital intercourse. The implication of this is *not* that people who were sexually abused cannot work in this field but that they will need to work on their own feelings. Unless it is dealt with, the implications for clear judgment and decision making by the worker are in question.

For all of us – however senior and experienced we are – the emotions that are stirred up need a place and some time for consultation and discussion. The principal need is to be able to hold on to the capacity to think, to observe, assess, evaluate and to be in touch with the range of feelings; and to go on thinking. Very often these cases get right inside and workers can take it home, their own sexual relationships being affected. Professionals can all too easily become caught up and enmeshed and often take the side of the child, losing sight of the family, the parents and the offender. Workers need strength and emotional resilience.

The provision of good support and supervision for all professionals is vital and yet is a rare commodity. By supervision is meant more than management, administration or discussion. It means time for the exploration of the process of the case, the emotional impact on the professional as a way of understanding the case. There is a need to consider the verbal, non-verbal and unconscious communications that get inside the mind of the professional. Very often what is going on inside the worker or between workers, or between agencies reflects what is happening in the family in a way that no other part of the contact does, so it is essential for good practice. It is also essential to free the worker so that they do not remain caught up, as this may lead to their becoming drained and burnt out.

Helps (1995) also found that the opportunity for teachers to talk in an interview setting helped some to disclose their own experience of sexual abuse in childhood. One teacher recalled the sense of trauma and the emotional impact of 'trying to keep things hidden, and the fear of talking to people'. This finding is consistent with INSET courses held for Fife teachers, where about 10 per cent of teaching staff attending the courses disclosed their own childhood sexual abuse (Campbell and Wigglesworth 1993).

The interview technique also helped teachers to talk through their experiences of teaching children whom they thought had been abused, and showed that many teachers continued to feel concerned about children they had taught in the past. It is evidently important that teachers have access to both emotional and practical support when dealing with an abused child, and to reassurance that there is no one solution to helping these children. Many teachers stressed that they would need somebody experienced outside the school to talk to as a source of emotional support. Unless there is such a supportive network available, many teachers could be carrying with them additional burdens of blame and guilt.

Lack of understanding of the professional network outside the school and of the role of the designated teacher emerged as a prominent area of concern in this study, and only one half of the teachers involved felt confident with it. We have presented the following examples of school-based concerns about children who were likely to have been sexually abused in order to illustrate some of the processes leading to referral and treatment.

Case Examples

The following example is of an 11-year-old boy who was referred to the Tavistock Clinic for 'counselling'. The class teacher's initial suspicion that all was not well in the child's home situation was later confirmed when a link was made with social services involvement. This case illustrates how myths still prevail among staff that it is preferable to maintain a co-operative relationship with parents rather than to try to ensure child protection. Another particular dilemma in this case was the issue of whether the child's psychological and mental health would be jeopardised if he remained in the home setting, or whether a residence order and another placement outside the home could preferably have been sought.

> Paul had attended his primary school for two years when his teacher became seriously concerned about his inability to concentrate in class and the 'detached' quality in his behaviour. The school was aware that Paul had lived in another European country prior to arriving in England. He was described as an intelligent child who had quickly become fluent in spoken English. He was slow to express ideas on paper, and his reading was erratic and difficult to assess with any consistency. Paul's teacher said he was quick to take offence, but could also try hard to please, and that it was difficult for Paul to concentrate on a subject for any length of time. The incident which led to this referral was that Paul set off a fire alarm in school, left the premises, and was later found wandering by the river nearby in a dazed condition.

> The headteacher made a formal referral to the social services department at this stage, as she felt concerned for Paul's safety. She also expressed her concerns to the school's educational psychologist. A

meeting was convened in school where it became apparent that the family were already known to social services. The circumstances were that Paul had been born and raised in an African country for the first two years of his life. He was then boarded with relatives, friends and stayed in state institutions in three different European countries. He eventually arrived in England to live with his mother, having experienced seven different homes, and had recently been rejected by his aunt to whom he had formed an attachment. Paul's mother had initially made a request to the school that she did not want any involvement with official agencies. The headteacher respected this as she realised that state intervention was regarded with fear and avoided at all costs in Paul's country of origin. In her letter to the social worker, the headteacher said she had realised that she could no longer 'protect' the boy from social services involvement.

This element of confusion about who was to be 'protected' from whom was a recurring theme of the intervention and involvement by different agencies. It became apparent that Paul had been physically and/or sexually abused in most of his previous placements. Paul's mother had known about this, and it seemed to have affected her perceptions of her child. It is a common reaction of family members to feel retribution towards the child when abuse has occurred, and this can be expressed in scapegoating, blaming and rejection. Paul was living a very isolated existence at home at the time of referral. He was deprived of toys and interests, and spent much of his time willingly looking after his three-year-old sister. Although Paul's mother recognised at a certain level that he needed help to overcome and make sense of his experiences, she also regarded him as a 'bad' child, and was ambivalent about his need for treatment.

During his first interview with a child psychiatrist, Paul kept his coat buttoned, even though the room was very warm. He was described in this interview as a forlorn and distant child who looked watchful and showed no sense of fun or vitality. It seemed as if everything he said or did was likely to be rejected, and it later emerged in psychotherapy sessions that Paul's personality seemed to have gone into retreat. Paul insisted that he had forgotten much of what had happened to him earlier in his life. In trying to forget some of the very painful memories of the sexual abuse, he had also managed to forget many other memories. He was helped to think about the abuse and to name verbally with the therapist's help what had been done to him. For the first year or so of therapy, Paul struggled with feelings that he was to blame for the abuse and also for the intervention, which still angered his mother.

Although the longer term outcome for Paul is uncertain, he has been enabled to make some sense of the several traumatic experiences which he was subjected to at an early age. He is now more able to use his thinking capacities, to express his feelings in drawings and he is less 'dissociated' and more involved in school activities. He is able to say to his therapist that he attends his sessions because of problems he experiences, and realises that he is unhappy at home. Paul still tends to see his mother as someone who might punish him for his feelings and behaviour. Although Paul's present circumstances may inflict further emotional damage, Paul's social worker has not yet thought it advisable to apply for a residence order. The upheaval and turmoil of Paul's first nine years are likely to have left him with a permanent sense of instability, and Paul is still anxiously attached to his mother, fearing further rejection. Another move into the unknown could not be considered at this stage, unless it had clear and demonstrable benefits for the child.

The second example concerns a seven-year-old girl, Sally, who lives with her mother, two sisters, brother and half-brother. Sally attended a social services day nursery at the pre-school stage, where concerns about language delay led to her being issued with a Statement of special educational needs. Both Sally's parents come from families where there has been intergenerational sexual abuse, and Sally's mother grew up in care after being rejected by her own mother at the age of five.

Although social services had an ongoing knowledge of Sally's home circumstances before she started school, the school and other involved agencies were not able to integrate their concerns until the educational welfare officer followed up Sally's absences from school. It then transpired that Sally was avoiding school because of fears of bullying. By meeting with Sally over a period of time, the educational welfare officer was alerted to suspicions that Sally was particularly troubled after visiting her father and step-brothers at the weekends. Sally was first able to confide that she was being teased by her step-brothers, whom she saw on the way home from school. When this was more fully investigated by other school staff it was possible to assemble a more detailed picture. Sally was being bullied mercilessly as her two older step-brothers told other children of imaginary sexual activities they had had with her.

A strategy meeting was convened which led to interviews with Sally's father and step-brothers by a social worker. Although there were strong suspicions at this stage that Sally was being sexually abused, the social worker subsequently referred Sally to the Tavistock on the grounds that she had been emotionally abused. Sally's mother was initially co-operative with the treatment plan and brought her to the Clinic on a weekly basis for therapy sessions. Later this required provision of a taxi and escort by social services, as the mother gradually withdrew her involvement.

Sally seemed a 'frozen' child, who responded dutifully to adults, spoke only when spoken to, and made little eye contact. She conveyed a feeling of being 'shut out', had little initiative and needed to be encouraged to play with the toys in the room. Sally was incapable of talking about what had happened to her and expressed her feelings in an idealised way – her wishes were that she could become a princess and live safely in a palace. Her thoughts were often disjointed and she seemed to suffer from unreasonable loyalty conflicts, as the approval of her mother was more important to her than the possibility of therapeutic change. This became quite an obstacle to her capacity to benefit from therapy, as her mother questioned her and sometimes slapped her when she returned home. She was still teased by her step-brothers who enviously accused her of having special treatment from the escort who took her from school to the clinic.

Sadly, Sally stopped attending therapy when her mother wanted no further involvement and was undermining Sally's treatment. Clinic staff continued to have serious concerns about Sally's existence in her family and requested that the social worker present a case for a care order to the court. However, the social worker response was: 'I cannot compel this family to co-operate with this department. As things stand, I doubt whether I can prove significant harm to Sally caused by her mother's neglect.'

Broader implications

This case has been chosen because it illustrates some of the difficulties staff have in thinking about the harm being done to a child, and in collaborating and working in a joint intervention. It exemplifies some of the myths which still prevail, that emotional abuse and neglect is difficult to 'prove' and is likely to be unsubstantiated in court. The strong likelihood of ongoing sexual abuse was denied in this instance even though family members had suffered abuse themselves. This is not an indictment of particular staff, but a common occurrence where there is under-resourcing, high turnover of staff and temporary contracts, inconsistent training, lack of supervision and low morale. In such circumstances, the tendency to blame the courts, the government or the mother is a palliative which is likely to make us feel individually better than taking difficult decisions which may incapacitate us even further.

In the above example, the social worker mistakenly believed that the onus was on him to provide the court with concrete examples of emotional abuse.

Establishing whether a child is suffering from 'significant harm' is now likely to involve seeking a child psychologist's assessment as the definition of harm needs to be set in the context of the child's physical, cognitive, socio-emotional and behavioural development. It is also important to note that the likelihood of future harm can be taken into account, which is in contrast to the previous legislation. Lindsey (1994) has drawn attention to some of the changes in the key principles in the Children Act, and their implications for different styles of work for practitioners. She emphasises the importance of co-operation between those who are skilled in listening to children and facilitating their communication, and those whose task is to prepare and apply for a Section 8 Order.

We have chosen both these examples as we felt they illustrated a number of key issues from a training perspective in how different staff groups are responding to the changes in practice implied in the Children Act. It is sometimes easier for staff to learn from areas of mutual misunderstanding which occur in practice. These tensions can represent live examples of the juxtapositions both between different styles of thinking implicit in the Act, and with former styles of working. It is still common to find that staff from different disciplines have not received adequate training in the fundamental principle of the Act, which is that the child's welfare is paramount. Adults are obliged to consider the child's perspective, and the Act contains a check-list of relevant factors to be taken into account when considering the welfare of the child in court proceedings. The first of these is 'the ascertainable wishes and feelings of the child concerned (considered in the light of his/her age and understanding)'. In both the examples we have considered here, difficulties in communicating about different styles of work, priorities, value systems, professional objectives, traditional ways of working and structures, and attitudes towards confidentiality meant that the child's interests and feelings were not able to be resolved in a way which produced a better outcome for the child concerned.

The motivation of staff to co-operate by debating and resolving differences and difficulties is a crucial aspect of being able to work together more effectively. Many able practitioners in their own fields do not fully understand or appreciate the roles and responsibilities of other professional groups. Although ACPCs have set up some joint training initiatives, the last ten years have seen a steady dismantling of some of the community-based systems which enabled multi-disciplinary placements during initial training to take place, for example in child guidance clinics, health-based multiprofessional teams, case conferences and other collaborative settings. This has occurred partly due to resource implications, and also because of compartmentalised styles of work which have arisen from tighter work specifications arising from contractual and statutory duties and under-staffing.

Educational and clinical psychologists are both examples of specialised staff groups who have not yet been able to develop their expertise fully with regard to children in need and child protection issues (Hodges 1994). Whereas they were formerly able to exercise professional autonomy in allocating and prioritising different areas of work, they are now more likely to be restricted to working within existing areas of statutory work and contractual demands laid down by their employers. The creation of internal markets and the separation of purchasers and providers is a further divisive force-field which prevents practitioners from collaborating effectively. There may actually be disincentives for managers to improve communication and shared practice between health, education, social services and voluntary agencies in the market place setting due to high costs and lack of clarity about who takes a major responsibility for the client, and therefore for the funding of the work.

Conclusions

In this chapter we have presented a school-based perspective to the understanding of child sexual abuse. We have emphasised the important roles of the class and designated teachers and of the educational psychologist in developing practical and emotional support systems for the early recognition of abuse within the school. We hope to have illustrated the complex, interactive nature of the knowledge and understanding which is required both of school and family functioning and also when teachers refer outside the school to the professional network. The emotional impact of this area of work on all staff is high, and staff are likely to be further incapacitated by under-resourcing and lack of opportunities for multi-disciplinary training. We hope to have provided a clarification of some of the issues involved in working sensitively with child sexual abuse, and to have illustrated the requirements for time, depth of thought, supervision and, above all, teams of highly motivated, well-trained staff working in adequately resourced settings. These are some of the basic elements which are required if staff are to be enabled to work more effectively together to protect children.

Resources

CATU – The Child Abuse Training Unit, National Children's Bureau, 8 Wakley Street, London EC1V 7QE. Tel: 0171 278 9441.

Has a database with publications on abuse, training, information on videos and training packages [need key words e.g. 'prevention', 'schools']. Directory of individual trainers prepared to offer training and consultancy; evaluative analysis of training programmes given in 'What's in the Box?'.

NSPCC, 67 Saffron Hill, London EC1N 8RS. Tel: 0171 242 1626.

Publications and Library Services (loans can be arranged through inter-library loan service).

The Community Education Department Centre's training guide. D. Braun (1988) 'Responding to Child Abuse: Actions and Planning for Teachers and Other Professionals'. Training Guide. £6.95.

- Gives exercises for professionals to explore their own feelings, attitudes and values.
- Practical ideas for teachers to work with pupils and parents on child protection.
- Information on publications, organisations, the law, etc.

CEDC, Lyng Hall, Blackcherry Lane, Coventry CV2 3VS. Tel: 0203 638660.

A. Peake 1989 – The Children's Society: CSA Prevention. Programme in Schools – information on preparation of such a programme in schools in details of curriculum areas. Also, 'My Book, My Body' (Teddie called Mousie with an account of sexual abuse; one day he tells someone and is believed).

Childline, Tel: 0171 239 1000. Free phone line: 0800 1111.

Since October 1986 has been operating on a 24-hour basis; it is a free and confidential service. Trained volunteers encourage children to confide in someone in their own lives.

Parentline – OPUS. Tel: 0181 645 0469.

Self-help group for parents. Various activity and picture/colouring books for young children to help them think of ways of getting out of dangerous situations – some about bullying, how the body works, telling secrets, safe forms of touching, etc.

Bibliography

Alvarez, A. (1991) 'Beyond the unpleasure principle.' In R. Szur and S. Miller (eds) *Extending Horizons*. London: Karnac.

Alvarez, A. (1992) *Live Company, Psychoanalytic Psychotherapy with Autistic, Borderline, Deprived and Abused Children*. London: Routledge.

Argyris, C. (1973) *Intervention Theory and Method: A Behavioural Science View*. Reading, MA: Addison Wesley.

Argyris, C. (1990) *Overcoming Organisational Defences*. London: Allyn and Bacon.

Argyris, C. and Schon, D. (1974) *Theory in Practice*. San Francisco, CA: Jossey-Bass.

Argyris, C. and Schon, D. (1987) *Organisational Learning: A Theory of Action Perspective*. Reading, MA: Addison Wesley.

Armstrong, D. (1992) 'Names, thoughts and lies: the relevance of Bion's later writing for understanding experiences in groups.' *Free Associations 2, 26*, 261–282.

Ashcroft, J. and Gray, I. (1993) 'Personal support in training: Trainee needs and course responsibilities.' *Clinical Psychology Forum 60*.

Aveline, H, and Shapiro, D. (1995) *Research Foundations of Psychotherapy Practice*. Chichester: Wiley.

Baker, A.W. and Duncan, P. (1985) 'CSA – A study of prevelance in Great Britain.' *Child Abuse and Neglect 9*, 4.

Barger, N. (1992) 'The management of change and personality type'. Oxford Psychologist presentation. June.

Barrett, M. (1994) 'Consultation to school sub-systems by a teacher.' In E. Dowling and E. Osborne *The Family and the School: A Joint Systems Approach to Problems with Children*. London and New York: Routledge.

Barrett, M. and Trevitt, J. (1991) *Attachment Behaviour and the Schoolchild. An Introduction to Educational Therapy*. London: Routledge.

Bentovim, A. (1992) *Trauma Organised Systems: Physical and Sexual Abuse in Families*. London and New York: Karnac Books.

Bichard, S. (1990) *Measures of Cognitive and Emotional development in the mentally retarded.'* London: Tavistock Clinic Paper No. 146.

Bick, E. (1968) 'The Experience of the skin in early object relations.' *International Journal of Psychoanalysis 49*, 484–486.

Bick, E. (1987) In D. Meltzer *The Collected Papers of Martha Harris and Esther Bick*. Perthshire: Clinic Press.

Binsted, D. (1986) *Developments in Interpersonal Skills Training.* Aldershot: Gower.

Bion, W. (1961) *Experiences in Groups and Other Papers.* London: Tavistock Publications. Republished Routledge 1989.

Bion, W. (1962) *Learning from Experience.* London: Heinemann.

Bion, W. (1974) *Brazilian Lectures.* Rio de Janeiro: Imago Editora.

Bion, W. (1984) *Second Thoughts: Selected Papers on Psychoanalysis.* London: Maresfield Reprints.

Black, D. (1993) 'Family intervention with families bereaved or about to be bereaved.' In D. Papadon and C. Papadatos (eds) *Children in Death.* London: Hemisphere.

Booker, R. (1991a) 'Responding to the needs of the context.' *Educational Psychology in Practice 7* 3–10.

Booker, R. (1991b) 'Continuing professional development.' Paper presented at the National Course for Educational Psychologists in Training, Tavistock Clinic and Brunel University, July 1991.

Bowlby, J. (1988) *A Secure Base: Clinical Applications of Attachment Theory.* London: Routledge.

Bronfenbrenner, U. (1979) *The Ecology of Human Development.* Cambridge, MA: Harvard University Press.

Bruggen, P. and O'Brian, C. (1986) *Surviving Adolescence: A Handbook for Adolescents and their Parents.* London: Faber.

Bruner, J. S. (1966) *Towards a Theory of Instruction.* New York: Norton.

Brunning, H. and Huffington, C. (1990) 'After the jump – what next? The thrills and spills of internal consultancy.' *Clinical Psychology Forum 35,* 33–35.

Brunning, H. and Huffington, C. (1990) 'Jumping off the fence: developing the consultancy model.' *Clinical Psychology Forum 29,* 31–33.

Brunning, H., Cole, C. and Huffington, C. (1990) *The Change Directory: Key Issues in Organisational Development and the Management of Change.* Leicester: The BPS (DCP).

Bryson, J. M. (1988) *Strategic Planning for Public and Non-profit* Organisations. London: Jossey-Bass.

Burden, R. (1980) 'The educational psychologist in schools.' In W. Gilham (ed) *Reconstructing Educational Psychology.* London: Croom Helm.

Burnham, K. (1992) *Family Therapy.* London: Tavistock Publications.

Campbell, D., Draper, R. and Huffington, C. (1988) *Teaching Systemic Thinking.* London: Karnac Books.

Campbell, H. and Wigglesworth, A. (1993) 'Child protection in schools: a survey of the training needs of Fife school teachers.' *Public Health 107,* 413–419.

Campion, J. (1984) 'Psychological services for children using family therapy in the setting of a school psychological service.' *Journal of Family Therapy 6* 1, 47–62.

Caplan, G. (1970) *The Theory and Practice of Mental Health Consultation.* London: Tavistock Publications.

Carter, E. and McGoldrick, M. (eds) (1991) *The Changing Family Life Cycle: A Framework for Family Therapy.* Second Edition. London: Allyn and Bacon.

Casement, P. (1985) *On Learning From the Patient.* London: Tavistock.

Cecchin, G., Lane, G. and Ray, W.A. (1992) *Irreverence – A Strategy for Therapists' Survival.* London: Karnac Books.

Children's Legal Centre (1993) 'Measures of control in adolescent psychiatric institutions.' *Childright 99.*

Clulow, E. (1994) 'Balancing care and control: the supervisory relationship as a focus for promoting organisational health.' In A. Obholzer and V. Roberts (eds) (1994) *The Unconscious at Work.* London: Routledge.

Copley, B. (1993) *The World of Adolescence; Literature, Society and Psychoanalytic Psychotherapy.* London: Free Association Books.

Dartington, A. (1995) 'Very brief psychodynamic counselling with young people.' *Psychodynamic Counselling 1, 2.*

Davis, H. (1993) *Counselling Parents of Children with Chronic Illness or Disability.* Leicester: British Psychological Society Books.

De Board, R. (1978) *The Psychoanalysis of Organisations.* London: Tavistock Publications.

De Vries, M. and Miller, D. (1984) *The Neurotic Organisation.* San Francisco, CA: Jossey-Bass.

Delaney, R. (1991) *Fostering Changes.* Fort Collins, USA: Walter J. Corbett Publishing.

Department for Education (1994) *Code of Practice on the Identification and Assessment of Children with Special Educational Needs.* London: HMSO.

Department of Health (1991) *Child Abuse: A Study of Inquiry Reports 1980–89.* London: HMSO.

Department of Health (1992) *The Health of the Nation: A Strategy for Health in England.* London: HMSO.

Dessent, T. (1980) 'The historical development of school psychology services. In W. Gillham (ed) *Reconstructing Educational Psychology.* London: Croom Helm.

DfE Initial Teacher Training (1992) 'Reform of Initial Teacher Training' Circular No 9/92. London: HMSO.

DHSS (1974) *Report of the Committee of Inquiry into the Care and Supervision Provided in Relation to Maria Coldwell.* London: HMSO.

Dicks, H. V. (1970) *50 Years of the Tavistock Clinic.* London: Routledge and Kegan Paul.

Dowling, E. and Osborne, E. (1994) *The Family and the School: A Joint Systems Approach to Problems with Children.* London and New York: Routledge.

Dryden, W. and Feltham, C. (1994) *Developing Counsellor Training*. London: Sage Publications.

Dryden, W. and Thorne, B. (1991) *Training and Supervision for Counselling in Action*. London: Sage.

Ellwood, J. and Oke, M. (1987) 'Analytic group work in a boys' comprehensive school.' *Free Associations 8*, 34–57.

Elton Report (1989) *Discipline in Schools*. Report of the Committee of Enquiry chaired by Lord Elton. London: HMSO.

Eraut, M. (1992) 'Developing the professions: training, quality and accountability.' Professorial lecture given at the University of Sussex, March.

Figg, J. (1994) 'Competent to practise.' *Educational and Child Psychology 2* 1.

Finkelhor, D. (1979) *Sexually Victimised Children*. New York: The Free Press.

Fisher, B. (1989) 'Differences between supervision of beginning and advanced therapists.' *The Clinical Supervisor 7*, 57–74.

Fotheringham, J. (1988) 'Sexual abuse – the teachers' perspective.' *Professional Development Initiatives*. Scottish Office Education Dept.

Freud, S. (1925) Foreword to A. Aichhorn *Wayward Youth*. New York: Viking Press.

Furniss, T. (1991) *The Multi-professional Handbook of Child Sexual Abuse: Integrated Management, Therapy and Legal Intervention*. London: Routledge.

Garland, C. (1991) 'External disasters and the internal world: An approach to psychotherapeutic understanding of survivors.' In J. Holmes (ed) *Handbook of Psychotherapy for Psychiatrists*. London: Churchill Livingstone.

Gilligan, C. (1982) *In a Different Voice: Psychological Theory and Women's Development*. Cambridge, MA: Harvard University Press.

Gilligan, C. *et al.* (eds) (1990) *Making Connections. The Relational Worlds of Adolescent Girls at Emma Willard School*. London: Harvard University Press.

Golby, M. (1994) *Case Study as Educational Research*. Exeter University: Michael Still.

Goodyer, I.M. (1990) *Life Experiences, Development and Childhood Psychopathology*. New York: Wiley.

Greenhalgh, P. (1994) *Emotional Growth and Learning*. London: Routledge.

Greenwich Education Psychology Service (1993) Annual Report. London: Greenwich EPS.

Gregory, R.P. (1981) 'Educational psychologists and innovation.' In I. McPherson and A. Sutton (ed) *Reconstructing Psychological Practice*. London: Croom Helm.

Grubb Institute (1988) *Professional Management*. London: Grubb.

Gustafson, J.P. and Cooper, L.W. (1990) *The Modern Context*. London: Norton.

Handy, C. and Aitken, R. (1986) *Understanding Schools as Organisations*. Penguin Books.

Harris-Hendriks, J. and Williams, R. (1992) 'The children's Act, 1989 – England and Wales: Implications for healthcare practice and schools.' *Association of Child Psychologists and Psychiatrists Newsletter 14*, 5, 213–220.

Harris-Hendriks, J., Black, D. and Kaplan, T. (1993) *When Father Kills Mother: Studying Children through Trauma and Grief.* London: Routledge.

Hawkins, P. and Shohet, R. (1991) *Supervision the Helping Professions.* Buckingham: Open University Press.

Helps, A. (1995) 'An investigation of primary school teachers' attitudes towards child abuse.' Dissertation for the MSc. in Educational Psychology. London: Tavistock Clinic.

Hirschorn, L. (1988) 'The workplace within, psychodynamics of organisational life.' Cambridge, MA: MIT Press.

HMSO (1989) *The 1989 Children Act.* London: HMSO.

Hodges, S. (1994) *Has the Children Act had any Effect on the Work of Child Clinical and Educational Psychologists: An Exploratory Survey.* London: Tavistock Library.

Hodgkinson, P.E. (1991) *Coping with Catastrophe – A Handbook of Disaster Management.* London: Routledge.

HQ, DOH, DES, WO (1991) *Working Together Under the Children Act 1989: A Guide to Arrangements for Inter-agency Co-operation for the Protection of Children from Abuse.* London: HMSO.

Huffington, C and Brunning, H. (1994) *Internal Consultancy in the Public Sector: Case Studies.* London: Karnac Books.

Huffington, C., Dowling, E. and Kennedy, L. (1993) 'Consultation: A course for psychologists.' *Clinical Psychology Forum 60*, 22–25.

Hyatt-Williams, A. (1975) 'Problems of adolescence.' In S. Meyerson *Adolescence and Breakdown.* London: George Allen and Unwin Ltd.

Jacques, D. (1984) *Learning in Groups.* London: Croom Helm.

Jennings, C. (1994) 'Challenges and opportunities: future training perspectives and the changing roles, tasks and contexts in educational psychologists' work.' *Educational and Child Psychology 12*, 2, 15–24.

Jennings, C. (1995) 'Child educational psychologists and the changing contexts in child and adolescent mental health.' In D. Indoe and A. Pecherek (eds) 'Therapeutic interventions.' *Educational and Child Psychology 12*, 4, 5–15.

Jewell, P. (1994) 'Multicultural counselling research: an evaluation with proposals for future research.' *Counselling Psychology Review 9*, 2, 44–50.

Jones, A. (1984) *Counselling Adolescents in School.* London: Anchor Press/Kogan Page.

Kelly, G. (1955) *The Psychology of Personal Constructs.* Vol. 1 and 2. New York: Norton.

Kempe, C. (1981) In P.B. Mrazek and C.H. Kempe (eds) (1981) *Sexually Abused Children and their Families.* Oxford: Pergammon.

King, M. and Trowell, J. (1992) *Childrens' Welfare and the Law: The Limits of Legal Intervention.* London: Sage.

Knowles, M. (1978) *The Adult Learner – A Neglected Species. Third edition.* London: Gulf Publishing Group.

Kolb, D. (1970) In D. Jacques (1984) *Learning in Groups.* London: Croom Helm.

Kraemer, S. (1988) 'Splitting and stupidity in child sexual abuse.' *Psychoanalytic Psychotherapy 3*, 3, 247–251.

Lawrence, G. (1977) In A. Obholzer and V.Z. Roberts (eds) *The Unconscious at Work.* London: Routledge 1994.

Lees, S. (1986) *Losing Out.* London: Hutchinson.

Leiper, R. (1994) 'Evaluation: organisations learning from experience.' In A. Obholzer and V. Roberts (1994) (eds) *The Unconscious at Work.* London: Routledge.

Lindsay, G. and Miller, A. (1991) *Psychological Services for Primary Schools.* London: Longman UK Ltd.

Lindsey, C. (1994) 'The Children's Act 1989 – Implications for the family and the School.' In E. Dowling and E. Osborne (1994) *The Family and the School: A Joint Systems Approach to Problems with Children.* London and New York: Routledge.

Lunt, I. (1993) 'Fieldwork supervision for educational psychologists in training: the findings of a 1984–5 survey.' In I. Lunt and M. Pomerantz 'Supervision and psychologists' professional work.' *Educational and Child Psychology 19*, 2.

MacKee, D. (1989) *Elmer, A Patchwork Elephant.* London: Anderson.

Maher, P. (1987) *Child Sexual Abuse: The Educational Perspective.* Oxford: Basil Blackwell.

McCarthy, M. (1992) 'Human resource development.' In S. Wolfendale (eds) (1992) *The Profession and Practice of Educational Psychology.* London: Cassell Education.

McLean, A. and Marshall, J. (1988) *Working with Cultures: A work book for People Working in Local Government.* Luton: Local Government Training Board.

Menzies-Lyth, I. (1960) 'A case-study in the functioning of social systems as a defence against anxiety.' *Human Relations 13,* 95–121.

Menzies-Lyth, I. (1988) *Containing Anxiety in Institutions.* Selected Essays Vol.1. London: Free Association Books.

Miller, A. (1983) *The Role of Violence in Child Rearing.* London: Virago.

Miller, A. (1990) *Banished Knowledge: Facing Childhood Injuries.* London: Virago Press.

Miller, A. (1991) 'Applied psychologists as problem-solvers. Devising a personal model.' *Educational Psychology in Practice 7,* 227–236.

Miller, A. (1994) 'Staff culture, boundary maintenance and successful "behavioural interventions" in primary schools.' *Research Papers in Education 9,* 1.

Miller, E. and Rice, A.K. (1967) *Systems of Organisations: The Control of Task and Sentient Boundaries.* London: Tavistock Publications.

Milner and Britton (1994) 'A workshop on skilled supervision.' *Clinical Psychology Forum 67,* 72–78.

Mitchell, J. (1983) 'When disaster strikes…critical incident stress debriefing process.' *Journal of Emergency Medical Services 8,* 1.

Moore, J. (1991) 'On being a supervisor.' In W. Dryden and B. Thorne *Training and Supervision for Counselling in Action.* London: Sage.

Morgan, G. (1986) *Images of Organization.* London: Sage Publications.

Mrazek, D. and Mrazek, P. (1981) In P.B. Mrazek and H. Kempe *Sexually Abused Children and their Families.* Oxford: Pergammon.

Nader, K. and Pynoos, P. (1993) 'School disaster: planning and initial interventions.' In R. Allen (ed) 'Handbook of post-disaster interventions.' *Journal of Social Behaviour and Personality 8,* 5, 299–320 (special edition).

Noonan, E. (1983) *Counselling Young People.* London: Routledge.

Noonan, E. (1988) 'The impact of the institution on psychotherapy.' In R. May (ed) *Psychoanalytic Psychotherapy in a College Context.* London: Praeger.

Norman, R. (1984) *Service Management.* London: Wiley.

Obholzer, A. (1992) *The Residential Setting in Psychotherapeutic Work with Adolescents.* Tavistock Clinic, Paper No. 124, London. (A paper given to the Joint USA-European Conference on 'The Facilitating Climate for Therapeutic Relations in Mental Health Services'. Perugia, Italy, 6th/7th June, 1992).

Obholzer, A. (1994) 'Authority, power and leadership: Contribution from group relations training.' In A. Obholzer and V.Z. Roberts *The Unconscious at Work.* (1994) London and New York: Routledge.

Obholzer, A. and Roberts, V.Z. (eds) (1994) *The Unconscious at Work.* London: Routledge.

Otway, O. and Peake, A. (1993) 'Empowering women: a self-help group for mothers of abused children.' *Educational and Child Psychology 10,* 3, 20–25.

Ovretveit, J. (1992) *Health Service Quality Measurement for Health Services.* Oxford: Blackwell Special Projects.

Ovretveit, J., Brunning, H. and Huffington, C. (1992) 'Adapt or decay: why clinical psychologists must develop the consulting role.' *Clinical Psychology Forum 46,* 27–29.

Palazzili, M.S. (1986) *The Hidden Games of Organisations.* New York: Pantheon.

Palmer, S. (1995) 'Stress management interventions in the workplace: a counselling psychologist's approach, experience and concerns.' *Counselling Psychology Review 10,* 1.

Palmer, S. and Dryden, W. (1994) 'Stress management: approaches and interventions.' *British Journal of Guidance and Counselling 22,* 1, 5–12.

Peake, A. (1991) 'Dealing with the suspicion of child sexual abuse: the role of the class teacher.' In G. Lindsay and A. Miller (1991) *Psychological Services for Primary Schools.* London: Longman UK Ltd.

Peckett, J and Shepherd, C. (1994) 'An evaluation of learning contract within the context of partnership in school-based training: implications for school-based mentoring.' *Mentoring and Tutoring 2,* 1.

Plowden Report (1967) Great Britain Central Advisory Council for Education (England) *Children and their Primary Schools. A Report of the Central Advisory Council for Education (England) Volume I: The Report.* London: HMSO.

Pomerantz, M. (1993) In I. Lunt and M. Pomerantz (1993) 'Supervision and psychologists' professional work.' *Educational and Child Psychology 10,* 2, 5–11.

Proctor, B. (1988) *Supervision, a Working Alliance.* (Videotape training manual) St Leonards on Sea, East Sussex: Alexia Publications.

Pynoos, R.S. and Eth, S. (1985) 'Developmental perspectives in psychic trauma in childhood.' In C. Figley (ed) *Trauma and Its Wake.* New York: Bruner/Mazel.

Raphael, B. (1983) *The Anatomy of Bereavement.* New York: Basic.

Reed, B.D. (1987) 'Professional Management.' ILEA course presentation. London.

Reed, B.D. and Palmer, B.M.W. (1972) *An Introduction to Organisational Behaviour.* London: The Grubb Institute.

Reynolds, D. (1994) 'Factors in school effectiveness.' Presentation to annual conference of educational psychologists in training. University of Durham, July.

Rice, A.K. (1963) *The Enterprise and its Environment. A Systems Theory of Management Organisation.* London: Tavistock Publications.

Rioch, M.J. (1975) 'The work of Wilfred Bion on groups.' In A. Coleman and W. Bexton (eds) *Group Relations Reader.* London.

Royal College of Psychiatrists (1993) *Child Psychiatry and Child Sexual Abuse.* London: Royal College of Psychiatrists.

Rushton, R. and Davis, H. (1992) 'An evaluation of the effectiveness of counselling training for health care professionals.' *British Journal of Guidance and Counselling 20,* 205–220.

Rustin, M. (1991) *The Good Society and the Inner World.* London: Verso.

Schein, E.H. (1969) *Process Consultation: Its role in Organisation Development.* Reading, MA: Addison-Wesley.

Schein, E.H. (1990) 'A general philosophy of helping: Process consultation.' *Sloan Management Review 4,* 57–64.

Schmidt, W.H. and Johnston, A.V. (1970) *A Continuum of Consultancy Styles.* Unpublished paper.

Schon, D.A. (1987) *Educating the Reflective Practitioner.* San Francisco, CA: Jossey-Bass Inc. Publishers.

Searles, H.F. (1955) 'The Informational Value of the Supervisors' Emotional Experience.' In *Collected Papers on Schizophrenia and Related Subjects.* London: Hogarth Press.

Sinason, V. (1992) *Mental Handicap and the Human Condition. New Approaches from the Tavistock.* London: Free Association Books.

Stern, D. (1985) *The Interpersonal World of the Infant.* USA: Basic Books Inc.

Stokes, J. (1994) 'Institutional chaos and personal stress.' In A. Obholzer and V.Z. Roberts *The Unconscious at Work.* London: Croom Helm.

Street, E. and Dryden, W. (1988) *Family Therapy in Britain.* Milton Keynes: OU Press.

Symington, N.C. (1986) *The Analytic Experience: Lectures from the Tavistock.* London: Free Association Books.

Szecsody, I. (1990) 'Supervision: A didactic or mutative situation.' *Psychoanalytic Psychotherapy 4,* 3, 245–261.

Szur, R. (1991) 'Thinking about adolescence.' In R. Szur and S. Miller (eds) *Extending Horizons: Psychoanalytic Psychotherapy with Children, Adolescents and Families.* London: Karnac Books.

Thomas, G. (1992) 'Ecological interventions.' In S. Wolfendale (ed) *The Profession and Practice of Educational Psychology.* London: Cassell.

Topping, K. (1992) 'Cooperative learning and peer tutoring: an overview.' *The Psychologist 5,* 4, 26–31.

Trist, E., Higgins, G., Murray, H. and Pollack, A. (1963) 'The assumption of ordinariness as a denial mechanism: innovation and conflict in a coal mine.' In E. Trist and H. Murray (eds) (1990) *The Social Engagement of Social Science, Volume I: The Socio-psychological Perspective.* London: Free Association Books.

Trist, E.L. (1970) 'Sociotechnical systems.' In P.B. Smith *Group Processes: Selected Readings.* Harmondsworth: Penguin Books.

Turquet, P.M. (1974) 'Leadership: the individual and the group.' In G.S. Gibbard *Analysis of Groups.* London: Jossey-Bass.

Waddell, M. (1994) *The Teenage Years: Understanding 12–14 year olds.* London: Rosendale Press.

Winnicott, D.W. (1956) 'The anti-social tendency.' In D.W. Winnicott *Through Paediatrics to Psychoanalysis.* (1978) London: Hogarth Press.

Winnicott, D.W. (1958) 'The capacity to be alone.' In D.W. Winnicott *The Maturational Processes and the facilitating environment.* London: Hogarth Press.

Winnicott, D.W. (1986) *Home is Where We Start From. Essays by a Psychoanalyst.* London: Penguin.

Wittenberg, I., Henry, G. and Osbourne, E. (1983) *The Emotional Experience of Learning and Teaching.* London: Routledge and Kegan Paul.

Wodarski, J.S. (1993) 'Maltreatment and the school-aged child: School performance consequences.' *Child Abuse and Neglect 17,* 581–589.

Wolfendale, S. (1988) 'Psychologists working with parents: context and skills.' In N. Jones and J. Sayer (eds) *Management and the Psychology of Schooling.* London: Falmer Press.

Yule, W. (1991) 'Work with children following disasters.' In M. Herbert (ed) *Clinical Child Psychology: Theory and Practice.* Chichester: J. Wiley.

Yule, W. and Gold, A. (1993) *Wise Before the Event. Coping with Crises in Schools.* London: Calouste Gulbenkian.

The Contributors

Roger Booker

Roger Booker is Principal Psychologist at Greenwich Education Department. His interests are in the development of systemic approaches to the management of professional services and in the training of professionals to become managers.

Su Burrell

Su Burrell is a clinical lecturer in Social Work/child protection in the Child and Family Department of the Tavistock Clinic. Most of her working life has been spent working in multi-disciplinary teams combining child and adolescent mental illness with a special interest in child protection. She is a founder member of SCOSAC, the networking organisation for professionals working in the field of child sexual abuse. She has a particular interest in multi-disciplinary child protection training and consultancy.

Enid Colmer

Enid Colmer is an experienced social worker and family therapist. She has worked for more than 10 years with children and families within a multi-disciplinary child guidance setting. Employed by Enfield Education Department as a Senior Child Guidance Social Worker she has been instrumental in developing consultation initiatives in schools. Her research dissertation for the MA in Systemic Therapy at the Tavistock Clinic focused on the different ways therapists work in post-trauma situations.

Jane Ellwood

Jane Ellwood has worked as a child and adolescent psychotherapist since 1976. Apart from ongoing psychoanalytic work, her interests include work with groups and staff consultations. She has helped to set up an MA in psychotherapy at Essex University. She has recently move to Glasgow, and now works at the Department of Child Psychiatry at York Hill Hospital.

Sue Holt

Sue Holt trained at the Tavistock Clinic as an Educational Psychologist and worked as an Educational Psychologist for the ILEA for eleven years before moving to Devon. She is currently an associate tutor on the Exeter MSc. in Educational Psychology and also works with JACAT, a joint agencies child abuse team specialising in treatment and consultation.

Clare Huffington

Clare Huffington is a Consultant Clinical Psychologist, Child and Family Department and Senior Consultant, Tavistock Clinic Consultancy Service. As well as working as a clinician, Clare consults to organisations in the public and private sectors both in child and family, mental health fields and in wider areas. She also organises a course entitled 'Consultation: A Course for Psychologists' within the Tavistock Clinic and has written several articles and books on the subject of consultancy.

Joyce Iszatt

Joyce Iszatt marks as Associate Tutor on the MSc Educational Psychology Training Course at the Tavistock Clinic and is a Senior Educational Psychologist in the London Borough of Enfield. Areas of interest include work with refugees and preventative approaches in the early years.

Carmel Jennings

Carmel Jennings is a Consultant Child Psychologist and Organising Tutor for the MSc. in Educational Psychology at the Tavistock Clinic. She is also a lecturer at Birkbeck College, University of London. Her current interests include consultation with multiprofessional services; personal professional development training practices and supervision; and ongoing work with children and families.

Elizabeth Kennedy

Elizabeth Kennedy is also Organising Tutor for the MSc in Educational Psychology at the Tavistock Clinic. She is Organising Tutor for 'Working in Partnership with Families of Children with Long Term Special Needs' and a Course Tutor for 'Consultation: A Course for Psychologists'. She is an educational psychologist in Westminster, and her special interests include 'working together' professional partnerships and on-going work with children and families.

Anton Obholzer

Anton Obholzer is a Fellow of the Royal College of Psychiatrists and a member of the British Psycho-Analytical Society. He is currently Chief Executive of the Tavistock and Portman NHS Trust, Associate Professor at Brunel University Department of Social Sciences and Associate Director of the Tavistock Institute Group Relations Training Programme. He is particularly interested in consulting to institutions from a psychoanalytic group relations perspective, and has done so for a variety of public and private sector organisations, both in the UK and internationally.

Eileen Orford

Eileen Orford is a child psychotherapist with a special interest in consultation to organisations whose primary work is with children in difficulty. She contributes to the training of child psychotherapists in the Tavistock Clinic and the British Association for Psychotherapy, and has also run the 'Consultation Course' in the Tavistock Clinic.

Judith Trowell

Judith Trowell is a Consultant Psychiatrist in the Child and Family Department of the Tavistock Clinic, and an acknowledged expert in the field of child and family mental health, specialising in child protection. She is currently Chair person at Young Minds and Chair of the ACPC in Camden, where she has initiated several training inputs for educational and multi-professional personnel.

Subject Index

Name Index